Ancient Wisdom for Today's World

Daniel L. Segraves

Ancient Wisdom for Today's World

A Commentary on the Book of Proverbs

Ancient Wisdom for Today's World
A Commentary on the Book of Proverbs

by Daniel L. Segraves

©1990 Word Aflame Press
  Hazelwood, MO 63042-2299

Printing History: 1992

Cover Design by Tim Agnew

All Scripture quotations in this book are from the King James Version of the Bible unless otherwise identified.

Printed in United States of America.

Printed by

Library of Congress Cataloging-in-Publication Data

Segraves, Daniel L., 1946–
      Ancient wisdom for today's world : a commentary on the Book of
   Proverbs / Daniel L. Segraves.
            p.   cm.
      Includes bibliographical references.
      ISBN 0-932581-60-9
      1. Bible. O.T. Proverbs—Commentaries.   I. Title.
   BS1465.3.S53   1990
   223'.707—dc20   89-29358
                                                                    CIP

Contents

Introduction

The Author of the Book of Proverbs

Even a cursory examination of the Book of Proverbs reveals that it was written by no ordinary man. The gracious influence of God was at work many years before the first proverb was penned to prepare the man who would be known as the wisest man in the world (I Kings 4:31).

Israel's King David, a man after God's own heart (I Samuel 13:14), desired to build a house for God (II Samuel 7:1-3). He was not permitted to do so because of the warlike nature of his reign (I Chronicles 22:1-16). But his son Solomon, whose name means "peaceable" and whose name was to reflect the nature of his reign, was to fulfill his father's ambition (II Samuel 7:12-15). While David was allowed to plan the construction of the Temple and even to amass the materials and provide the workmen, the actual building was carried out under the authority of Solomon.

As the Preacher was later to say, there is "A time to break down, and a time to build up . . . a time of war, and a time of peace" (Ecclesiastes 3:3, 8). The constructive work of building is best carried out in an atmosphere of peace. Jesus said, "Blessed are the peacemakers: for they shall be called the children of God" (Matthew 5:9).

Christians are to "follow after the things which make for peace, and things wherewith one may edify another" (Romans 14:19).

Edification, which means building up and strengthening, is a recurrent theme in the New Testament Epistles. Christians must take care to speak only words that edify (Ephesians 4:29). Even the gifts of the Spirit are to be governed by their edifying effect on the church (I Corinthians 14:12). If someone wishes to see the Lord, he is required to follow both peace and holiness (Hebrews 12:14). And Jesus is the Prince of Peace (Isaiah 9:6).

The wars under David's reign were necessary for that time; wickedness and evil must be rooted out. But the building of the Temple was reserved for the reign of peace.

While Solomon was not without fault, he had a basic love for the Lord (I Kings 3:3). And when the Lord appeared to him in a dream and gave him the opportunity to ask for anything he desired, Solomon made a wise decision. "Give therefore thy servant an understanding heart," he requested, "to judge thy people, that I may discern between good and bad" (I Kings 3:9). God was pleased that Solomon had not asked selfishly, so He granted Solomon's request and gave him a wise and understanding heart. The nature of this wisdom was to be so remarkable that none before or after Solomon could be compared to him (I Kings 3:12). In addition, God gave Solomon the riches and honor for which he did not ask (I Kings 3:13).

The result of this interchange between the Lord and Solomon is seen in I Kings 4:29-34:

And God gave Solomon wisdom and understanding exceeding much, and largeness of heart, even as the sand that is on the sea shore. And Solomon's wisdom excelled the wisdom of all the children of the east country, and all the wisdom of Egypt. For he was wiser than all men . . . and his fame was in all nations round about. And he spake three thousand proverbs: and his songs were a thousand and five. And he spake of trees, from the cedar tree that is in Lebanon even unto the hyssop that springeth out of the wall: he spake also of beasts, and of fowl, and of creeping things, and of fishes. And there came of all people to hear the wisdom of Solomon, from all kings of the earth, which had heard of his wisdom.

Since Solomon's reign was from 971–931 B.C., we may place the date of the Book of Proverbs as in the tenth century. The book has thirty-one chapters, 915 verses, and 15,043 words. While Solomon spoke three thousand proverbs, he was inspired of the Holy Spirit to record less than one thousand of them for inclusion in this book.

By and large, proverbs compare one thing to another. God's wisdom is taught as the Holy Ghost compares spiritual things with spiritual things (I Corinthians 2:13). The Book of Proverbs, being Scripture, is spiritual. It is inspired of God, and therefore it is profitable for doctrine, reproof, correction, and instruction in righteousness (II Timothy 3:16; II Peter 1:21).

That it is possible to know the right thing to do and yet fail to do it is sadly illustrated in the life of the man who wrote the proverbs. He was not always successful in translating his theoretical wisdom into practice, and he paid for his failure by the loss of his privileged relationship with God. Though he warned of the dangers of liaisons with ungodly women, Solomon was heedless to his own advice. He loved many foreign women, and his wives turned away his heart after other gods (I Kings 11:1-13).

As we study these proverbs, let us remember the solemn lesson that even the man who was moved by God to write them was not immune from the penalty of breaking them.

The Nature of Hebrew Poetry

While much modern poetry depends upon rhyme or rhythm, the Book of Proverbs presents a poetry of ideas. That is, rather than a parallelism of phonetics or meter, there is a parallelism of thought.

In Hebrew poetry, this parallelism is traditionally identified in three categories: synonymous, antithetic, and synthetic. Some think it more precise, however, to identify this parallelism as completive, contrastive, and constructive.[1]

The *completive parallel* refers to poetry in which the second phrase completes the first in the sense of agreement and further development. This type of parallel occurs primarily in the Book of Psalms. Psalm 92:12 provides an example:

The righteous shall flourish like the palm tree: he shall grow like a cedar in Lebanon.

The first phrase introduces the subject of the prosperity of the righteous; the final phrase agrees and develops the idea further by illustrating how he will prosper, or describing his strength in prosperity. The term *completive* seem to be superior to *synonymous* in this case, for the second phrase is not simply synonymous with the first; it actually develops the idea further.

The *contrastive parallel* is common in the Book of Proverbs. In this case, the latter phrase actually contrasts with the first, not necessarily in a negative way but in a way that develops the thought further. An example is Proverbs 3:1:

My son, forget not my law; but let thine heart keep my commandments.

The first phrase is essentially negative: it is a commandment not to forget. The second is essentially positive: it is a commandment to remember. While the proverb is thus contrastive, the contrast does develop further the idea of the importance of not forgetting the law.

In this case, the term *contrastive* seems superior to *antithetic,* for the latter term implies opposition. And the final phrase of Proverbs 3:1 is certainly not opposed to the first.

The *constructive parallel* consists of a series of parallel ideas that are added one to the other until a whole is formed. One example spans four verses—Proverbs 30:11-14:

There is a generation
that curseth their father,
and doth not bless their mother.
There is a generation

that are pure in their own eyes,
and yet is not washed from their filthiness.
There is a generation,
O how lofty are their eyes!
and their eyelids are lifted up.
There is a generation,
whose teeth are as swords,
and their jaw teeth as knives,
to devour the poor from off the earth,
and the needy from among men.

The subject of this constructive parallel is a corrupt generation. Step by step, the thought is developed from their disregard for parental authority, to their self-righteousness, to their pride, and finally to their violence.

The term *constructive* seems superior to *synthetic* here, for the latter term implies reasoning that proceeds from established principles. That does not actually occur in proverbs such as these. It is not so much a matter of reasoning from principles, but rather the gradual development of an idea in much the same way that a building is constructed: block upon block.

In the various forms of poetry, the parallelism serves as a means of interpretation. That is, if the first phrase is somewhat obscure, the second will clarify. The first may be figurative; the second literal. The first may be positive; the second negative.

The Nature of a Proverb

The word *proverb* comes from the Latin *proverba (pro:* for, before; *verba:* words) and implies a short, concise statement that in few words expresses the thought of many words. *Webster's Dictionary* defines a proverb as "a short saying in common use that strikingly expresses some obvious truth or familiar experience; adage; maxim." While most of the proverbs in the Book of Proverbs are indeed proverbs in this modern English sense of the word, the Hebrew word translated "proverbs," *mishle,* is broader in scope. It reaches out to include truths expressed in a more lengthy and complex manner.

A proverb is often based upon a comparison or a similarity. It expresses a general principle or gives advice that has general application. Often it explains the typical outcome in a certain kind of situation. While a particular experience may not fulfill a relevant proverb in every respect, what the proverb says about human nature and society is true.

The Structure of the Book of Proverbs

The Book of Proverbs can be broadly divided into three major sections. The first, chapters 1 through 9, does not in the strictest sense consist of proverbs, but rather sonnets and monologues in praise of wisdom itself.

The second section, chapters 10 through 24, includes both proverbs and epigrams (terse, witty, pointed statements) that deal with the practical expressions of wisdom in daily life.

The third section, chapters 25 through 31, includes additional proverbs and epigrams that were copied by the men of Hezekiah, king of Judah. In addition, this section contains thirteen sayings of Agur (chapter 30), an oracle of Lemuel's mother (chapter 31:1-9), and an acrostic on the virtuous woman (chapter 31:10-31). The last twenty-two verses are an acrostic because each verse from 31:10 to 31:31 begins with a letter of the Hebrew alphabet, so that the first letter of each verse lists the entire alphabet from beginning to end.[2]

Here is an outline of the Book of Proverbs.[3]
  I. In Praise of Wisdom (chapters 1–9)
      A. Introduction (1:1–9) (sonnet)
      B. Enticements of Sinners (1:10–19) (sonnet)
      C. Wisdom's Warning (1:20–33) (monologue)
      D. Wisdom the Deliverer (2:1–22) (sonnet)
      E. The Reward of Obedience (3:1–10) (sonnet)
      F. Wisdom the Supreme Reward (3:11–20) (sonnet)
      G. Wisdom and Safety (3:21–26) (sonnet)
      H. Wisdom and Perversity (3:27–35) (sonnet)
      I. Wisdom's Tradition (4:1–9) (sonnet)
      J. The Two Paths (4:10–19) (sonnet)
      K. Wisdom and Health (4:20–27) (sonnet)
      L. The Strange Woman (5:1–23) (sonnet)
      M. Co-Signing (Suretyship) (6:1–5) (sonnet)
      N. The Sluggard (6:6–11) (sonnet)
      O. The Sower of Discord (6:12–19) (sonnet)
      P. Adultery (6:20–35) (sonnet)
      Q. Wisdom and the Strange Woman (7–8) (monologue)
      R. The Houses of Wisdom and Folly (9) (sonnet)
  II. Practical Expressions of Wisdom in Daily Life (10–24)
      A. 375 Proverbs (10–22:16)
      B. Sixteen Epigrams

Notes

[1]J. Sidlow Baxter, *Explore the Book* (Grand Rapids: Zondervan, 1966), 3:19.

[2]Ibid., 135.

[3]This outline closely follows the one suggested by Baxter in *Explore the Book,* but it is modified for the sake of simplicity and to update some of the terms.

Chapter One

Solomon the author (verse 1). The Book of Proverbs opens with the clear statement that Solomon, the son of David, is the author. There is no question that the first twenty-nine chapters are proverbs of Solomon. (See Proverbs 25:1.) Some suppose, however, that chapters 30 and 31 were authored by others, because of the statements at the beginning of those two chapters.

Proverbs 30:1 reads, "The words of Agur the son of Jakeh, even the prophecy: the man spake unto Ithiel, even unto Ithiel and Ucal." It is possible that the names in this verse are transliterations rather than translations. (To transliterate is to change the letters of one language into corresponding or equivalent characters of another alphabet or language. For example, the word *baptize* is a transliteration of the Greek word *baptizo*.) In this case, a literal translation of Proverbs 30:1 would read, "The words of the collector of wise sayings, the son of the obedient one: even the prophecy: the man spake unto With Me Is God, even unto With me Is God and I Shall Be Completed." Thus it is possible that this verse refers to Solomon rather than an actual person by the name of Agur. Jewish rabbis identify Agur as another word for Solomon and the obedient one as David.

Proverbs 31:1 reads, "The words of king Lemuel, the prophecy that his mother taught him." The name "Lemuel" means "devoted to God." It is possible that this also is a term for Solomon, whose mother, Bathsheba, taught him. II Samuel 12:25 is an example of such a name being given to Solomon. There, "Jedidiah" means "beloved of the LORD."

Regardless of whether the last two chapters of Proverbs were authored by Solomon, we know they are inspired Scripture. The entire book was included in the Hebrew canon (the collection of books accepted as inspired) before the time of Christ, and He gave His stamp of divine approval to the entirety of the Old Testament, including Proverbs (Luke 24:44). In the Hebrew Bible, the Book of Proverbs was included in the section known as Psalms, which we call the poetry and wisdom literature.

Wisdom the chief subject (verse 2). The second verse of the Book of Proverbs introduces the major subject of the book: wisdom. From its origin to its practical application in the daily situations of life, wisdom glows deeper than the reddest ruby on every page of the book. *Webster's Dictionary* defines wisdom as "the right use or exercise of knowledge." Bill Gothard has suggested that wisdom is "seeing and responding to life from God's point of view." The English word *wisdom* is the translation of several Hebrew words in the Book of Proverbs; the most common is *hokmah.* This word speaks of the skill with which craftsmen, sailors, singers, mourners, administrators, and counselors perform their duties. Thus, being wise means "being skilled in godly living. Having God's wisdom means having the ability to cope with life in a God-honoring way."[1]

The word *wisdom* appears over fifty times in the Book of Proverbs. Proverbs 4:7 declares, "Wisdom is the principal thing; therefore get wisdom: and with all thy getting get understanding." Wisdom is the *principal* thing. It is more valuable than gold, silver, or rubies.

While wisdom is the first quality mentioned in verse 2, instruction follows closely. The Book of Proverbs is designed so that one who studies it will receive both wisdom and instruction. The word "instruction" is translated from the Hebrew *muwcar* and implies chastisement, reproof, warning, instruction, and restraint. The Book of Proverbs was one of the chief elements in the educational curriculum of ancient Israel. Parents used it to teach their children. When the first elementary schools for boys began about two centuries before the time of Christ, it was one of the main resources used by the teachers. It is a book of instruction, and a large part of the instruction is accomplished by reproof, rebuke, correction, and discipline. Later, the book declares, "Reproofs of instruction are the way of life" (Proverbs 6:23). (See also Proverbs 9:8; 12:1; 15:10; Psalm 119:71.)

A genuine education is a painful process; there is no such thing as "easy" learning. At some point in the process, the student must apply himself diligently to the subject at hand and do so at the expense of other, more pleasant, pursuits. A teacher in the classroom knows that even a test is to be a learning tool. In the same way, we receive instruction through the reproofs of life. It is a wise man who learns from painful experiences.

The proverbs are designed not only to give wisdom and instruction but to enable the student to "perceive the words of understanding." The Holy Spirit has elected to give us truth and wisdom by use of words. (See II Peter 1:19-21; Proverbs 30:5-6; Psalm 12:6-7.) Some 2,500 times the Old Testament declares, "Thus saith the LORD." During the nineteenth century, rationalism suggested that the Bible was inspired in thoughts or concepts but not in its words. The Bible nowhere suggests, however, that God communicated merely by general ideas, thoughts, or concepts. Rather, it declares that He has spoken in words.

The Bible identifies "understanding" with departing from evil (Job 28:28). The words of Scripture will cause a person to depart from evil and to go in the right way.

To receive instruction (verse 3). The instruction of verse 2 comes from four basic sources: wisdom, justice, judgment, and equity. In verse 3 the Hebrew word translated "wisdom" is *sakal,* which means to be circumspect and hence insightful. Webster defined the word *circumspect* as "looking on all sides . . . cautious; prudent . . . examining carefully all the circumstances that may affect a determination." As a person becomes more observant, as he opens his eyes to take a broader view, he receives instruction. A narrow vision begets a narrow mentality. It is possible for a person to deny reality because of his limited perspective.

Justice, from the Hebrew *tsedek,* is the ability to discern what is right. Human reasoning is deceptive in determining what is right and what is wrong. When Adam and Eve ate of the tree of the knowledge of good and evil, they basically were seeking to decide for themselves what was right and what was wrong. But God never intended for man to struggle with this decision. Man was to know what was right, and he was to do right. God reserved the determination of right and wrong for Himself.

In eating of the tree of the knowledge of good and evil, man attempted to play God. But the human mind is inadequate to this task. Only by the Word of God can man discern right and wrong. "Strong meat belongeth to them that are of full age, even those who by reason of use have their senses exercised to discern both good and evil" (Hebrews 5:14). The ability to discern between good and evil is called "strong meat," and this ability belongs only to those who are of "full age." Clearly, it is something developed over a period of time in conjunction with diligent study and prayer. Those who are able to make such decisions have received the instruction of justice.

Judgment has to do with a verdict rendered. Judgment is the enacting of justice, or the pronouncement of justice.

Equity speaks of evenness or straightness. The implication is that equity is evenhanded judgment based upon true justice. It has been suggested that the modern secular concept of fairness is often the enemy of true justice and mercy. "If . . . we attempt to reach fairness apart from God's laws, fairness becomes distorted. God knows and sees everything, and His just laws are the only door to true, eternal fairness. God is no respecter of persons. He shows no favoritism but gives to every man according to his motives, thoughts, and deeds."[2] True justice and equity have been contrasted with the secular notion of "fairness" as follows:

- Justice is the application of the principles of God's Word, which are totally consistent with His holy character.
- The principles of justice are universal and are not optional.

- Justice reveals the true nature of God and the rebellious nature of man.
- Justice requires full payment for every violation of God's holy law.
- "Fairness" is lowering God's standards to the level that can be achieved with our human will and ability.
- "Fairness" is based on man's value system and man's timetable. It is the product of human comparisons.
- "Fairness" is looking at a situation from the viewpoint of each person rather than from the viewpoint of God.
- Equity is the application of justice to situations not covered by the law.
- Equity always follows justice. Therefore, principles of justice must be understood before equity can be determined. For this reason, Scripture lists equity after justice, such as in Colossians 4:1.
- Equity is applying God's general principles to a specific situation.[3]

It is wonderful to see how current and up-to-date, how timeless, the Book of Proverbs is. One of the major concerns in today's world is for justice. The courts are playing an ever larger role, especially in North American society. True wisdom, justice, judgment, and equity come only from the wisdom and instruction of God's Word, from the words of understanding it contains.

To give subtilty, knowledge, and discretion (verse 4). The proverbs of Solomon are designed also to give subtilty to the simple. Subtilty is a combination of prudence and knowledge, resulting in a discernment that enables a person to judge critically what is correct and proper, united with caution.

Knowledge and discretion may commonly be thought of as the domain of those with years of experience in life. But these qualities are available to the young person who will apply himself to a diligent study of the Book of Proverbs. "I understand more than the ancients, because I keep thy precepts" (Psalm 119:100). The word *discretion* speaks of sagacity, which is "quickness or acuteness of discernment or penetration; readiness of apprehension; the faculty of readily discerning and distinguishing ideas, and of separating truth from falsehood" *(Webster's Dictionary).*

The Book of Proverbs, then, will help a young person to quickly grasp a situation, to accurately evaluate what is really happening. He will be able to see past the fog of surface problems to root causes.

Willingness to listen is a sign of wisdom (verse 5). Learning is a lifelong process. One of the first indications of a person's wisdom is his willingness to listen. Only a foolish person will assume that he knows it all. As someone confessed, "The more I learn the more I realize I don't know." As we learn and grow mentally, new vistas open up before us that we did not even realize existed.

Ignorance is not bliss; it can be deadly. God declared to ancient Israel, "My people are destroyed for lack of knowledge: because thou hast rejected knowledge, I will also reject thee" (Hosea 4:6). "Also, that the soul be without knowledge, it is not good," Solomon said (Proverbs 19:2). As a young boy, Jesus grew mentally, physically, spiritually, and socially (Luke 2:52). James offered this counsel: "Let every man be swift to hear, slow to

23

speak" (James 1:19). A wise man will hear.

The result of a wise person's hearing is an increase in learning. This "hearing" goes beyond the perfunctory politeness of waiting until another person is finished speaking before one starts talking. It describes intense listening—listening so attentive that it results in grasping not only the words but also the underlying principles and even the spirit of the speaker.

No learning occurs without hearing, whether hearing God or hearing other people. The hearing may be the actual process of listening with the ears to spoken messages, or it may be "hearing" by reading or observing. But learning will never occur where there is no hearing. If a person wishes to learn, he must be willing to hear.

Listening is a neglected and quickly vanishing skill in our world. We must practice diligent and attentive listening. We must make a genuine effort to break through the inertia of an undisciplined and inattentive mind. The mind has marvelous ability to comprehend, to reason, to think, but the use of the mind is up to each individual. The brain is one of the members of the body just as the hand or the eye. It does not act independently of the will. We must apply the brain and mind to hearing, just as we apply the eye to seeing, the tongue to speaking, and the hand to writing. "Incline thine ear unto wisdom, and apply thine heart to understanding" (Proverbs 2:2).

Wisdom and understanding go hand-in-hand (Proverbs 4:7). The person who hears and increases learning is a person of understanding. He will attain wise counsel. He will seek after, and find, wise counsel. Three times the Book of Proverbs indicates that wisdom is found in a "multitude of counsellers" (Proverbs 11:14; 15:22; 24:6). A wise person will seek this kind of counsel. He will not make the mistake of Solomon's son, Rehoboam, who rejected the counsel of the elders and accepted only that given by his peers. (See I Kings 12:8-15.) He will realize that wisdom is found in the counsel of a cross-section of godly people. Rather than rejecting counsel until he finds a counsellor who agrees with him, he will take the consensus of counsel from a broad spectrum of unbiased individuals.

To understand proverbs, wise words, and dark sayings (verse 6). A further purpose of the Book of Proverbs is to provide a vehicle whereby the student can learn to understand the meaning of proverbs and the words spoken by wise men, including their "dark sayings." The Hebrew word translated "dark sayings" has reference to something that has been tied in knots, as when we say we have a "knotty problem." This phrase does not speak of mere mental gymnastics but of the ability to grasp the real issue.

The source of knowledge (verse 7). The beginning of true knowledge is "the fear of the LORD," which means reverence, respect, and awe for God and His Word. A person who does not fear God may know certain facts, but his knowledge is corrupted by his lack of regard for the Lord. For example, both the unbeliever and the believer may say, "The world is round." But a closer examination will reveal that each mean different things by this statement. The believer is speaking of a world created by God to be inhabited by humans. Even when he says "round" he is testifying to the existence of a definite standard by which measurement can be made. The unbeliever, on the other hand, is speaking of a world that is the chance result of an accident in the cosmos, a world that came into being without purpose or design and that is inhabited by animals of various levels that are also the product of random evolution. He does not believe in absolute standards; everything is relative.

Similarly, both the believer and the unbeliever may say, "It is raining." But to the unbeliever the rain is simply condensation. It is the chance result of unpredictable weather patterns. If anyone is thanked or accused, it is the mythical "Mother Nature." The believer, however, recognizes rain as the blessing of God, given by Him as a witness of His goodness. A person who does not fear God has, at best, limited and corrupted knowledge.

The close relationship between wisdom and knowledge is shown also in Psalm 111:10: "The fear of the LORD is the beginning of wisdom: a good understanding have all they that do his commandments: his praise endureth for ever." There is no true wisdom outside the fear of the Lord.

The word *philosophy* comes from two Greek words, *phileo,* meaning "to love" and *sophia,* meaning "wisdom." A philosopher is a lover of wisdom. But all philosophy that is not centered in Christ is corrupt. There may be some truth in it, but it will be contaminated by a lack of regard for the true God. It will be impossible to interpret facts accurately and to come to sound spiritual conclusions. Paul warned the Colossians, "Beware lest any man spoil you through philosophy and vain deceit, after the tradition of men, after the rudiments of the world, and not after Christ. For in him dwelleth all the fulness of the Godhead bodily. And ye are complete in him, which is the head of all principality and power" (Colossians 2:8-10). Christless philosophy is a corrupt and dangerous philosophy. Jesus Christ is the Cornerstone, the Foundation, the very Wisdom of God. (See I Corinthians 1:24.) He must have the preeminence in *all* things (Colossians 1:18).

Later in the Book of Proverbs Solomon said, "The fear of the LORD is the beginning of wisdom: and the knowledge of the holy is understanding" (Proverbs 9:10). A person does not have genuine understanding without a knowledge of the holy. Faith in God is not an optional diversion for those with time on their hands. It is the absolute central feature of all of life. A person who does not fear God is missing the whole point of life. Regardless of how high his goals may be or what he reaches in the pursuit of them, his life at the core is aimless, shiftless, without rhyme or reason.

Long before the days of Solomon and David, Job observed, "Behold, the fear of the Lord, that is wisdom; and to depart from evil is understanding" (Job 28:28). God is the source of all knowledge and wisdom. There is none outside of Him. Much that people believe to be true and have learned in secular educational systems to be true is not really truth at all. Truth does not evolve, but what humans proclaim as truth may change from day to day. Some Christians have been influenced by the claims of secular knowledge to believe that the Bible is not scientific or historically accurate. But there is no division between secular truth and spiritual truth. Truth is truth. The proper foundation for true knowledge in any area, including "natural" phenomena, is the fear of the Lord. When people remove the Bible from the total education of their children, they yank the foundation from beneath their social structure.

The Book of Proverbs lists several characteristics of a fool. One of them is seen in this verse: a fool will despise wisdom and instruction. He has no heart for the discipline of learning and attaining wisdom. He is comfortable with the way he is; he does not want to be changed. All he can stomach is the pablum dished out by the secular world.

Instruction and law from parents (verse 8). The phrase "my son" appears at least twenty-two times in the Book of Proverbs. The book was written by a wise father, Solomon, to his son, offering the wisdom necessary for genuine success in many areas of life. It is sad that Solomon's son Rehoboam did not follow his father's counsel. As a result of his refusal to listen to wisdom, his kingdom was torn apart and he was left with only a small portion.

The first appeal to the son is an appeal to recognize the value of the counsel and direction given by a father and mother. This admonition demonstrates that the things most valuable are often found at home rather than in some distant, exotic place. The invitation is not to find a "holy man" or guru to follow, but to hear a father's instruction and a mother's law. The individual who turns away from the counsel offered by godly parents rejects one of the most valuable sources of wisdom and direction he will ever find.

The father is said to give instruction, while the mother is said to give the law. Similarly, Proverbs 6:20-23 says that the father gives the commandment and the mother gives the law. Perhaps a distinction between the two can be made on the basis of Proverbs 6:23: "For the commandment is a lamp; and the law is light; and reproofs of instruction are the way of life." A lamp is the source of light;

it is an object that emits light. The light is the product of the lamp. In the family relationship, the father is responsible to give the commandment—the ultimate object or purpose in view. The mother is to give the law— the outworking of that purpose, the practical means by which the objective will be achieved.

For example, a father may say to his young son, "I want your room clean when I come home tonight." To enable the child to fulfill this task, the mother may say, "Now the first thing to do is pick up your dirty clothes and put them in the hamper." When that is accomplished, the mother may say, "Now make your bed." In this way, the child, led by his mother's law, will accomplish his father's commandment.

Attractive adornment (verse 9). The young person who listens to his father's instruction and abides by his mother's law will find that they develop in him a genuine attractiveness. (See Proverbs 4:9; 25:12.) They provide him with a depth of character not seen in those who walk in stubborn rebellion against parental authority. This is the kind of ornamentation or adornment that sets a Christian apart from the unbeliever. (See I Peter 3:1-7; I Timothy 2:9-10.)

The proper response to sinners' enticement: Don't consent (verse 10). It is a mistake to wait until temptation presents itself to decide whether or not to yield. Temptation will be resisted successfully only by those who have, in advance, without the intense pressure of enticing temptation, made up their minds they will not consent under any circumstance. Some of the ways that sinners seek to entice believers are in person, and through the television, music, advertisements, books, and magazines. The antidote is found in the practice of Psalm 1.

The mob mentality of sin (verses 11-14). The mob spirit is dangerous. People often do things as a part of a larger group that they would never do individually. The underlying humanistic philosophy is that the majority determines what is right and wrong. (See Exodus 23:2.) But God alone determines what is right and wrong. Whether one person or all people oppose Him, God is still true and the opposition is lying. (See Romans 3:4.)

Don't walk in the same direction with sinners (verse 15). Not only are we not to participate with sinners in their sin, but we are not even to set our foot on the wrong path they are taking. If we do, we run the risk of being guilty by association. There is also the danger that familiarity will result in a relaxed attitude toward their sin, as Alexander Pope stated so well in *An Essay on Man:*

> Vice is a monster of so frightful mien,
> As to be hated needs but to be seen;
> Yet seen too oft, familiar with her face,
> We first endure, then pity, then embrace.

Sinners dig their own pit (verses 16-18). Sinners condemn themselves by their sins; they bring judgment upon themselves by their own actions. This will certainly be evident at the last judgment, and it is often apparent in this life. Even a bird knows to avoid a net spread while it watches, but sinners do not seem to realize that their own actions will condemn them.

The wisdom of the Golden Rule is evident in that people frequently are the recipients of the same kind of treatment they give others (Matthew 7:12). The person who digs a pit for his enemy will fall in it himself (Proverbs 26:27). The story of Mordecai and Haman is a classic example. Haman was hanged on the very gallows he had prepared for Mordecai.

Not only is it unwise to initiate evil; it is also foolish to repay evil with evil. (See Romans 12:14, 17-21.) It is a simple matter to know how to treat others: we should ask, "How do I want to be treated?"

Greed: the thief of life (verse 19). There is nothing inherently evil about money. But there is something desperately wrong with greed. The person who is motivated by greed will find that it exacts its pound of flesh. Greed's currency is the life of the person who practices it. (See Proverbs 13:7, 11; 23:4-5; I Timothy 6:7-10.)

Wisdom personified as a woman (verses 20-21). Two women are pictured in Proverbs: wisdom and folly. Wisdom does not play hard to get. Even in the streets, where common people jostle, her voice is heard. She is not available only beneath the high-vaulted ceilings of research libraries or in the conclave of scholars. She is available for all.

Wisdom's message (verse 22). Wisdom asks, "Why stay where you are? Why not grow? Why not learn? Do you plan for the rest of your life to be an aimless repeat of what has gone before? Why not change?"

Wisdom's promise (verse 23). The first step from foolishness to wisdom is to turn. If someone keeps doing what he has always done, if he changes nothing about his attitude toward life but keeps responding to it in the same way, he will be no better off ten years later than he is today. In fact, he will probably be in worse shape. Before there can be any improvement, there must be a turn. All the New Testament preachers, including John the Baptist, Jesus Christ, Peter, and Paul, proclaimed this message, using the word *repent*. Literally, this word means "an about face." Repentance is a turn. It is a recognition that one has been going in the wrong direction and a commitment to do something to change it.

We should note the relationship between wisdom and reproof. Throughout the Book of Proverbs the value of reproof is seen. It is foolish to reject reproof. There can be no learning, no instruction, without reproof. Indeed, "reproofs of instruction are the way of life" (Proverbs 6:23). The person who is never reproved, or who never accepts reproof, never grows. He can only deteriorate.

The turn made at wisdom's reproof will not be in vain. When wisdom observes a person turning from foolishness to her, she does two things: (1) she pours out her spirit; and (2) she makes known her words to that person. Wisdom is not merely a matter of the intellect; it is first a matter of the spirit. Before words of wisdom can be received, the heart must be prepared by the Spirit of God. (See I Corinthians 2:11-14.)

Wisdom uses words to communicate her insights. Once again, we are reminded that the Bible is the very Word of God. God communicated by words, not merely by general concepts, ideas, or thoughts. The Bible is not the product of men putting some sort of cosmic principle into the best words they can find with their limited vocabulary; it is actually God's words to us.

Wisdom's warning (verses 24-28). Wisdom has made every effort to attract the attention of people. But many of them place no value at all on her counsel; they refuse to accept her reproof. Because they have rejected her and the principles she would have taught them, she is power-less to help them in their time of trouble.

Her laughter and mocking at their calamity and fear is not the expression of a perverse desire to utter the final, cosmic, "I told you so." Rather it is a way of saying that those who reject wisdom will remember her voice; they will recall her invitation, an invitation that if accepted would have spared them from desolation, destruction, distress, and anguish. The wisdom they rejected will mock them. The people who have rejected wisdom will dis-cover—when they finally decide they need it—that it is too late. Again, it is not that wisdom obtains perverse pleasure out of watching her enemies suffer; it is simply because wisdom cannot be obtained in a moment of time. It cannot be grabbed on the run, like a hamburger at the drive-in window of a fast-food restaurant. It comes as the result of a committed, diligent, faithful, lifelong pursuit.

Rejection of knowledge is rejection of God (verse 29). As in verse 6, the fear of the Lord and knowledge are inseparably entwined. At the very root, all good things come from the fear of the Lord; all evil springs from a disregard of Him.

Reaping the results of rejecting wisdom (verses 30-32). There is no way to avoid the consequences of rejecting wisdom. A person can eat the satisfying fruit of wisdom, or he can eat the fruit of foolishness. He can be filled with wisdom, or he will be filled with his own devices, which is the ultimate expression of "doing my own thing" and having it "my way."

In the final analysis, rejection of wisdom is deadly. When a person makes a decision to turn away from wisdom, he has signed his own death warrant. To the eyes of other fools, it may appear for a brief time that he made the right decision. But his prosperity and complacency are empty and deceitful. Some may be deceived into thinking that the prosperity is genuine, but when the real test comes, it fails. It is as useless in the real test as a papier-mache axe to a woodchopper. (See Psalm 73.)

Wisdom's reward (verse 33). The person who listens to wisdom and acts on her principles will discover a life of safety and quietness. He will be free of worry. Wisdom will enable him to see beyond the immediate circumstance. He will understand the law of cause and effect. (See Psalm 37:1-11.)

Notes

[1]John F. Walvoord and Roy B. Zuck, eds., *The Bible Knowledge Commentary* (Wheaton, Ill.: Victor Books, 1985), OT: 902.

[2]*The Unexpected Enemy of Justice and Mercy* (Oak Brook, Ill.: Institute in Basic Youth Conflicts, 1982), 4.

[3]Ibid.

Chapter Two

The path to understanding and knowledge (verses 1-5). In Proverbs 1:7, Solomon declared the fundamental truth that "the fear of the LORD is the beginning of knowledge." Here he listed for his son eight steps that lead to understanding the fear of the Lord and finding the knowledge of God: (1) receive my words; (2) hide my commandments within you; (3) incline your ear to wisdom; (4) apply your heart to understanding; (5) cry after knowledge; (6) lift up your voice for understanding; (7) seek understanding as you would seek silver; and (8) search for understanding as you would search for hidden treasures.

In each of these steps, the responsibility rests with us. Wisdom has already made herself available (1:20-25). All that remains is for a person to receive her counsel. It will not be forced upon him; that is contrary to the nature of wisdom. Folly is aggressive (7:6-21); she catches men (7:13). Wisdom calls to people; she even stretches out her hand (1:24). But she waits for them to turn before she pours out her spirit and makes known her words (1:23).

The first step to attaining understanding and knowledge, Solomon told his son, is to "receive my words." This is the first rung on the ladder. Before any further progress can be made, the student must receive the words. If he rejects them, the other seven steps will escape him altogether. Step one provides for and makes possible the other steps.

Paul congratulated the Thessalonicans for taking this first step: "For this cause also thank we God without ceasing, because, when ye received the word of God which ye heard of us, ye received it not as the word of men, but as it is in truth, the word of God, which effectually worketh also in you that believe" (I Thessalonians 2:13). Things that would prevent someone from taking this first step include skepticism, which doubts that the words really are the words of God, and a careless attitude, which underestimates the incomparable significance of the Word. The Christian must never be guilty of underestimating the value and importance of the Word of God. The name of God is of awesome significance (Matthew 6:9), but God has magnified His Word even above His name (Psalm 138:2). The first, all-important step to knowledge and understanding is to accept the words of Scripture as they are in truth, the very words of God Himself.

The second rung up the ladder is to hide the words within us. After accepting or receiving the words, it is necessary to transfer them from the page to the heart. Not only is this a step toward understanding and knowledge, it is an essential key to resisting temptation. David said, "Thy word have I hid in mine heart, that I might not sin against thee" (Psalm 119:11). We hide the Word in our heart when we become so thoroughly conversant with it that it becomes a part of us and its principles are interwoven into our very thought processes.

The way to hide God's Word in our heart is by memorization and meditation. Memorization imprints the Word indelibly on our heart (mind). In meditation we reflect on the Word to plumb the depths of its meaning and application.

As we hide the Word in our heart on a faithful and consistent basis, our thoughts begin to follow the paths established by the Word. For this reason, the person who meditates in the law of the Lord day and night will prosper (Psalm 1:2). David prayed, "Let the words of my mouth, and the meditation of my heart, be acceptable in thy sight, O LORD, my strength, and my redeemer" (Psalm 19:14).

This kind of prayer is necessary because the fall of man corrupted man's thoughts. Thus Isaiah declared, "Let the wicked forsake his way, and the unrighteous man his thoughts. . . . For my thoughts are not your thoughts, neither are your ways my ways, saith the LORD. For as the heavens are higher than the earth, so are my ways higher than your ways, and my thoughts than your thoughts" (Isaiah 55:7-9).

The corrupting influence of the Fall on man's thoughts is so pronounced that even the new birth does not totally reverse it immediately. The new birth reverses the damage done to our spirit (John 3:6), but it does not instantaneously transform our thought patterns. This is why it was necessary for Paul to write to the church at Rome, "And be not conformed to this world: but be ye transformed by the renewing of your mind, that ye may prove what is that good, and acceptable, and perfect, will of God" (Romans 12:2). Unsaved people walk "in the vanity of their mind" (Ephesians 4:17), but Christians must "be renewed in the spirit of [their] mind" (Ephesians 4:23). The ultimate expression of the Christian mind, which each Christian should reach for, is the mind of Christ (Philippians 2:5).

Verse 2. The person who has begun to hide the Word in his heart is prepared to take the third step toward understanding and knowledge: to incline his ear to wisdom. Inclining the ear alludes to the physical act of turning or leaning in the direction of the speaker, the better to hear his words. This action indicates that the student is making a decision to receive wisdom. He is intentionally and purposefully making every effort humanly possible to hear wisdom's faintest whisper. Of course, he is to incline not only the physical ear but also the ear of the spirit. (See Revelation 2:7.) It is not strange to speak of inclining an ear toward the inanimate entity of wisdom when we remember that wisdom is personified as a woman and that wisdom speaks through the Word of God.

The Word of God is spirit and life (John 6:63). God cannot be separated from His Word. (See John 1:1-2, 14.) It is not that the Word has a life of its own; it has the very life of God in it. "For the word of God is quick, and powerful, and sharper than any twoedged sword, piercing even to the dividing asunder of soul and spirit, and of the joints and marrow, and is a discerner of the thoughts and intents of the heart" (Hebrews 4:12). This verse attributes the following qualities to the Word: (1) It is quick (alive); (2) It is powerful; (3) It is sharper than the sharpest sword; (4) It pierces in such a keen and precise way as to distinguish between the soul and spirit and the joints and marrow; (5) It discerns the thoughts and intents of the heart. These qualities help us understand why the Word is something to which we must incline our ear. We must purposefully listen to wisdom as she speaks to us from the Word.

The fourth rung up the ladder is applying the heart to understanding. The word *heart* is often used in Scripture as a synonym for *mind.* Just as the student must purposefully incline his ear to wisdom, so must he purposefully apply his heart, or mind, to understanding. He must consciously, intentionally, relentlessly apply himself to the pursuit of understanding.

Verse 3. The practical aspect to his pursuit is seen in the following steps. The fifth thing the student must do is cry after knowledge. It would be a mistake to dismiss this phrase as mere symbolism. True knowledge is not just a dusty accumulation of facts. If it were, it would certainly be foolish and useless to cry after it literally; doing so would be as unrewarding as standing in the midst of the public library while calling aloud for all the knowledge residing in the books to come. But true knowledge is also spiritual in nature. It is the knowledge of God. Therefore the student must literally cry out in prayer for knowledge. "If any of you lack wisdom, let him ask of God, that giveth to all men liberally, and upbraideth not; and it shall be given him. But let him ask in faith, nothing wavering. For he that wavereth is like a wave of the sea driven with the wind and tossed. For let not that man think that he shall receive any thing of the Lord. A double minded man is unstable in all his ways" (James 1:5-8).

Not only is the student to cry out for knowledge, he is to lift up his voice for understanding, which is the sixth rung up the ladder. Just as he prays for knowledge, so he is to pray for understanding.

Verse 4. The next two steps make it clear that the promise of James does not mean that God will respond to a prayer for wisdom by pouring it into one's mind as with a funnel, but that He will so order a person's diligent search that wisdom will be found. The seventh step is to seek knowledge and understanding as one would seek silver. The eighth step is similar: the student must search for knowledge and understanding as he would search for hidden treasure.

The diligence needed to seek out knowledge and understanding is evident in the methods of a trained and disciplined treasure hunter. He does not just set out aimlessly, going first in one direction and then another in hopes of finding treasure in obvious places. He researches legends and history; he examines maps with meticulous care. He outfits himself with the proper equipment. When he finds the treasure he does not treat it carelessly; he has made provision for its protection and safekeeping. Understanding and knowledge are of far greater value than gold and rubies (Proverbs 20:15), and they must be sought with equivalent care.

Verse 5. The key word of verse 5 is the first word: *then.* The student will understand the fear of the Lord and find the knowledge of God only by taking the eight steps.

There are at least twenty-four benefits of fearing the Lord. The fear of the Lord enables us to (1) overcome sinful habits (Proverbs 16:6); (2) begin learning knowledge (Proverbs 1:7); (3) start being wise (Proverbs 9:10); (4) have a longer life (Proverbs 10:27); (5) discover the fountain of life (Proverbs 14:27); (6) learn contentment (Proverbs 15:16; (7) grow in wisdom (Proverbs 15:33); (8) get riches, honor, and life (Proverbs 22:4); (9) participate in true worship (Psalm 5:7); (10) have no want (Psalm 34:9); (11) experience God's salvation (Psalm 85:9); (12) receive daily provision (Psalm 111:5); (13) experience strong confidence (Proverbs 14:26); (14) have a satisfying life (Proverbs 19:23); (15) share the secrets of the Lord (Psalm 25:14); (16) experience God's goodness (Psalm 31:19); (17) have constant protection (Psalm 33:18-19); (18) be delivered from trouble (Psalm 34:7); (19) be looked to for truthfulness (Psalm 60:4); (20) receive a spiritual heritage (Psalm 61:5); (21) be given God's mercy (Psalm 103:11); (22) have the Lord's pity (Psalm 103:13); (23) bring delight to the Lord (Psalm 147:11); (24) become a special treasure of God (Malachi 3:16-17).[1]

There are at least eleven consequences of not fearing the Lord. Where there is no fear of the Lord, there is no (1) restraint of evil (Romans 3:10-18); (2) effective church discipline (Acts 5:5; I Timothy 5:20); (3) guard against false church members (Acts 5:11-13); (4) perfecting of holiness (II Corinthians 7:1); (5) scriptural submission (Ephesians 5:21); (6) maturity in salvation (Philippians 2:12-13); (7) entering into God's rest (Hebrews 4:1); (8) influence on unsaved husbands (I Peter 3:1-2); (9) effective witnessing (I Peter 3:15); (10) fulfilling of godly desires (Psalm 145:19); and (11) effective ministry to the lost (Jude 23).[2]

There are two aspects of the knowledge of God: (1) knowing Him and (2) knowing what He knows. The knowledge of the holy is equated with understanding (Proverbs 9:10). The lack of knowledge darkens counsel (Job 38:2). The lack of knowledge is destructive (Hosea 4:6).

The entire sacrificial system of the law of Moses was designed to give people a knowledge of God. But the people became more enamoured with the system than with the God who gave it. God is disappointed when His children major in minors and minor in majors (Hosea 6:6).

Jesus accused the lawyers of taking away the key of knowledge (Luke 11:52). Knowledge is a key. This means it is essential; it must be used to open the door to a relationship with God. The knowledge of God will never be exhausted by humanity (Romans 11:33-36). But God wants to use His children to distribute His knowledge (II Corinthians 2:14). Our enemy is everything that exalts itself against the knowledge of God (II Corinthians 10:4-5).

All the treasures of wisdom and knowledge are hidden in Christ (Colossians 2:3). Knowledge is a treasure. We are to grow not only in grace, but in the knowledge of our Lord and Savior, Jesus Christ (II Peter 3:18). Every person has some level of the knowledge of God (Romans 1:20-21). The ultimate result of rejecting this knowledge is to be given over to a reprobate mind (Romans 1:28).

We should pray faithfully for God to give us the spirit of wisdom and revelation in the knowledge of Him (Ephesians 1:17). One of the chief purposes of the gift ministries is to bring the church to the knowledge of the Son of God (Ephesians 4:13). We should also pray that we would increase in the knowledge of God (Colossians 1:10).

When a person is born again, he is renewed in knowledge after the image of God (Colossians 3:10). Grace and peace come to us through the knowledge of God (II Peter 1:2). All things that pertain to life and godliness come to us through the knowledge of Him (II Peter 1:3). The knowledge of God in us should produce fruitfulness

(II Peter 1:8), and it is through the knowledge of the Lord that we escape the pollutions of the world (II Peter 2:20).

The Scripture has much more to say about the importance and nature of knowledge, but these things are sufficient to show us the importance of diligently taking the eight steps that lead to understanding the fear of the Lord and finding the knowledge of God.

God is the source of wisdom, knowledge, and understanding (verse 6). There is no other ultimate source. Christians should reject the myth that truth can be divided into two separate categories of secular and sacred. All truth is ultimately of God. Regardless of the academic discipline, truth is rooted in God Himself.

This understanding has profound implications for Christians in every field. "Christians are committed to understanding . . . information as it really is in light of God's revelation, and non-Christians are committed to misconstruing the world in terms of their allegiance to independence. . . . Whether in psychology, biology, history, mathematics, philosophy, theology . . . the facts of the science are understood differently by Christians and non-Christians."[3]

Whether revealed in God's Word, through His creation, or in the hearts of people, all truth finds its source in God.

God is the giver of wisdom and our defender (verse 7). Those who are righteous may be certain that God has sound wisdom (as opposed to human wisdom) reserved for them. Those who walk uprightly may be sure He will be a buckler to them. The buckler was a type of shield, a piece of defensive armor. It was made of wood, covered with skin or leather, strengthened with plates of metal, and worn on the left arm. In the middle of the buckler was a protrusion that was useful in causing stones and darts to glance off. The buckler was often four feet long and covered the whole body.[4]

God is the keeper of paths and the preserver of ways (verse 8). The person who follows the Lord does not need to worry about his future. God is in control. The believer will discover that God makes no apologies for dealing with His children differently from those who reject Him (Exodus 11:7).

Another benefit of taking the eight steps (verse 9). Not only will the eight steps outlined in verses 1-4 result in the student's understanding the fear of the Lord and finding the knowledge of God, but they will lead to an understanding of righteousness, judgment, equity—indeed, everything good.

The results of wisdom and knowledge (verses 10-22). Lest the student think that the blessings of wisdom and knowledge are merely mental, Solomon listed the practical results of these qualities. Wisdom cannot be head knowledge only; it must enter into the heart. It must become a part of the person. And one's relationship with knowledge cannot be merely academic; it must be pleasant to his soul. He must love knowledge.

The first result (verse 11). The first benefit of wisdom and knowledge is preservation. Discretion here means sagacity, which is quickness or acuteness of discernment or penetration; readiness of apprehension; the faculty of readily discerning and distinguishing ideas and of separating truth from falsehood. It will keep an individual from making destructive mistakes. Understanding, which is defined in Scripture as departing from evil (Job 28:28), will also work to keep a person from being destroyed.

The second result (verse 12). Solomon had already warned his son against being enticed by sinners (1:10). Here he told him that the way to avoid being enticed by the evil and froward person is to gain wisdom and knowledge. The word *froward* means "perverse, that is, turning from, with aversion or reluctance; not willing to yield or comply with what is required; unyielding, ungovernable; disobedient; peevish" (Webster). Wisdom and knowledge will enable a person to detect the error in the evil person's way and words.

The first characteristic of the evil person (verse 13). There is no middle ground between good and evil. A person either walks in the light or in the darkness. (See Matthew 7:13-14; I John 1:6-7.)

The second characteristic of the evil person (verse 14). An evil person can be easily identified by what delights him, by the things in which he rejoices. This is the exact opposite of love's characteristic (I Corinthians 13:6).

The third characteristic of the evil person (verse 15). The evil person's ways (motives) are crooked, and his deeds (paths) are perverse.

The third result (verse 16). Wisdom and knowledge will not only deliver from the evil man, but also from the strange woman. The "strange woman" can be a literal woman who entices to evil, or she may be a figurative representation of spiritual folly in contrast to wisdom.

Flattery is *the first characteristic of the strange woman.* Flattery means "false praise; commendation bestowed for the purpose of gaining favor and influence, or to accomplish some purpose" (Webster). (See Psalm 12:3; Proverbs 20:19; 29:5.)

The second characteristic of the strange woman (verse 17). She forsakes the guide of her youth, or in other words, the husband she married while young.

The third characteristic of the strange woman is that she forgets the covenant she made with God earlier in her life. At some point she made a covenant with God to remain pure, to live according to God's principles. Marriage is certainly a holy covenant. When a woman forgets her marriage covenant and forsakes the godly training she had when young, she becomes a "strange woman."

The strange woman's house is on an incline (verse 18). The man who visits a strange woman has taken the first step downward to death and destruction. To walk to her house he must leave the paths of righteousness, the plain path, the even way. The paths that lead to and from her house are deadly paths. (See Proverbs 6:32-35.)

The deadly grip of the strange woman (verse 19). Nothing short of a miracle from God can redeem an individual who yields to the temptation of a strange woman. It is not within human power to break the viselike grip of moral impurity. The man who walks on the paths of death finds it quite impossible to step over into the paths of life. Only the miracle of redemption can help him.

A better way to walk (verse 20). Only through wisdom and knowledge can a man walk with good men and keep to the righteous paths.

The divergent destinies of the upright and the wicked (verses 21-22). Though circumstances may temporarily indicate otherwise, we may be certain that, in the final analysis, the upright will receive the promises of God and the wicked will be rejected by Him.

Notes

[1]See *The Overlooked Requirements for Riches, Honor, and Life,* supp. alum. vol. 13 (Oak Brook, Ill.: Institute in Basic Youth Conflict, 1987).

[2]See ibid.

[3]Richard L. Pratt, Jr., *Every Thought Captive* (Phillipsburg, NJ: Presbyterian and Reformed Publishing Company, 1979), 59-60.

[4]See *Webster's Dictionary,* facsimile edition; 1928 (Anaheim, CA: Foundation for American Christian Education, 1967), s.v. "buckler."

Chapter Three

An appeal to remember (verse 1). In order to not forget the law, study and memorization is necessary. Keeping the commandments in one's heart seems to speak of meditation.

Three benefits of obedience (verse 2). The first blessing of obedience is length of days, which seems to speak of the quality of life. The second blessing is long life. The third blessing is peace. People attempt to obtain these blessings by counterfeit currency, but they can be obtained only by careful attention and obedience to the Word of God.

Mercy and truth, in that order (verse 3). Mercy without truth would have no standards within which to operate. Truth without mercy is hard and unbending. (See Psalm 57:3; 61:7; 85:10.) Even judgment must be tempered by mercy (James 2:13). Mercy and truth must balance and complement each other. They must be so closely held as to be bound around one's neck or written on his heart.

The result of balancing mercy and truth (verse 4). The approval of God is our utmost concern. Even the study of the Scriptures must be approached from the balanced position of mercy and truth. God cannot approve a deficiency in either area. The result of a balance in mercy and truth is that both God and man will be favorable toward those who have found that balance.

Which way do we lean? (verse 5). We will either "lean" on the Lord by trusting in Him with all our heart, or we will lean on our own understanding. There is no middle ground. Verse 5 is an appeal to reject humanism; we must not walk by our feelings, or by what seems right to us. (See Proverbs 14:12.)

How to have God direct our paths (verse 6). We should acknowledge God in *all* our ways. Instead of falling for the myth that life can be divided into the secular and the sacred, we should submit every area of life to the lordship of Jesus Christ.

Refusing to think we are wise (verse 7). When we begin to think that we are wise, then we have taken the first step to deception. We must never put confidence in our own ability. Instead, we must keep walking in the fear of the Lord and keep departing from evil.

The promise of health (verse 8). A life lived in total submission to the Lord is physically and spiritually beneficial. Conversely, a life lived without regard to the Lord is physically and spiritually detrimental.

The promise of provision (verses 9-10). Our substance is our possessions, all that we own. We should use everything we have in a way that brings glory to the Lord. We should honor the Lord in the way we use our home, automobile, clothing, everything. We should specifically give the firstfruits of all our increase, or the tithe, to Him. (See Genesis 4:4; 14:20; 28:22; Exodus 13:2; Numbers 3:13; Deuteronomy 26; I Kings 17:13; Malachi 3:8-12; I Corinthians 9:13-14; Philippians 4:10-19.) If we seek God first, He will supply our needs (Matthew 6:33), and as a general principle, when we follow God's plan of giving we can expect blessings even in this life.

God's purpose in correcting His children (verses 11-12). Permissiveness is not love. As Dr. James Dobson says, "Love must be tough." If we can understand God's motive in chastening us, it will help us not to despise His chastening and not to be weary of His correction. God chastens His children because He loves them, just as a wise and loving father disciplines the son in whom he delights. Loving parents do not discipline their children to hurt them or to keep them from having fun. They discipline them because of the inherent danger of unwise acts and in order to develop in them the character necessary to be strong adults.

None of God's sons is exempt from chastisement (Hebrews 12:5-11). While the "fathers of our flesh" basically corrected us with respect to our physical life, God is the "Father of spirits" and His discipline is primarily concerned with our spirits. One of the major instruments God uses in His discipline of the human spirit is the Word of God, which is spirit and life (John 6:63).

One of the chief aims of God's discipline is that we might be partakers of His holiness (Hebrews 12:10). When a person receives discipline in the right way, with the right spirit, though it is painful temporarily, in the long run it will produce the "peaceable fruit of righteousness" (Hebrews 12:11). Chastening and learning go hand-in-hand (Psalm 94:12). Though God may "break some bones" in the process of discipline, the proper response to His discipline will result in those bones, now healed and stronger than before the breaking, "rejoicing" (Psalm

51:8). The psalmist recognized that, in the long run, it was good for him to be afflicted, for it resulted in his learning God's statutes (Psalm 119:71). Our response to God's chastisement should be, "Turn me, Lord; change me." (See Jeremiah 31:18.)

Sometimes in the process of discipline, especially if a person refuses to respond to God's attempts to accomplish His purposes, it will become necessary for Him to chasten "with the rod of men" (II Samuel 7:14). Many times God will use other people and circumstances in an effort to bring about change in us.

Parents can learn many lessons about the proper discipline of children by studying the manner in which God disciplines His children. (See Deuteronomy 8:5.) Love, rather than anger, produces the desired result in discipline. (See Psalm 6:1.) And though the Lord's chastisement may be painful, it will not extend to death to those who have a heart after Him (Psalm 118:18).

The source of true happiness (verse 13). Genuine happiness, not temporary thrills or pleasure, comes to the person who finds wisdom and understanding. This truth helps us appreciate the true value of wisdom and understanding. They bring lasting happiness to the human condition, which nothing materialistic can do.

Wisdom and understanding are profitable (verse 14). The Hebrew word translated "merchandise" speaks specifically of profit. Gold and silver, the two most precious metals in the ancient world, are a poor second and third to the value of wisdom and understanding. There is always a market for wisdom and understanding, even in the secular world. People who have these qualities are in demand everywhere. Those who possess them will never find themselves on the shelf.

The greatest desire (verse 15). Nothing we can think of is worth more than wisdom and understanding.

The relative value of wisdom's three blessings (verse 16). The three blessings of wisdom are length of days, riches, and honor. Length of days seems to mean the quality of life. (See verse 2.) It is the most important of the three blessings, for it is pictured as being in wisdom's right hand. In Scripture, the right hand is the preeminent place, the place of greatest honor and power. Riches and honor are held in wisdom's left hand.

Pleasant ways and peaceful paths (verse 17). Where there is wisdom, there will be pleasantness and peace. Wisdom never results in strife and contention. "Only by pride cometh contention: but with the well advised is wisdom" (Proverbs 13:10). (See James 3:13-4:1.)

Wisdom is a tree of life (verse 18). The first mention of the tree of life is in Genesis 2:9. (See also Genesis 3:22-24.) If the tree of the knowledge of good and evil represents sinful choices and carnal "wisdom," possibly the tree of life represents true, spiritual wisdom. It is necessary to "lay hold" on wisdom and to "retain" her. Fallen human nature tends toward ignorance and folly; a disciplined effort to pursue and retain godly wisdom is necessary.

Even God used wisdom (verse 19). If wisdom and understanding were useful to God Himself in creation, surely they will be useful to us in dealing with the everyday affairs of life. In fact, by the proper use of wisdom, we can "create" good things as well.

The true identity of "nature" (verse 20). What humans call "nature" is really God's knowledge at work. Unfortunately, to a large degree, modern science is an attempt to discover the secrets of "nature" without the key of God's wisdom.

More benefits of wisdom and discretion (verses 21-26). When wisdom and discretion are retained, they produce life, grace, safety, absence of fear, rest, and confidence.

Giving others their due (verse 27). We are responsible for the payment of our debts. But there are other debts we owe besides money. When we have the ability to do so, we are to perform good for those to whom it is due. We owe honor to the elders who labor in the Word and doctrine (I Timothy 5:17). We owe tribute, custom, fear, and honor to human governments (Romans 13:7-8).

Don't postpone neighborly help (verse 28). Societies are strengthened when neighbors feel a strong obligation to one another. Instead of merely decrying the general decay of neighborliness, we should be willing to take steps to correct that problem with those who live around us. (See Matthew 5:42.)

Don't seek to harm a neighbor (verse 29). Neighbors must support and protect one another. A person who protects and helps his neighbor will find ultimately that he is strengthening his own position, but someone who devises evil against his neighbor will find that he is hurting himself. (See Proverbs 26:27.)

Don't contend with someone without cause (verse 30). (See also Psalm 15:3; Matthew 5:22; James 5:9.) We should not provoke a quarrel or cause strife. Moreover, it is foolish and dangerous to involve ourselves in strife that has nothing to do with us. Not infrequently, third parties will think, If I will step into this situation, I can resolve it. But just as frequently, the third party will discover that he incurs the wrath of the two who are in disagreement. His involvement unites the two who were formerly antagonists. (See Proverbs 26:17.)

Don't follow the example of those who oppress others (verse 31). When we hear of how others have profited by taking advantage of people, we may be tempted to do the same, but we must resist this temptation. For example, a man may boast that he made extra profit by substituting inferior, cheap materials for the quality he agreed to install. Another may "pull a fast one" under the theory that what people do not know won't hurt them. But the Lord feels very keenly about the oppression of people by people. (See Psalm 62:10; James 5:1-6.) He desires for everyone to live by the Golden Rule (Matthew 7:12). He gave the parable of the Good Samaritan to illustrate how we are to treat others (Luke 10:25-37).

God's response to the perverse and the righteous (verse 32). God abhors the froward. The word *froward* means perverse, that is, turning from, with aversion or reluctance; not willing to yield or comply with what is required; unyielding; ungovernable; refractory; disobedient; peevish. On the other hand, God is so intimately close to the righteous that He even shows them His secrets.

Is our home blessed or cursed (verse 33)? The blessings and cursings of the Lord are specified in Deuteronomy 28. The wicked is cursed, but the righteous is blessed. Thus, a just person need not worry about someone putting a curse on him or his home. That it is impossible for Satan to curse what God has blessed is illustrated in the story of Balaam (Numbers 22-24).

God responds to people according to their attitudes (verse 34). God deals with people on the basis of the way they respond to Him. The greatest secret to being blessed and used by God is to have humility; the greatest hindrance to being blessed and used by God is pride. James 4:6 and I Peter 5:5 quote this verse.

The results of wisdom and foolishness (verse 35). We should not look at others and declare their fortunes or misfortunes to be the result of the mythical Lady Luck. There is a law of cause and effect. Ultimately, the spiritual will receive glory, while spiritual fools will receive shame.

Chapter Four

Education is primarily the father's responsibility (verses 1-2). God holds the father responsible for the education of his children. Throughout both testaments, education was home-centered. While ancient Israel did develop elementary schools for boys, these schools were conducted often in the synagogues and depended upon the fathers to supply their student body and their financial support. The teachers actually served the homes; the school was an extension of the values and beliefs taught in the homes. The decline of educational quality in the United States of America began when the influence of the home and the church was minimized.

Solomon, the son of David and Bathsheba (verse 3). The son born of the adulterous relationship between David and Bathsheba died; Solomon was the next son born to them. The gladness and joy with which Solomon mentions his father and mother indirectly illustrates that God does not hold a child responsible for his parent's sins and that both David and Bathsheba had been forgiven by God and were fully restored to an honorable position.

Solomon's teacher (verse 4). Evidently David taught Solomon personally. He made certain that he fulfilled his responsibility to instruct his son in spiritual wisdom.

David's curriculum when teaching Solomon (verse 5).
The curriculum used by David to instruct his son was simple: wisdom and understanding. He did not explore humanistic theories or situation ethics. He taught him the truth, as resident in God Himself. Without wisdom and understanding, "education" is dangerous.

Wisdom will do what a diploma will not (verse 6).
Wisdom will *preserve* and *keep* a person. Book learning or degrees from educational institutions are no substitute for wisdom. Even in an economic sense, employers seek workers who have wisdom and understanding. They need trustworthy, creative, understanding employees, not merely people who have degrees or diplomas.

The most important thing in the world (verse 7).
Wisdom—seeing life from God's point of view—is more important than anything else. The chief aim of our "getting" should not be money, prestige, or fame, but wisdom. Wisdom will bring with her all that is worthwhile.

The source of promotion and honor (verse 8). When a person puts wisdom first, when he is so intimately involved with wisdom that he can be said to "embrace" her, she will reciprocate by giving promotion and honor. Ultimately, promotion is not a matter of luck or having the right connections; it is the result of having the right attitude toward wisdom.

Wisdom's "cap and gown" (verse 9). When a graduate participates in commencement exercises, he wears a cap and gown that indicates his level of achievement. When wisdom is exalted, she gives an "ornament of grace" and a "crown of glory." Grace is the desire and power to do the will of God. The wise person will grow in grace. As his level of wisdom grows, so will his desire and power to do God's will. The wise person will also be held in high esteem by those whose opinions matter.

The secret to a long life (verse 10). Like the fifth commandment, the admonition to hear one's father and to receive his sayings is accompanied by the promise of long life. (See Exodus 20:12; Ephesians 6:1-3.) The reason such a promise can be made is that obedience to parental authority will save a son or daughter from many foolish and disastrous mistakes, both natural and spiritual, that take lives and shorten lifespans.

Different ways; different paths (verse 11). There is a "way of wisdom" to follow and "right paths" to take. Clearly, there must also be a "way of ignorance" and "wrong paths," but neither David nor Solomon thought it necessary to teach error in order to equip their sons to deal with it. They taught what was right. When truth only is taught, error is readily recognized when it presents itself.

Wisdom provides a firm, solid footing (verse 12). The word *straitened* means "made tense, tight, narrow, confining." When a person walks in wisdom, he will not stumble through life, lurching from one failure to another. He will not feel pressured, tense, and confined. He will have liberty, freedom, and joy.

Instruction is life (verse 13). Many people develop such a distaste for instruction that they cannot wait to stop learning. But instruction is life! Life is a great learning process, a vast school. The person who stops learning will find himself frustrated and thwarted, with a sense of aimlessness and purposelessness.

A lesson from wisdom (verse 14). A wise person will not walk the same path as evil people. Not only is there the danger of guilt by association, but there is also the detrimental influence of the ungodly. (See Psalm 1:1.) This admonition does not imply that we should not attempt to win evil people to the Lord; it rather prohibits our uniting with them for common purposes that could lead us into evil. (See II Corinthians 6:14-18.)

Stay as far away from evil as possible (verse 15). Not only is the wise person not to walk on the path of the wicked, he is to avoid it totally; he is not even to walk by it. One of Eve's first mistakes was getting close enough to the forbidden tree to carry on a conversation with the serpent. (See Proverbs 14:7; Romans 13:14; Ephesians 4:27.)

How to discern a wicked person (verse 16). The wicked and evil person does not feel his day is complete unless he has perpetrated some kind of mischief. He especially delights in causing some innocent person to fall into sin.

The contrast between the wicked and the just (verses 17-18). Wickedness and violence characterize the lifestyle of evil people. On the other hand, those who are just are continually growing in God. Day by day, they see things more clearly, they learn more about His Word, and they desire to be more like Him. The phrase "shining more and more unto the perfect day" refers to the manner in which the day grows constantly brighter until noon. At the earliest hours of morning, only the vaguest shapes and outlines may be seen. But as the morning progresses, these things take on more definition until they can finally be seen in their greatest detail. Similarly, the just person sees more clearly every day; he understands more and more what God is doing in his life. He walks more perfectly as he goes along.

Ignorance of the cause-and-effect relationship (verse

19). While the just person sees more clearly all the time, the wicked walk in black darkness. Their path is so dark they do not even know what is causing them to stumble. They do not recognize the law of sowing and reaping. They fail to see the connection between their previous actions and the resulting circumstances.

Purposeful attention (verse 20). In an entertainment oriented society, many have the idea that something must be entertaining to be worthy of attention. This is of course not true. Some of the things that are most entertaining to the eye and ear are the least worthy of attention, while often what is least entertaining is most important. The point of this verse is that paying attention is a choice. One can discipline himself to be attentive to anything he chooses.

Reading, memorizing, meditating (verse 21). Words of wisdom should regularly be read ("Let them not depart from thine eyes") and memorized and meditated upon ("Keep them in the midst of thine heart").

Words of life and health (verse 22). The words of wisdom are more than human words. They possess life. (See John 6:63.) They produce health in those who digest them. Instead of a vitamin deficiency, some people have a Word deficiency.

Protect the source of life (verse 23). It is essential to guard the heart diligently, for it determines our life. Often in Scripture, the word *heart* speaks, as it does here, of the soulish part of man: his mind, will, and emotions. The words *heart* and *mind* are often interchangeable. The importance of a disciplined, well-ordered mind can never be underestimated. (See Matthew 15:18-20; Romans 12:2; II Corinthians 10:4-5; I Peter 1:13.)

Control your words (verse 24). There is a direct relationship between a person's heart and his words. (See Matthew 12:34-35.) It is important to our spiritual life to control our speech. (See James 3.)

Control your eyes (verse 25). Many temptations enter the heart (mind) through the eye-gate. (See Job 31:1.) Literal application of this verse can be a major step to victory over moral impurity. We must learn to submit our eyes and our other members to God (Romans 6:12-19).

Look where you are going (verse 26). We should examine the path we are taking. Where does it lead? Are there any obstacles to progress? Our ways will be established only as we give great attention to our path. (See Ephesians 5:15.)

Follow the map (verse 27). We are to follow the words of wisdom exactly, without improvising or looking for a shortcut. The Bible is a divine, infallible, inerrant road map. It charts the precise course to life, health, happiness, and heaven. Those who follow it will never be lost. Those who ignore it will never be saved.

Chapter Five

The need for purposeful attention restated (verse 1). Repeatedly the Book of Proverbs appeals for purposeful attention. (See 2:2; 3:1; 4:20; 7:1.) This admonition emphasizes the necessity of a disciplined effort to grasp what might otherwise be overlooked. A New Testament parallel is the repeated invitation: "He that hath an ear, let him hear what the Spirit saith unto the churches" (Revelation 2:7, 11, 17, 29; 3:6, 13, 22).

The result of purposeful attention (verse 2). The aim of the repeated appeal to be attentive to wisdom and understanding is that the student will regard discretion and his lips will keep knowledge. The proper attitude toward discretion and knowledge will come only to the person who has first disciplined himself to listen carefully to wisdom and understanding.

A person's lips should keep knowledge, which implies the importance not just of knowing truth but of speaking it. The Book of Proverbs has a great deal to say about the significance of words. They can be a blessing or a curse, both to the one speaking them and to those who hear him. (See 10:19; 14:23; 18:8, 21; 21:23; 26:20.) Of course, many other books of the Bible address the same subject. (See Ecclesiastes 5:3; Matthew 12:36-37; Titus 1:10; James 1:26.)

The seeming sweetness of temptation (verse 3). The remainder of this chapter deals with the danger of yielding to moral impurity. While this is a warning about literal temptation to physical involvement, it is also an allusion to the temptation of spiritual folly in general, with folly pictured as an immoral woman just as wisdom is pictured as a virtuous woman.

The first warning is against the immoral woman's use of words. (See 6:24.) She is a master of flattery, of smooth words. She is a liar, and she will say anything necessary to seduce her victim. She has no commitment to the truth. Her temptations seem to be very desirable.

The bitterness of sin (verse 4). The attractiveness of temptation contrasts sharply to the actual result of yielding. Yielding to temptation is deadly.

The result of sin is death (verse 5). (See Romans 6:23; James 1:14-15.) The immoral woman is headed in the direction of death and hell. The man who is seduced by her joins her in her journey.

Sin cannot be rationalized (verse 6). Some people with analytical minds think that they can study sin sufficiently so as to participate in it without reaping its bitter reward. They tell themselves that they will participate in it until just before the moment of destruction, until just before it is too late, and then they will get out of it. But this is not the way sin works. Its course cannot be charted; it cannot be put on a graph. It is slippery and deceptive. There is only one safe way to deal with temptation, and that is revealed in the following two verses.

Stay as far away from sin as possible (verses 7-8). The only safe thing to do is to remain totally faithful to the words of wisdom and to stay as far away from temptation as possible. One should not approach the door of temptation's house even out of curiosity. Eve may never have had a problem with the tree of the knowledge of good and evil had she stayed completely away from it. The serpent tempted her as she approached the tree.

The consequences of moral impurity (verses 9-11). If a person is tempted with moral impurity, he should write these six consequences on a card and carry it with him. When he is tempted, he should review these results of yielding to temptation: (1) loss of honor, reputation, respectability, and dignity; (2) shortened life, and trouble while alive; (3) loss of wealth to others; (4) loss of the fruits of labor to others; (5) sorrow; and (6) physical disease.

One of the most remarkable and frightening aspects of the physical results of moral impurity today is Acquired Immune Deficiency Syndrome (AIDS). World health officials, including U.S. Surgeon General Koop, estimated that about one hundred million people worldwide will die from AIDS before the disease has run its course.

Bitter regret, too late (verses 12-14). The cry of the person who reaps the bitter results of moral impurity is, "Why didn't I listen?" The way to avoid this dilemma is to do just the opposite of the example of these verses: (1) love instruction; (2) love reproof; (3) obey teachers; (4) incline the ear to those who instruct.

It is not uncommon for the immoral to take great delight in committing their wickedness in the presence of those who are saved; it seems to heighten their perverse pleasure. They love to shock the sensibilities of others. But this action is one of the very things they mourn later in life.

Don't be deceived by the myth of the greener grass (verse 15). This verse and those that follow stress the importance of turning one's attention to one's lawful companion. If a man will forget about the other man's cistern and well and give up trying to sneak a drink from them, he will find his own cistern and well are fully satisfying.

Tend to your own fountains (verses 16-17). These verses may refer to the offspring of lawful relationships: children. There should be no doubt as to the parentage of one's children; the marriage relationship should not be complicated and contaminated by the involvement of strangers.

Rejoice with your wife (verse 18). A man should forget about other possible romantic relationships and concentrate on developing the fullest relationship with his lawful mate. (See Ecclesiastes 9:9.)

Satisfy yourself with legitimate love (verse 19). God created man and woman to enjoy a full relationship spiritually, socially, and physically. There is nothing wrong with the marital relationship and its physical dimension. (See I Corinthians 7:3-5; Hebrews 13:4.)

What purpose is served by moral impurity (verse 20)? When a satisfying relationship is possible in a fully legitimate way, why would someone turn from his lawful companion to develop a furtive, fruitless, and frustrating relationship with another?

The Lord observes all we do (verse 21). "The eyes of the LORD are in every place, beholding the evil and the good" (Proverbs 15:3). God's knowledge is complete; He is omniscient. (See Psalm 139:1-12.) Everyone will one day stand before Him to answer for the deeds done in the body (Romans 2:6; Revelation 20:12).

The sinner brings about his own death (verse 22). People die spiritually for their own sins, not the sins of others. It is impossible for someone to escape the results of his sin, unless he confesses and forsakes it. (See Proverbs 28:13.)

The final result of sin (verse 23). The sin described here started by listening to the smooth and sweet words of a strange woman, but it ends with death. Without instruction, people die. The ultimate consequence of spiritual folly is destruction.

Chapter Six

The dangers of co-signing (verses 1-5). Several passages in Proverbs warn against surety. (See also 11:15; 17:18.) The definition of *surety* is, in law, "one that is bound with and for another; one who enters into a bond or recognizance to answer for another's appearance in court, or for his payment of a debt or for the performance of some act, and who, in case of the principal debtor's failure, is compellable to pay the debt or damages; a bondsman; a bail" (Webster). The Hebrew word translated "surety" is *arab,* which means "to braid, i.e. intermix; also to give or be security." The person who is a surety involves himself with the life of another in the same way that strands of a rope are braided together. These and other verses in Proverbs warn against being a guarantor or security for someone else's debts.

The most common way of being a guarantor today is co-signing. This practice is dangerous because a lender that requires a co-signer is indicating that the borrower is possibly not in a sound enough financial position to pay the debt. In other words, he is possibly borrowing beyond his means. The lender is saying, "We are not confident that he is qualified to pay the debt." The one who co-signs is in the final sense himself the lender.

Thus, according to Proverbs, co-signing for an unlimited amount, for an amount beyond one's means, or for an uncertain future amount is wrong. (See Proverbs 22:26-27.) It appears that co-signing for a limited amount is appropriate only if one is genuinely willing and able to loan this amount of money and, if necessary, to pay it and consider it as a gift, with no regrets.

It is not a sin to loan or borrow money (See Matthew 5:42; 25:27). Of course, the law of Moses prohibited people from charging interest on loans to their brethren or to the poor, and it limited loans to about six years.

In short, co-signing can be a dangerous snare. Being a guarantor is so dangerous that Solomon recommended a formula for extricating oneself. The first step to take is to humble oneself, which implies an admission of folly or wrongdoing, and plead with the friend for release. The second step is to refuse sleep until the matter is resolved. Tomorrow could bring disaster; it should be taken care of today. The third step is to escape as an animal would from a hunter by cancelling the agreement if possible or by otherwise limiting liability. If the person for whom one co-signs defaults on the loan, the co-signer will be the hunted.

The example of the ant (verse 6). Lazy people can learn from the example of the ant. The ant is mentioned only twice in the Old Testament, here and in Proverbs 30:25. The Scripture uses many illustrations from the animal kingdom, for we can learn valuable lessons from God's creation. The ants, for example, operate purely by God-given instinct. Humans also have instruction from God, but they often subordinate it by laziness and carelessness. The lesson for the sluggard is that the ant provides for her needs by industrious work and wise storing in reserve, and she does not have to borrow unwisely or depend upon the work of others.

No employer, no supervisor, no training (verse 7). The ant has no guide, no one to train her to do her job. She has no overseer, no supervisor to tell her what to do and to make sure she has done what she should. She has no ruler, no employer to whom she must ultimately answer. How much would the average person accomplish if he had none of these? People have abundant opportunity to make wise use of the counsel of those in authority, but they often ignore it. They think they would like to be free of restraint, but if they were free, they would often resort to anarchy.

The ant works at the right time and prepares for the future (verse 8). Even though she has no one to tell her what to do and when to do it, the ant works hard at the right time and prepares for the time when no food will be available. She knows how to budget and save. She is industrious. Whenever we see the ant, she is working.

Too much sleep is a sign of sluggishness (verse 9). Sleep is not wrong, but lack of activity and industry is. The question is not, "Why do you sleep?" but "Why do you sleep so long?" (See Proverbs 13:4; 19:24; 20:4; 21:25.)

A love of sleep results in poverty (verses 10-11). Those who love sleep, those who are lazy, will fall into poverty. The implication is that poverty will overtake them as a person who travels quickly overtakes one who walks slowly, or like an armed robber.

These and other passages of Scripture teach us it is not wrong to save, but wise. Our level of spending should not automatically rise to meet the level of our income. Rather, we should set aside some of our income for future needs. Saving and paying cash for needed purchases is much wiser than borrowing, presuming on the future, and paying high interest rates.

A person's character is revealed by his words (verse 12). This truth is stated repeatedly in the Book of Proverbs and elsewhere in the Scriptures. It is possible to tell what kind of a person someone is by the words he speaks. Someone with a froward—self-willed, independent, rebellious—mouth is a worthless, wicked person.

The wicked person is deceptive (verse 13). He sends misleading, deceptive signals. For example, winking has long been a signal that one is deceiving a person and for others not to interfere. To many people today, the crossing of the fingers supposedly nullifies any promises made while they were crossed. Basically, this person does not mean what he says. He will say anything to get what he wants, but he has no intention of keeping his word.

His is a heart problem (verse 14). Since his heart is lawless, he has no reservations about doing wrong. His full-time business is planning evil or trouble. He plants discord, which God hates. (See Proverbs 6:19.)

Seven things God hates (verse 16). The wording of this verse indicates that there are fully seven things God hates, but He particularly despises the seventh.

Pride, lying, and violence (verse 17). Pride was the original sin of Lucifer. (See Isaiah 14:12-16; Ezekiel 28:11-19.) Pride the root of all sin, for it exalts self above the will of God. Pride is the first step to shame (Proverbs 11:2). It is the cause of contention (Proverbs 13:10). It is the prelude to destruction (Proverbs 16:18). It is, in itself, sin (Proverbs 21:4).

Lying is also a sin. Satan is the father of lies (John

8:44). All liars will share a common destiny with him in the lake of fire (Revelation 21:8). Those who love and make lies will share the destiny of being barred from heaven (Revelation 22:15).

The third warning is against violence, particularly against hands that shed innocent blood. God abhors murder. In the Old Testament God gave instructions concerning capital punishment (Genesis 9:5-6) and commanded Israel to war against the enemies of God on many occasions, but these were people whom He had judged guilty of violating His law and fighting against His chosen nation and plan. The warning here is against shedding innocent blood.

This is precisely the sin committed by abortionists. The blood of innocent babies runs freely in the United States of America every day, as literally thousands of them are murdered in their mothers' wombs.

Wicked thoughts and plans (verse 18). God gave us the marvelous ability to imagine, to visualize, to be creative. He hates for us to prostitute this God-given ability by devising wicked plans. The people of Noah's day did so (Genesis 6:5), and because of this intense misuse of the power of imagination, God destroyed most of the human race at that time. God has given humans the power to invent, but He hates the practice of using His gift to invent evil (Romans 1:30).

God gave people feet to be able to run to the aid of those in need and to be yielded to Him as an instrument of righteousness. (See Romans 6:13.) He hates for His gift to be perverted so that the feet carry people swiftly to do wrong.

False witness and sowing discord (verse 19). The ninth

commandment specifically prohibits the bearing of false witness against one's neighbor (Exodus 20:16). A false witness can be instrumental in convicting an innocent party, which can ultimately result in the death penalty. To protect the innocent, under the law one witness was never sufficient to condemn someone to death. Two, and preferably three, were required. (See Deuteronomy 17:6.) To further protect the innocent, even after guilt was declared, the accusers had to place their hands on the accused and declare in the presence of all the people that he was indeed the guilty party. Then the accusers had to be the first to cast the stones to put the accused to death. (See Deuteronomy 13:9.) All of these protections gave a false witness maximum opportunity to reverse his testimony. Only the most callous and hardened person could maintain a false witness through all the required developments in the trial.

To this day it is a dangerous sin to bear false witness against an innocent party. Even the secular court system demands that the witness pledge to tell the absolute truth. The person who prevaricates is himself guilty of perjury with its attendant penalties.

It is better to err on the side of mercy than on the side of judgment. Even those who have seen or heard something that seems to affix blame should be cautious, for things are not always what they seem. It is very possible to misinterpret what we see or hear.

The seventh thing God hates and the one which, by implication, He hates most of all is sowing discord among brethren. The New Testament also addresses this sin. (See Galatians 5:20; II Thessalonians 3:11; I Timothy 5:13; I Peter 4:15.) It is God's desire that people walk in harmony and unity; the person who sows discord works directly against God's plan. The most common way discord is sown is when one person tells something harmful to the reputation of another person—whether true or false—to someone who has no need or authority to hear it.

Father's commandment; mother's law (verse 20). This verse reiterates the teaching of Proverbs 1:8. The father and mother are partners in training children.

Keep them constantly in mind (verse 21). These instructions are obviously symbolic terms to describe the constant attention that should be given to the father's commandment and the mother's law. The Pharisees, by their strict literalism, attempted to fulfill similar commands in the law of Moses by physically attaching phylacteries to their forearms and foreheads when praying. But it is possible to have copies of the Scriptures attached to one's person and still not have the Word hidden in one's heart.

Three blessings of obedience to parents (verse 22). The commandment to honor and obey one's parents is not given to cramp one's lifestyle or to rob a person of legitimate pleasure. Actually, obedience to one's parents provides: (1) direction in life; (2) safety; (3) instruction, which includes a sense of belonging and a freedom from loneliness and purposelessness.

Lamp and light (verse 23). The commandment, given by the father, is like a lamp. It is the source of illumination. The law, given by the mother, is like the light that issues forth from the lamp. A lamp without light is useless, and there will never be light without a source. The lamp and the light together give reproof. Instruction will almost always involve reproof, and wise teachers know how to reprove in a nonoffensive manner (Proverbs 16:21, 24).

Submission to parents is a guard against moral impurity (verse 24). In general, before children disobey God they first disobey their parents. And disobedience to parents is generally disobedience to God also. The young person who obeys godly parents will never fall into the grievous sin of moral impurity. In contrast to their godly instruction and admonition, the evil woman uses flattery to seduce her victim.

The false beauty of immorality (verse 25). There is a beauty in holiness (Psalm 29:2). There is a false beauty in immorality, a beauty that depends on the artificial attraction of suggestive actions, seductive clothing, and makeup. *The Pulpit Commentary* says, "The eyelids are the instruments by which the amorous woman beguiles or catches her victims. She allures him by her glances. . . . Allusion may possibly be made to the custom of Eastern women painting the eyelids to give brilliancy and expression; II Kings 9:30." (See also Jeremiah 4:30; Ezekiel 23:40.) The wise man will not separate the immoral woman's "beauty" from her person; her "beauty" is simply a subterfuge to trap the unwary.

Immorality is a thief and a killer (verse 26). Immorality will gradually take from a person all he has gained, until at last he has nothing and is forced to beg even for food. The immoral person hunts, which means there is a prey. Ultimately, someone who falls to moral impurity will pay with his life. The devil is the enemy, and he will do anything possible to trap and destroy God's children. Just as a hunter stalks his prey, so does the evil one. This is not honorable warfare; it is guerrilla warfare.

The penalty for moral impurity is certain (verses

27-29). It is impossible to dabble in moral impurity and to emerge unscathed. Involvement in moral impurity is compared to fire and hot coals. It may look alluring and attractive, but once embraced it burns and destroys. The Hebrew word translated "toucheth" means to "lay a hand upon." (See I Corinthians 7:1.) The refusal to touch is a guarantee that purity will be maintained. Touching another man's wife results in the breaking down of barriers that guard against immorality.

Thievery is more honorable than sexual immorality (verses 30-31). Thievery is wrong under any circumstances. But if someone steals because he is genuinely hungry, people do not despise him, though they will make him pay with a severe penalty.

Adultery destroys (verse 32). Involvement in sexual immorality is a sign of a lack of understanding. While it may be momentarily pleasurable to the body, it is destructive to the soul.

Adultery damages permanently (verse 33). While God will forgive the sin of adultery if it is confessed and forsaken, the adulterer lives under a permanent reproach in society. While all sin brings condemnation, some sins have more severe earthly, social consequences.

Adultery invites violence (verse 34). A man who commits adultery with another man's wife sets himself up for revenge and possibly even violent death.

Nothing will appease in the case of adultery (verse 35). The man who has been sinned against cannot be paid off. No matter how many gifts are given, he will never forget his humiliation and anger until he has gotten vengeance. For example, during 1986 in the metropolitan area of Toronto, Ontario, Canada, which had a population of 3.2

million, there were thirty-seven murders, and thirty-four of them resulted from domestic problems. The person who commits adultery violates numerous scriptural passages, including those that teach the importance of protecting one's neighbor and not devising evil against him. This sin is instrumental in the breakdown of families, neighborhoods, communities, and nations. A violation of the marriage vow is a violation of the most basic foundation of society.

Chapter Seven

Keep your eye focused upon truth (verses 1-2). It is necessary to go beyond academic knowledge to actual practice: "Keep my words." The commandments should be "laid up" as one would store a valuable commodity, and then they should be kept. Those who move beyond academic knowledge to experiential knowledge will find that the commandments, when obeyed, produce life.

Bind and write (verse 3). Binding the commandments on the fingers and writing them on the heart is obvious symbolism; it is not satisfied by placing portions of Scripture in little boxes to wear on one's person. A person's fingers are generally always in front of him; thus, the Word of God should be kept always before a person. Writing the Word upon the tables of the heart speaks of meditation and memorization.

Identifying with wisdom (verse 4). It is important for a person to be closely identified with and related to wisdom and understanding. In his mind, speech, and actions he should ally himself with wisdom, saying, "Wisdom, you are my sister. Understanding, you are my kinswoman."

The right woman will keep a man from the wrong woman (verse 5). The strange woman can represent two things: (1) a literal woman who is immoral; (2) folly, in contrast to wisdom as a virtuous woman. The first step in this strange woman's attempt to seduce is flattery.

The behavior of one who lacks understanding (verses 6-7). If wisdom is not considered a sister and understanding a kinswoman, the chances are very high that a person will enter into an immoral, sinful relationship with folly.

The first mistake of an ignorant young man (verse 8). The first step in laying aside every weight and sin that so easily besets us (Hebrews 12:1) is to avoid the places, people, or circumstances that prey on one's weakness. If the young man of this passage had remembered the admonition of Proverbs 5:8 to stay far away from the immoral woman's house, he would never have fallen into her trap. If Eve had stayed away from the forbidden tree, she would never have succumbed to temptation. Temptation usually comes in cycles, and it is usually related to certain times, events, places, or people. The wise person will anticipate these temptations and avoid them to the extent possible.

Evil loves darkness (verse 9). While the evildoer foolishly thinks darkness is a cloak for his sin, he forgets that God can see just as clearly in the darkness as He can in the light. (See Psalm 139:12; John 3:19-21.)

Two signs of moral impurity (verse 10). While some scoff at the idea that one's dress is of any significance, this verse refers to specific attire that identifies a harlot. It is at the opposite end of the fashion spectrum from that of godly women. (See I Timothy 2:9-10; I Peter 3:3-4.) The key concept for godly appearance and dress is modesty. Modesty does not draw the wrong kind of attention to itself. It does not invite lustful looks. It does not provoke lewd imaginations. It is not extravagant, ostentatious, or artificial, but moderate and self-controlled. It encourages respect and wholesome admiration for one's character, rather than emphasizing merely the physical appearance.

One aspect of immodest attire is makeup, for it appeals to the lust of the flesh and lust of the eyes, seeking to create artificial "beauty" on the basis of sexual allure. Not too many years ago prostitutes and other immoral women were known euphemistically as "painted women." The source of this identification and the feeling that garish painting of the face is improper is the Holy Scriptures, which always associate the use of artificial paint in an attempt to make oneself attractive with an immoral woman. (See II Kings 9:30; Proverbs 6:25; Jeremiah 4:30; Ezekiel 23:40.) Although many women who wear makeup today do not seek to be immoral, makeup is still immodest in its emphasis, values, and effects.

The second sign of this woman's moral impurity is her subtilty of heart. Subtilty is not necessarily identical to wisdom; here it indicates craftiness. The immoral woman is a schemer who traps the unwary.

Two additional signs of moral impurity (verses 11-12). The immoral woman is loud and stubborn. These characteristics are exactly the opposite of those of the godly woman as described in I Peter 3:4-5. In addition, the immoral woman will not stay at home. She refuses a home-centered life and rejects it in favor of the aggressive pursuit of evil. She does not wait for her victim to come to her; she actively seeks opportunities for immorality.

The aggressiveness of the morally impure woman

(verse 13). She is bold, impudent, and brazen. When we view the morally impure woman as a symbol of folly, it becomes apparent why it is so easy not to follow God's Word and God's will. Wisdom is not aggressive—it must be pursued and cultivated—but folly is.

Hypocritical righteousness (verse 14). Those who are involved in moral impurity often make an outward show of religiosity, and they are inventive at justifying their actions. (See Proverbs 16:2.) But no excuse will suffice when a person stands before the holy God in judgment.

The lying tongue of the morally impure (verse 15). She flatters her victim by saying she was looking specifically for him. But this statement is a lie. She would have said the same to anyone.

The beautiful picture painted by sin (verses 16-18). Temptation is enticing and alluring. Like a whited sepulchre, sin puts on a false front. It does not mention the certain results of moral impurity. (See Proverbs 5:9-11.)

The false assurances of sin (verses 19-20). The characteristic statement of temptation is "No one will ever know."

The power of words (verse 21). Sin uses flattering, deceptive words to entrap its victim. Words are basic to life. One will listen either to God's words or to the devil's. It is important to read the right words, listen to the right words, and speak the right words.

Forsaking the path of wisdom (verse 22). As an ox to the slaughter, the man who yields to the immoral woman walks to his own destruction. As a fool to the stocks (an ancient punishment), he has chosen his path by his actions. In other words, the results of forsaking wisdom are detrimental and predictable. When one forsakes the path of wisdom, he behaves with the ignorance of an animal or the folly of a fool.

Wisdom too late (verse 23). He sees only the beautiful picture; he does not see or hear the dart slipping through the air. He hurries to sin in the way that a bird hurries to get the food in a trap. He does not realize until it is too late that he will pay with his life for a few moments of physical pleasure.

Controlling the heart (verses 24-25). Instead of following the heart into immoral ways, we are to heed the words of wisdom and order our heart to follow the right paths. (See Proverbs 18:2; 28:26.)

Learning from others' mistakes (verse 26). Everyone who is deceived by folly is destroyed. There are no exceptions, but there are many examples. Only a fool says, "I must see for myself."

The road to death and hell (verse 27). The person who chooses folly has made his decision to walk toward hell and death.

Chapter Eight

The availability of wisdom (verses 1-4). The basic message of the opening verses of chapter 8 is that wisdom is available. She does not play hard to get. Even those with the least ability can find her.

Wisdom cries aloud in public; understanding puts forth her voice. She does not stand passively; she offers an open invitation to all who would hear. She stands at the top of high places. She waits at the side of the paths. She stands by the roads where people travel from one city to another. She also stands at the entrance of cities, still calling. Scripture never pictures wisdom as unavailable to those who sincerely seek her. (See James 1:5-8.)

The reference to high places may simply be another example of the general availability of wisdom, or it may have a more specific meaning. Generally, the Scriptures speak negatively of high places, since they were most frequently associated with the worship of false gods. Occasionally Israel worshiped the true God in the high places, but even this worship often seemed to be in periods of spiritual compromise, although God sometimes met His people and spoke to them in high places. (See Numbers 33:52; II Kings 23:5; II Chronicles 1:1-13; 31:1; 33:3, 17.) The meaning in Proverbs 8:2 could be that even in the place where people worship false gods, wisdom stands in an attempt to turn them to the true God.

People do not have to remain foolish (verse 5). Wisdom is not just for those with advanced education. It is not just for those who are high in society. It is available to simpletons and fools.

Excellent and right things (verse 6). Every word of wisdom is excellent and right. It is necessary only to hear, to listen to her.

Truth only (verse 7). Every word of wisdom is true; she cannot mouth words of wickedness. (See James 3:13-18.)

Righteousness contrasted with frowardness and perversity (verse 8). Frowardness has to do with self-will, stubbornness, and rebellion. Perversity has to do with twisting or warping what is right and good. In contrast, righteousness submits to the will of God and walks in His ways. A person who speaks with a rebellious or perverse mouth discloses that he lacks wisdom.

Why wisdom is obscure to some (verse 9). If a person has understanding and knowledge, wisdom's words are plain. They make sense. They are clear. But to the person without understanding and knowledge, they are obscure and difficult to grasp.

Wisdom is superior to silver and gold (verse 10). This verse does not tell the godly person to refuse silver and gold; they were the biblical media of exchange. But it compares instruction with silver and knowledge with choice gold in order to illustrate the value of these qualities. If we must make a choice, it is more profitable to choose instruction than silver, knowledge than gold.

Nothing is as valuable as wisdom (verse 11). What do

people of the world desire? Wealth, fame, long life, happiness. But wisdom is more desirable than them all. Wisdom so far outdistances all the other things people pursue that there is no comparison. Yet sadly, most spend their entire lives pursuing the less desirable things.

Discretion and sagacity (verse 12). Prudence here indicates discretion. Webster defines discretion as "prudence, or knowledge and prudence; that discernment which enables a person to judge critically of what is correct and proper, united with caution; nice discernment, and judgment, directed by circumspection, and primarily regarding one's own conduct."

"Witty inventions" seems to speak of sagacity, which is "quickness or acuteness of discernment or penetration; readiness of apprehension; the faculty of readily discerning and distinguishing ideas, and of separating truth from falsehood." Wherever we find wisdom, we will find discretion and sagacity; they dwell together.

The first step of the fear of the Lord (verse 13). The Book of Proverbs elsewhere defines the fear of the Lord as the beginning of wisdom and knowledge. According to this verse, then, the first step toward the attainment of either is to hate evil. As long as we are fond of the knowledge of evil, either through a desire for respectability in the eyes of the world or through ignorance of its dangers, we will never gain wisdom. We should hate evil because it is an affront to God and a snare to humanity. Wisdom hates pride, arrogance, evil ways, and the perverse mouth.

We must allow the Bible to identify evil, for our human judgment is faulty. If the decision as to what is evil is left to us, we will often excuse evil as good and call good evil.

True counsel is found only in wisdom (verse 14). People need counsel. True counsel imparts strength, not weakness.

But not all counsel is of God. The world offers counsel in the form of a humanistic psychology that is inadequate for spiritual needs and often incompatible with the Scriptures, as the following points demonstrate: (1) It does not consider the spiritual nature of man at all. (2) It does not provide assurance of a cure. (3) It offers no absolute standards of right and wrong, no basis for moral judgment. (4) It endorses the world's standard of behavior. (5) It often offers scapegoats for people's actions instead of emphasizing their moral responsibility for their actions. (6) It has no uniform convictions. (7) It offers no uniform treatment.

Counselling is important and useful when it is based on the true wisdom of God's Word. But ungodly counsel has no place in the Christian's life. And the person who meditates on the Word of God, serves God faithfully, attends church regularly, and is consistent in prayer will need relatively little counselling.

Prosperous governments rely on wisdom (verses 15-16). Wisdom will teach kings how to reign and princes how to decree justice.

Mutual respect (verse 17). Wisdom will not reject any who love her. On the other hand, she will not force herself on those who do not love her. As a magnetic field attracts iron filings, so wisdom will attract those who love her.

The word translated "early" has the connotation of "dawn." One must not wait until he has exhausted all other possibilities before he turns to wisdom; he should go to wisdom first.

Genuine riches (verse 18). While wisdom is more desirable than gold, silver, and rubies, by her a person can receive riches and honor. In particular, she grants the truly durable riches, which include such things as peace, joy, and love. By contrast earthly, material riches will not last (James 5:1-3).

The fruit of wisdom (verse 19). What could be better than fine gold and silver? Yet wisdom's fruit is superior to either. Wisdom is not just an inert quality; it bears invaluable fruit in a person's life.

Where wisdom leads (verse 20). Wisdom leads in the way of righteousness; genuine righteousness will never be known apart from her. She directs in the paths of judgment, giving the ability to make right decisions. Without wisdom, it is impossible to do so.

A lasting inheritance (verse 21). Wisdom's inheritance is solid, genuine, true. Wisdom fills the treasuries of those who love her. By contrast an inheritance gained quickly (dishonestly) is not lasting (Proverbs 20:21).

Wisdom was with God before creation (verses 22-31). Wisdom is an attribute of God, and as such it was with Him from the very beginning, even before the dawn of creation. God delights in wisdom as does a wise parent in his child. Wisdom rejoices particularly in those human beings who receive her. She is above the reach of the animal kingdom, and she has no purpose in dwelling in the uninhabited parts of the earth.

Some people use this passage in an attempt to make wisdom a second person "in" the Godhead. But it obviously personifies the attribute of wisdom as a woman in contrast to folly, as throughout this section of Proverbs. The Bible clearly teaches the absolute oneness of God and excludes the concept of plural divine persons (Deuteronomy 6:4; Galatians 3:20). Moreover, it never describes God or a supposed "member" of the Godhead as a woman.

The blessing of wisdom (verse 32). The person who keeps the ways of wisdom will find that he is blessed.

We must not refuse instruction (verse 33). Instruction may be painful. It may cross our preferences, but we must accept it to gain wisdom.

We must seek wisdom daily (verse 34). The attainment of wisdom is not a once-in-a-lifetime affair. We must pursue it day after day.

Wisdom's fruit (verse 35). The supreme blessing of wisdom is life and favor with God.

Why some love death (verse 36). The person who rejects wisdom only hurts himself. It is impossible to be neutral in this area. Those who hate wisdom actually love death, because a lack of spiritual wisdom surely leads to destruction.

Chapter Nine

The two houses (verse 1). Both folly and wisdom are pictured as having a house. Folly has a house to which she seduces her victims through sensual promises. Wisdom has a house to which she invites pupils for instruction. The house of wisdom has seven pillars. The number seven symbolizes divine fullness, perfection, and completeness. It comes from a Hebrew word meaning "to be complete, to be full, to be satisfied, to have enough." By contrast, the house of folly is incomplete, imperfect, unsatisfying.

Wisdom's banquet (verse 2). Wisdom has a satisfying and attractive banquet prepared for all who will come and dine. (See also Psalm 23:5.)

Wisdom's invitation (verses 3-6). Wisdom, both directly and through the delegated efforts of others (such as evangelists, pastors, teachers, witnesses), invites and actually urges people to come to her banquet. (See Matthew 22:2-4.) With such an invitation, there is no need for anyone to stay "simple" or to continue to "want [lack] understanding." But the person who would gain wisdom must "turn in." He must make the turn. (See Isaiah 55:1-3; John 6:51-63; I Corinthians 1:24, 30.)

Only those who have wisdom really live. Anything else

is a living death. It is mere existence. To live spiritually, a person must forsake something, namely spiritual foolishness. It is not merely a matter of forsaking, however. There is no place for inactivity or stagnation. After he forsakes, he must go. He must pursue wisdom. Understanding is a way of life.

When there is no point in reproof or rebuke (verse 7). It does no good to reprove a scorner or to rebuke a deliberately wicked person. Prudence, caution, and tact are needed in dealing with this kind of person. Such a scorner or wicked person, when reproved or rebuked, will often resort to finding supposed inconsistencies and sins in the person who is so reproving and rebuking him. Jesus addressed this situation in Matthew 7:6.

Different responses to reproof and rebuke (verse 8). A person's reaction to reproof and rebuke reveals whether he is a scorner or a wise person. The former will hate the one who tries to correct him; the latter will love such a person instead.

Growing in wisdom (verse 9). A wise and just person does not resist learning new lessons in life. He looks upon every situation, whether pleasant or unpleasant, as an opportunity to learn yet more wisdom, to put God's principles to work.

Definitions of wisdom and understanding (verse 10). The starting point for wisdom is the fear of the Lord. Understanding is connected with the knowledge of the holy. The ways of God should not be a complete mystery to us. We should know not only His works or acts, but His ways, or the principles that guide His actions. Then we can begin to understand what God will do in a given situation.

The secret of a longer life (verse 11). Following wisdom will increase the life span because it will keep a person from doing foolish things that shorten life, and it will prompt him to do wise things that lengthen life.

Personal responsibility (verse 12). Wisdom is good for us; it is not just a vague intellectual pursuit. (See I Corinthians 3:8.) A scorner is alone responsible for his sin. No one else can force someone to be a scorner.

A difference between folly and wisdom (verse 13). Wisdom is calm, dignified. Folly is clamorous, which means "turbulent, animated by passion." The woman who follows the lead of wisdom, who studies to be quiet, will be admired and respected. The woman who follows folly and is loud-mouthed and boisterous will be disdained. In this case, the word "simple" indicates that she is unable to resist temptation; she has no moral fiber. Moreover, she "knoweth nothing": folly is naturally accompanied by ignorance.

The house of folly (verse 14). Folly also has a house, but she does not need to send out maidens as wisdom does, because people are more easily tempted to sin than persuaded to righteousness. Her house is in the highest and most conspicuous part of the city, and she sits immodestly before her door, plying her immoral trade shamelessly.

Folly's universal call (verse 15). As people walk in the path of right and duty, she tries to turn them aside. Those who walk the narrow path are not immune from the seductive call of folly.

Folly's counterfeit invitation (verse 16). Folly mimics wisdom, giving the same invitation. (See verse 4.) Spiritually ignorant people find it hard to distinguish between good and evil, false and true, especially when their

sensual appetite is aroused and sides with the temptress.
(See Hebrews 5:14.)

Folly's banquet (verse 17). Wisdom offers meat and
wine; folly offers bread and water. Wisdom invites openly to a well-furnished table; folly calls to a secret meal
of the barest supply. Wisdom offers something full and
satisfying; folly gives something that does not fill.

It is a trait of corrupt human nature to think that forbidden things are attractive simply because they are
unlawful. Most violence and destruction is senseless, that
is, done with no motive other than the thrill of doing what
is forbidden. But things gained without effort or danger
or discipline soon lose their charm.

Folly's guests (verse 18). None of those in the house
of folly can be said to be "living." They are dead, the
merest shadow of living people. Those who accept the invitation of folly are already in the depths of hell (hell on
earth), and the only way they can be redeemed is by a
miracle of God.

Chapter Ten

This chapter begins the actual proverbs written or spoken by Solomon. The word *proverb* means "to set, or place side by side" or "by comparison." Contrast is used throughout the proverbs to demonstrate the difference between wisdom and folly.

The source of parental gladness or sorrow (verse 1). To a large degree, children are entrusted with their parents' happiness. A father who has a wise son will be glad; a mother with a foolish son will be heavy with sorrow. Especially when they are young, children do not fully understand their influence on their parents' emotional well-being. But when sons and daughters are older, when they are married and have their own families, they should recognize even then the importance of making their parents glad. If for no other reason than this, they should seek wisdom.

A man may, when his son is small, think of the boy's future success, fame, or wealth. But as the years go by these things fade into insignificance, and he realizes that the most important quality his child could have is wisdom.

Sometimes, in their desperation for their children to be wise and avoid mistakes, parents will do unwise things and actually drive their children toward the very things they hope to help them avoid. A parent must find a delicate balance between protecting and guiding children and releasing the children. At some point, parents must be willing to release their children to make mistakes.

Nothing a parent can do will guarantee his children will always make right decisions. Even God, the perfect father, who had two children and placed them in a perfect environment, saw both of them fail. If He had never released them to fail, they would actually have been puppets, without the power of choice. The most powerful impact for right a parent can have on his child is the example he sets before him. Formal teaching is of little value without the actual demonstration of what is taught.

Empty treasures (verse 2). All of the soft living, lavish spending, and "the good life" purchased at the expense of morality is unprofitable. But righteousness, regardless of the presence or absence of the so-called good life on this earth, is profitable in the only area that matters: it delivers from death.

Is God for you or against you? (verse 3). The Lord does not allow those who live for Him to go without the things necessary for life. (See Psalm 37:25; 84:11.) On the other hand, true happiness does not elude wicked people by accident. God is actively involved, casting away from them what they think will satisfy them.

The sure way to poverty and riches (verse 4). The "slack hand" speaks of an open, ineffective hand or palm. The slack hand neglects to maintain what it presently has, both physically and spiritually. (See Proverbs 24:30-34.) A slack hand is wasteful. Valuable things that are often wasted include (1) time (our most precious asset); (2) resources; (3) energy (on worthless pursuits); (4) money. A person with a slack hand gets too much sleep, which is as bad as too little (Proverbs 19:15). He uses imagined excuses to justify his lack of effort (Proverbs 22:13). He will say, "There's no need to try." A person with a slack hand makes signs of activity, but he never gets anywhere (Proverbs 26:14). He neglects the things that obviously need doing (Ecclesiastes 10:18). A person with a slack hand will not use what he has. He reasons that if he had as much as someone else he would do something, but since he has only a little, he will do nothing (Matthew 25:24-25). Dealing with a slack hand will surely bring a person to poverty, regardless of how much he begins with.

The "hand of the diligent" speaks of a hand that is braced for work. The diligent hand is the opposite of the slack hand. The diligent person will do what is necessary to maintain his present position, both spiritually and physically, and to improve his lot. The diligent person is not wasteful. He conserves time, resources, energy, and money. He neither sleeps too much nor too little. He does not use excuses to justify lack of effort. His activity is purposeful and will accomplish results. He will do the things that need doing. He will use what he has, not worrying about others who have more.

A time to gather (verse 5). Wisdom prompts a person to gather in the time of harvest, to do the right thing at the right time. Some suppose it is simply luck that puts a person in just the right place at just the right time, but usually it is wisdom. When opportunity knocks, some people are so drowsy that they cannot hear it.

Blessings or violence? (verse 6). The just are blessed and cannot be cursed. But the wicked bring many curses upon themselves by the violence of their mouths. Contrary to popular opinion, people die as they have lived. If they lived cursing, they die cursing. People form habits that are virtually impossible to break even when those habits are destroying them.

The lessons of history (verse 7). Eternity and to some extent even human history reveal the ultimate blessing of righteousness and the shame of wickedness. For example, the name of George Washington or Abraham Lincoln evokes praise, but the name of Adolf Hitler causes abhorrence.

A mark of wisdom (verse 8). A wise person will not resist learning yet another lesson. He loves reproof. He is teachable. The person with loose lips will trip on them and fall. One of the marks of a fool is his prating, which means chatter, idle talk, constant and foolish speech.

The importance of walking right (verse 9). A person who is living right and doing right has the greatest security in the world. Sin will be found out, however, and it will be exposed. If it is not uncovered now, it will be at the judgment.

Being careful about the winkers (verse 10). Winking with the eye here indicates craftiness and concealment. (See Proverbs 6:12-15.) Again the warning is given: a chattering fool shall fall.

The mouth is a well (verse 11). It brings forth attitudes and thoughts from deep within a person's spirit. With the words of our mouth we have the ability to impart life or death, both to ourselves and others. (See Proverbs 18:21.) Again the warning is given: violence covers the mouth of the wicked. We must not speak words of violence, for words have a powerful impact upon thoughts and expectations. For this reason, it is not appropriate to threaten to "kill" someone or "break someone's neck." Above all, we must not take it upon ourselves to pronounce damnation upon anyone. Only God can make pronouncements about eternity, and even He is not willing that any should perish.

The source of strife and the attitude of love (verse 12). What stirs up strife? It may be called many things, such as "concern," but it is actually hatred. By contrast, someone who truly loves another person will not look for an opportunity to expose his errors for public ridicule but will seek to restore him as privately as possible. (See Proverbs 17:9.)

Where wisdom is found (verse 13). Wisdom will be demonstrated in a person's words. A person who lacks understanding will suffer the consequences in externally imposed discipline or in punishment.

How to tell if destruction is near (verse 14). As some people collect butterflies, stamps, or coins, a wise person collects and stores knowledge. But a foolish person's words will cause him to be on the brink of disaster.

Where the rich and poor meet (verse 15). The overriding problem with wealth is the tendency to trust in it. (See Mark 10:24; I Timothy 6:6-10.) The poor man may be pitied by many, but the rich man is really in no better shape. His confidence is in something that could very well be taken from him tomorrow. The poor man may be destroyed by his poverty, but the rich man may be destroyed by his wealth. (See Proverbs 19:7; 30:7-9.)

Results of righteousness and wickedness (verse 16). The efforts of the righteous and wicked produce two different things. The efforts of the righteous produce life; the efforts of the wicked produce sin, the wages of which is death.

The way of life (verse 17). There are only two ways, death and life. The person who lives according to wise instruction is on the way of life, but the person who refuses reproof makes a serious mistake. Even if some reproof is unmerited, it can help a person to learn much about self-control and grace.

Marks of a fool (verse 18). Two characteristics of a fool are: (1) he pretends to love those he hates; and (2) he slanders. Slander is "a false tale or report maliciously uttered, and tending to injure the reputation of another by lessening him in the esteem of his fellow citizens, by exposing him to impeachment and punishment, or by impairing his means of living; defamation" (Webster).

A sign of a sinner and of a wise man (verse 19). A "big talker" is sure to sin with his lips. A wise person, however, guards his lips. He does not say all he could say; he does not tell all he knows; he does not say all he thinks; he does not speak impetuously or rashly.

A valuable tongue and a worthless heart (verse 20). The tongue of a just person is extremely valuable; but even the heart of a wicked person is worth little. How can a tongue be valuable? By speaking upbuilding, encouraging, edifying things and by not speaking hurtful things. How can a heart be worthless? By not harboring mercy or grace and by entertaining revenge, bitterness, and malice.

Food from lips (verse 21). Words feed people with strength. How important is wisdom? Many have died because they did not have it.

Riches without sorrow (verse 22). The momentary thrills of the world are followed by disappointment, regret, remorse, emptiness, and sorrow. In contrast, God's blessings make us truly rich, and they are not followed by regret and remorse.

The wicked sportsman (verse 23). A fool delights in evil, in harmful acts and breaking rules. He thinks it is great fun. A person of understanding will avoid such destructive practices.

Faith and fear (verse 24). In many ways, faith and fear are two sides of the same coin. In the spiritual realm, both of them produce the object of their focus. (See Hebrews 11:1.)

The transitory nature of wickedness; the permanence of righteousness (verse 25). The wicked are as unstable as a whirlwind; the righteous are solid and enduring. The righteous person will not be a "flash in the pan." His light will continue to burn through test and trial.

Do not send a sluggard (verse 26). Just as a person is annoyed by smoke in his eyes or vinegar on his teeth, so the man who uses a sluggard will regret his action. Things of importance should be entrusted only to faithful people. Faithfulness is demonstrated in small things (Luke 16:10). (See also II Timothy 2:2.)

Long life or short life? (verse 27). The life of those who fear the Lord will be prolonged because their fear of Him will prevent them from doing harmful things that tend to shorten life. The years of the wicked will be shortened because, in their wickedness, they will do risky things that tend to shorten life.

Goals fulfilled and unmet (verse 28). The godly desires of the righteous will be fulfilled, causing gladness. The expectations of the wicked will vanish before he obtains them, like a mirage.

The sources of strength and destruction (verse 29).

Walking in God's way makes a person strong, but sin leads to destruction. Someone who feels weak should check the way he has been walking.

The unmoveable (verse 30). The righteous are stable and secure; the wicked may make a big splash, but they will pass away without an eternal inheritance.

What the mouth indicates (verse 31). A sign of a just person is what his mouth brings forth. Those who use their tongues in a rebellious, self-willed way abuse a gift of God, and they will be judged for it.

Knowing what to say (verse 32). A righteous person will know the right things to say at the right time. He will not have to regret what he has said. The wicked person does not have this ability. He blunders on, speaking unacceptable and perverse things.

Chapter Eleven

A false balance and a just weight (verse 1). The prohibition against false or substandard weights and measures teaches honesty in all pursuits, and in ancient societies it was the foundation of economic soundness. (See Leviticus 19:35-36; Deuteronomy 25:13-16; Proverbs 20:10; Ezekiel 45:9-12; Hosea 12:7 [where the word *oppress* means "to press upon, violate, or defraud"]; Micah 6:10-11.) It is not enough for people to refrain from using false weights and measures; they are not permitted even to own them. A modern example of this sin is the practice of used car dealers turning back mileage odometers several thousand miles, making it appear as though the car has been driven fewer miles than it actually has. Dishonest adulteration of goods is another example. (See Isaiah 1:22.)

After pride, shame (verse 2). The proud person will surely be brought to shame. Wisdom will not be found with the proud, but with the humble. But while a person should not think of himself more highly than he ought to think, he should not continually berate or belittle himself as if that were humility. (See Romans 12:3.)

The guiding quality (verse 3). Many decisions that sinners worry and fret over for days can be made in a moment by a person with integrity. Life is not as complicated as it seems; there are a limited number of principles at work. When a principle is compromised, a person with integrity will know automatically not to get involved in the situation.

"Discerning God's Direction in a Business Decision," published by the Institute in Basic Youth Conflicts in 1973, applies this concept to business and investment. For example, a person with integrity learns to beware of incredible "deals," get-rich-quick schemes, "opportunities" that involve his money rather than the money of the one who approaches him, gains that come through the misfortunes of others, and deals that require immediate decisions without the opportunity for reflection, counsel, and confirmation. Such approaches are at the root of most schemes to cheat a person out of his money.

No genuine profit in riches (verse 4). Riches may serve to make life softer and easier on this earth, but they will be of no value in the day of judgment. The Supreme Judge of the universe cannot be bribed. The only thing that will profit in that day will be righteousness. All humanity will stand before God equally on the basis of their deeds, not their wealth. (See Revelation 20:12-13.)

How destinies are determined (verse 5). This is a companion verse to verse 3. A person who is righteous will be able to make the important decisions of life. The principles by which he lives will guide him. In the same manner, the wicked person will make decisions based upon his wickedness, which will ultimately destroy him.

The source of deliverance (verse 6). The theme of verses 3 and 5 continues here. The righteous will find that their righteousness results in deliverance from destruction, while the evil desires of the wicked will result in their fall.

No hope for the wicked dead (verse 7). While they live, wicked people may harbor lofty ambitions; they may have great dreams and plans. But death is final for the wicked. There is no hope in hell. There will be no goal setting, no positive thinking for the wicked in eternity.

A stand-in for the righteous (verse 8). Though trouble may appear inevitable, the righteous person will ultimately be delivered from it. He will be replaced in that troubled situation by a wicked person. (See Proverbs 21:18.)

The destructive mouth (verse 9). The Book of Proverbs repeatedly discusses the power of words both for good and evil. The hypocrite's major weapon is his mouth. A hypocrite is a pretender. For example, he pretends to love his neighbor, especially to his face, but behind his neighbor's back he gossips, slanders, and spreads rumors. The just person is not at the mercy of the hypocrite, however. He can be delivered through right knowledge, specifically the knowledge of God's Word. A person who has a knowledge of the Word of God will know what to do, how to do it, and when to do it in order to be delivered.

How a city is blessed (verses 10-11). A city will be blessed when the righteous are in positions of authority and influence. (See Proverbs 29:2.) But if the wicked capture these positions, the city will suffer. (See Proverbs 29:8.) Many cities, states, and nations suffer a leadership crisis today because God's people are unwilling to involve themselves in civic affairs.

In the Old Testament, God's people sometimes held positions of authority and influence. Moses was both a religious and civil ruler. Daniel was the first of three presidents set over 120 princes, and he answered directly to Darius the king (Daniel 6:1-3). His friends Shadrach, Meshach, and Abednego served directly under him (Daniel 2:46-49). Joseph was the governor of Egypt, serving directly under Pharaoh (Genesis 41:41-44). There were saints in Caesar's household (Philippians 4:22). At least one early Christian, Erastus, held a very responsible civic position: city chamberlain, or treasurer (Romans 16:23).

In a republican form of government, such as the United States and Canada have, it is the duty of every citizen to vote. It is also their privilege to become informed, influence other voters, attempt to convince those in office of their views, and run for office themselves. Christians who refuse to vote have no place to criticize the actions of those in office. One thing that made America great in its early days was that many of its founders and leaders were God-fearing men, men of high moral standards. When the quality of elected officials has declined, the nation has been brought to dishonor.

Lack of wisdom (verse 12). When a person despises his neighbor, it is a sign that he lacks wisdom. A central biblical principle is that people are to be concerned about the welfare of their neighbors. Not only does this attitude promote strong and secure neighborhoods, it provides an opportunity for Christian witness. (See Proverbs 3:29.) A person who despises and mistreats his neighbor lays the groundwork for his own destruction.

On the other hand, if a person knows how to abstain from contention or retaliation, even in the face of imagined or real wrongs, it is a sign that he has understanding. One of the greatest evidences of genuine strength of character is the ability to refrain from saying damaging things that could be said.

The sure sign of a talebearer (verse 13). When a person confidentially offers to share secret or privileged information, he is a talebearer. No matter what he promises, he will pass on any secrets someone tells him to others. It is foolish to tell this person anything of significance, for he will not keep a confidence. He will often offer to share confidential information in order to give him leverage and to obligate others to reciprocate by sharing confidential information with him. It is easy to distinguish a talebearer from a person with a faithful spirit: the talebearer reveals secrets, but the faithful person conceals them. (See II Timothy 2:2.)

The value of counsel (verse 14). There is safety in godly counsel. (See Psalm 1:1.) Those who reject counsel are sure to fail. When facing a major decision a person should seek counsel from a number of wise people in order to obtain a general consensus. Otherwise, he may overlook some important point. The person who declares, "Nobody is going to tell me what to do" is headed for destruction.

Dangers of co-signing (verse 15). Surety means agreeing to stand good for another's debt if the borrower fails to pay. The common form today is co-signing. The Book of Proverbs repeatedly warns of the dangers associated with this practice. (See Proverbs 6:1-2; 17:18; 20:16; 22:26; 27:13.) It is unwise because the need for this practice usually indicates that the borrower is unqualified for the loan; he has already borrowed all he can afford to repay, or he has no demonstrable means of repaying the debt, or he has already demonstrated a failure to be faithful in repaying obligations. It removes an incentive to correct his lack of qualification and to seek God for His provision, supply, and direction. In short, one of the wisest steps a person can take to secure his own financial position is to refuse to stand good for the debts of others. If he thinks the borrower has a genuine need, it may be better to give him the money outright.

Honor or riches? (verse 16). A gracious woman (one who is full of grace) will never be dishonored. She will also bring honor to her husband. (See Proverbs 31:11-12.) On the other hand the "strong"—or, as the Hebrew indicates, the terrible and violent—retain riches. Of course, honor is more valuable than riches (Proverbs 22:1).

Doing ourselves a favor (verse 17). When someone has mercy on others, he strengthens his own soul. Someone who is cruel and refuses to show mercy, however, brings trouble to his own body. It is good for a person, spiritually and physically, to be merciful and kind. It is damaging, spiritually and physically, to be hard, unbending, and cruel.

One of the great contributing factors to the state of a person's health is his attitude. The person who looks at life through eyes of flint and whose heart is cold as stone opens the door to physical damage, emotional trauma, and spiritual death.

Why "sure things" fail (verse 18). The wicked person develops a scheme that he thinks is foolproof. He believes he has all the angles covered. It is a sure thing in his mind. But it is a deceitful work. While it may appear to be certain to succeed, actually it is doomed to fail. But the person who does right can be certain of his reward; it is a sure reward. It is always right to do right.

Life or death (verse 19). The righteous person by his

nature tends to perform things that tend to promote life. The places he goes, the things he does, the words he says, and even what he eats and drinks will tend to life. The evil person will naturally do things that tend to promote death. The places he goes, the things he does, the words he says, the people he has fellowship with, and what he eats and drinks will tend to death.

Abomination and delight (verse 20). The rebellious, lawless person is an abomination—something detestable or loathsome—in God's eyes, while He delights in the upright. God instructed Israel not to bring an abomination into their house (Deuteronomy 7:26). Even today there is the danger of contamination by an abominable thing. Christians must guard their homes against abominable influences. (See Psalm 101:2-7.) They must prevent rebellious, lawless people from influencing their homes by means of television, wrong books and magazines, ungodly video or audio tapes or records, wrong radio programs, or any other way. Instead, they should actively seek to have their homes influenced by upright people.

No safety in numbers (verse 21). Humanism teaches that right is determined by majority rule. But if every person on earth agreed in opposition to God, God would still be true (Romans 3:4). No matter how many people do evil together or how strong their covenant, their combined strength and agreement will not spare them punishment. Compared with the number of those who oppose God, it may appear that the righteous are only a "seed." But regardless of how small the number of those who do right, they will be vindicated and delivered.

Gold, swine, and discretion (verse 22). This verse tells us something about the value of gold, the nature of swine, and the need for women to practice discretion. Discretion relates to proper taste, reason, and discernment. Beauty is wasted on a woman who lacks discretion. (See Proverbs 31:30.)

Right and wrong desires (verse 23). The righteous person wants only what is good. But the wicked man has wrong values, wrong goals, wrong desires. His future is tainted by his character. He does not care if a thing is good or not; he wants what he wants.

The key to plenty (verses 24-25). Generosity produces plenty. There is an eternal law that works regardless of economic policy or conditions. Giving produces a return, just as planting produces a harvest. (See Malachi 3:10-12; Luke 6:38; II Corinthians 9:6-7.) Stinginess produces poverty.

It is helpful to think of money or other goods as seed. This analogy certainly does not mean that money is to be thrown to the winds in a careless, thoughtless fashion. Rather it should be sown carefully in good ground. The Christian should be just as concerned about the integrity of the ministry in which he invests as the farmer is about the condition of the field in which he plants. The person who gives directly to one who is genuinely in need has planted his seed in good soil.

Free enterprise (verse 26). The Bible endorses the concept of free enterprise and private ownership. The commandment "Thou shalt not steal" would have no meaning if there were no private property. However, enterprise should be conducted according to basic rules of not by unrestrained greed. The person who withholds basic necessities from the marketplace in hopes of creating a shortage and thus increasing the price and his profits will be cursed by the people. The merchant who freely sells necessities at a just price will prosper. This admonition particularly applies to people who are engaged in providing goods or services basic to human life.

Why good things happen to good people (verse 27). A person who sincerely and diligently seeks to do right will find favor with God and humans, but if a person is intent on evil, it will come back to him. This verse states another form of the law of sowing and reaping. Every deed is a seed that will potentially produce a harvest.

The wrong attitude toward money (verse 28). The question we must ask ourselves is, "Where is my trust?" The person who trusts in money will certainly fall. A person does not have to have money in order to trust in it. If he thinks money would solve his problems if he had it, then he is trusting in money. The person who is overcome with fear, worry, and doubt because of the loss of a job or a bad economy demonstrates that his trust is in money. (See Mark 10:24.)

Regardless of economic trends or personal fortunes, the righteous person will flourish in the same way that a branch flourishes. In other words, he recognizes he is not his own source of life and strength, for a branch depends solely on the vine for life. (See John 15:4-5.) The righteous person worries no more than a branch worries. His responsibility is not to originate life or fruitfulness but to simply let the life of the vine flow through him.

The danger of troubling one's own house (verse 29). The person who does things that trouble his own family is courting disaster. He will gain nothing of substance; he will be left grasping the air. The first place Christianity must be demonstrated is in the home. Wise people will

111

be promoted; fools will be demoted.

The tree of life (verse 30). In Scripture, the tree of life is connected with wisdom. (See Proverbs 3:18.) If the forbidden tree in the Garden of Eden was the tree of wrong knowledge, it is reasonable to assume that the tree of life would have given right knowledge. The "fruit of the righteous" speaks of what the righteous person produces. He will produce wisdom, both by his words and his deeds. One of the fruits of wisdom is the winning of souls, and wisdom is a necessity in this endeavor. In this Old Testament context, the winning of souls seems to refer to the ability to establish lasting friendships and to persuade others to right points of view.

Compensation (verse 31). Not only will the righteous reap what they sow in this present world, but so will the wicked and even more so. (See I Peter 4:18.) Nothing we do is in a vacuum. Every action will be followed by a reaction. Ultimately, God's justice will prevail in every life.

Chapter Twelve

Instruction, knowledge, and reproof (verse 1). Not only do we see the relationship between instruction and knowledge in this verse, but also the relationship between these two and reproof. Instruction and knowledge go together. There will be no knowledge where there is no instruction. Instruction can come from the school of life, but often an actual human teacher will be involved. In fact, human teachers are necessary in the church. (See Romans 12:4-7; I Corinthians 12:28; Ephesians 4:11-12.)

The latter part of Proverbs 12:1 declares that the person who hates reproof has characteristics of a brute beast. His basic tendency is to despise being told what to do. This person will never have true knowledge, for instruction often takes the form of reproof. For example, when an answer on a test is marked wrong, that is both reproof and instruction. When a trainee has to be shown again how to do his job, that is both reproof and instruction. A person who is willing to accept reproof will find that it contributes greatly to his education.

The most valuable blessing (verse 2). What could be superior to obtaining the Lord's favor? When a person chooses to do good, the blessings of the Lord will be upon him. Genuine spiritual goodness comes only from the presence of the Holy Spirit. (See Galatians 5:22-23.) The good person will have no need of wicked tactics. He does not have to rely on favoritism, under-the-table activities, or good-luck charms. Indeed, God will judge the person who relies on anything or anyone other than Him for blessings, prosperity, and provision.

No stability in wickedness (verse 3). As a continuing development of the theme begun in verse 2, this verse declares that wickedness will never establish a person. As Asaph realized at last, though the wicked may seem to prosper for a time, his feet are in slippery places. (See Psalm 73, especially verse 18.) But righteousness roots a person so that he cannot be moved. It may take some time before the evidence of a deep root is visible. The wicked may, during that time, appear to be accomplishing more than the righteous, for the wicked spends little time developing a root system. What he does is on the surface, visible only to the human senses.

This truth is illustrated in the story Jesus told of a foolish man who built his house directly on the sand, while a wise man took the time to build on a solid foundation. While the house of the wicked may have gone up quickly, it was destroyed just as quickly. (See Matthew 7:24-27.)

A woman's influence on her husband's reputation and health (verse 4). A virtuous woman brings honor to her husband. (See Proverbs 31:10-31 for a description of a virtuous woman.) A woman should realize that her character and behavior have a great influence on her husband's health. A woman who brings shame to her husband damages his well-being like rottenness in his bones.

Diseased bones have unhealthy bone marrow. The bone marrow plays a vital role in the production and condition of the blood, and the life is in the blood. (See Leviticus 17:11.) Similarly, the woman who shames her husband is disastrous to her husband. Just as a virtuous woman is a public crown to her husband, an unhappy, immoral woman is a public disgrace to him.

Right thoughts, wrong counsel (verse 5). Righteous people start at the right place: the thoughts. Not only are their words right, but their inmost thoughts are right. All else is born of the thoughts. An old adage declares: "Sow a thought; reap a deed. Sow a deed; reap a habit. Sow a habit; reap a character. Sow a character; reap a destiny." It all begins with the thoughts. If one's thoughts are right, his actions will be right. If his actions are right, he will be right. This is why every thought must be brought into captivity unto the obedience of Christ (II Corinthians 10:4-5).

While the righteous think right thoughts, the wicked not only think evil but also speak evil. They give wrong and deceitful counsel. In the multitude of godly counsellors there is safety (Proverbs 11:14), but wicked counsel simply compounds wickedness. While there is safety in the multitude of right counsel, there is destruction in the multitude of wicked counsellors.

Words tell all (verse 6). How is it possible to discern if a person is wicked? His conversation betrays him. He is constantly discussing "getting even" with someone or taking advantage of someone. The theme of his conversation will be to "lie in wait for blood."

How is it possible to discern if a person is upright? His conversation will reveal him also. The theme of his conversation will be how to rescue another or how to help some person in need. And his honest and proper speech will deliver him from much trouble.

The fate of the wicked; the future of the righteous (verse 7). Continuing the theme of verses 2 and 3, this verse reveals that the wicked will be overthrown. The house they have built will come down. But the structure erected by the righteous will endure. No storm will be able to destroy it.

Commended or despised (verse 8). A person will receive commendation according to his wisdom. The wiser he is, the more he will be commended. But if a person's heart is perverse, he will be despised. Wise people will commend wisdom and despise perversity. Of course, those who are perverse will not commend the wise; they will commend the perverse. Thus, what kind of person someone is, is often revealed by what kind of people admire him and what kind of people he admires.

Humility is better than pride (verse 9). This verse speaks of someone who is lightly esteemed or held in contempt, perhaps because of his humility. If he is able to provide for his needs and has someone to serve him, then he is in a much better position than the proud person who lacks the basic necessities of life. By exalting himself, he may drive away those who would help him.

Humility tends to draw the right people; pride tends to drive them away. No one was more humble than Jesus, yet He had many willing to serve Him. At the same time, He was despised by those who do not value humility. (See Isaiah 53:3.)

The treatment of animals reveals character (verse 10). A righteous person will regard life wherever he finds it, for he realizes that all life is from God, including the life of animals. This does not mean that a righteous person will not hunt for food; God created animals and gave them to humanity for food. (See Genesis 9:2-4.) But a righteous person will treat his animals (whether working animals or pets) with respect and dignity. He will see that they are fed and properly protected and cared for.

While the righteous person is kind even to animals, the wicked person finds it difficult to be tender and kind in any situation. Even in his attempted expressions of tenderness and mercy he will be cruel.

Working and loafing (verse 11). A person who works diligently will not lack the basic necessities of life. But the person who turns away from honest work for worthless, frivolous pursuits displays a lack of understanding. It is possible to tell much about a person by observing what he does more: working or talking.

A net or a root (verse 12). A net is something by which people catch their prey. Wicked people admire the way other evil people attain wealth and pleasure, and they determine to do the same thing. A root is something through which life comes. A righteous person will produce lasting fruit as a natural product of his high principles. A net may or may not catch prey. Even if it does, it must be used again. The net itself cannot produce. Its catch will soon be used up; it produces nothing lasting. But a root continues to produce satisfying fruit season after season. The net, in this context, represents wicked methods. It captures what belongs to another. By contrast, the root represents honorable and honest gain.

The snare of words (verse 13). The wicked person's mouth brings him more trouble than anything else. A trap is always just a word away. While the Bible nowhere guarantees the just person exemption from conflict, it

117

does promise him he will come out of it safely. (See Psalm 34:19; John 16:33.)

The fruit of right words and honest labor (verse 14). While a wicked person is snared by the words of his mouth, as seen in the previous verse, the righteous person will be satisfied with the results of his words. (See Proverbs 18:21.) What a person is by his speech and conduct will bear positive fruit in his life. The law of sowing and reaping is a divine law: people ultimately receive the proper reward for their labors. (See Galatians 6:7.)

The fool's way (verse 15). A mark of a fool is that he does what seems right to him without considering God's will or seeking advice from others. He does not realize that this approach leads to death. (See Proverbs 14:12.) Rather than rushing into a course of action simply because it seems right to him, the wise person seeks and acts on godly counsel.

The fool's temper (verse 16). Another mark of a fool is that he has no control over his anger. (See Proverbs 25:28.) A prudent person will not bring shame to himself by a foolish public display of temper. He rules his spirit; he does not tell all he knows, do all he feels like doing, or say all he thinks.

The relationship between words and character (verse 17). A person's words publicly reveal his inner character. They will either display his righteousness or his deceitfulness. A person who speaks the truth demonstrates his righteousness; a false witness reveals his deceitfulness. The term "false witness" specifically describes someone who gives an untrue report about the activities of another. This sin was prohibited in the Ten Commandments (Exodus 20:16).

The influence of words on well-being (verse 18). Repeatedly the Book of Proverbs stresses the power of words. (See Proverbs 18:21.) It is possible to speak words that pierce others like swords. Wrong words can have very damaging effects. (See Proverbs 18:8; 26:22.) But the wise person will use the tongue to help, to strengthen, to encourage. (See Ephesians 4:29.) In doing so, he will contribute positively to the physical, mental, and spiritual health of others.

The relationship between words and stability (verse 19). Like verses 2-3 and 7, this proverb reveals that those who speak truth will be permanently established. Those who speak lies may appear to prosper, but it will be only for a moment.

The condition of the heart (verse 20). Deceit is a destructive force that resides in the heart of the person who imagines or devises evil. In time, it will kill him. But joy resides in the heart of the wise—those who counsel peace rather than devising evil—and joy is a life-giving force.

No evil for the just (verse 21). A just person can be assured that nothing will happen to him that God does not permit, and if God permits something, the end results will not be evil or harmful. Some situations may be painful and even tragic, but the just person knows that ultimately God will work all things together for his good (Romans 8:28). The wicked, however, will experience one troublesome event after another with no assurance that good will ultimately prevail! His life is full of evil and calamity.

The importance of honesty (verse 22). God hates dishonesty and delights in honesty. In describing the person who "deals truly," this verse speaks of a way of life, not just of words. If a person wants God to delight in him, he must be honest.

The prudent person and the fool (verse 23). The prudent person knows more than he tells. The fool tells more than he knows. In describing the prudent person who "concealeth knowledge," this verse does not speak of dishonesty or deceit, but of discretion and humility. A wise person does not disclose information inappropriately or harmfully, nor does he try to flaunt or boast of his knowledge.

The diligent rule; the slothful serve (verse 24). In general, people rise to positions of authority through diligence; they sink into servanthood through slothfulness. The slothful tend to explain away the manner in which people in authority rose to their positions. They attribute it to luck or favoritism. The slothful also tend to resent those who are over them and to detest having to answer to others.

To ancient Israel, Moses declared, "The LORD shall make thee the head, and not the tail; and thou shalt be above only, and thou shalt not be beneath; if that thou hearken unto the commandments of the LORD thy God, which I command thee this day, to observe and to do them" (Deuteronomy 28:13). Asaph asserted, "For promotion cometh neither from the east, nor from the west, nor from the south. But God is the judge: he putteth down one, and setteth up another" (Psalm 75:6-7).

The role of words in emotional health (verse 25). This verse is a companion to Proverbs 15:13 and 17:22. Depression or despondency has a negative effect upon mental and even physical health. But a good word, a good report, has a positive effect upon the emotions and thereby even on physical health.

One of the greatest factors that contributes to overall health is attitude. For this reason, it is wise not to become preoccupied with evil reports but to focus on what is cheerful, positive, pleasant, helpful, and encouraging. We are to think on things that are of "good report" (Philippians 4:8). This teaching does not mean we should ignore the reality of problems, suffering, and human needs. But rather than allowing these things to conquer our minds, we should become actively and positively involved in overcoming problems and in helping the hurting through their sorrows.

Influence on neighbors (verse 26). This proverb shows the importance of choosing the right friends. A righteous person sets an example for his neighbors that encourages them to raise their standards. But a wicked person seduces his neighbors by his negative influence. He tempts and deceives them into lowering their standards as they observe his godless lifestyle.

Wastefulness and diligence (verse 27). This verse uses the person who does not roast an animal that he killed in hunting as an example of slothfulness. Lazy people typically waste valuable resources and start projects without ever finishing them. A sign of diligence is the careful preservation of resources. Diligence produces quality items that will last; slothfulness produces shoddy items that are soon discarded.

No death on the righteous path (verse 28). Righteousness is a way of life. It is a matter of choosing right, of doing right. It tends to life, for it keeps one out of situations and places that tend to death. And ultimately the righteous will inherit eternal life and be forever triumphant over death.

Chapter Thirteen

Hearing right (verse 1). It is a wise son who listens to and acts on his father's instruction. Even when a son attains adulthood, he is wise to seek his father's counsel as long as his father is alive. Part of honoring one's parents is to consider their advice respectfully even as an adult.

The person who refuses to listen to rebuke is a scorner. This verse presumes a relationship between instruction and rebuke. Rebuke is instruction, and instruction often takes the form of rebuke.

Eating right (verse 2). The fruit of a person's mouth is his words. Someone will "eat good"—things will go well with him—as a result of his speaking good words from a good heart. But the sinner, whose heart is evil and who speaks wrong words, will find that things will not go well with him spiritually. His soul—his mind, will, and emotions—will "eat violence." Ultimately, he will face destruction.

Speaking right (verse 3). A person's life is preserved as he learns to restrain his mouth, his words. But the person with unrestrained words invites destruction. This principle is certainly true spiritually, and in many situations it is true of physical life as well.

Desire and diligence (verse 4). Desire alone is impotent. Positive thinking alone is of little value. Desire must be completed by diligence, and then goals will be attained. The problem with the sluggard is not that he has no ambition. (See Proverbs 21:25.) It is that he refuses to do what is necessary to realize his ambitions. He begins to look for shortcuts, which often lead to dishonesty and crime. Right mental attitude must be completed by right actions.

Hating sin (verse 5). A righteous person will hate sin. (See Proverbs 8:13.) He does not hate sinners, but he hates the sin that destroys sinners. When people do not hate sin it is because they do not focus their attention on the results of sin; they look only at the temporary pleasures. (See Hebrews 11:25.)

A righteous person must hate dishonesty in every form. Since Satan is the father of lies (John 8:44), deception finds its roots in him. Much can be discerned about a person's character by his attitude toward dishonesty, even in others. A wicked person thinks nothing of lying, and this attitude makes him loathsome. Eventually, he will be brought to shame by his dishonesty.

The source of preservation or destruction (verse 6). The way of life an individual chooses will either preserve or destroy him. From a spiritual perspective there is no such thing as fate or luck.

False and true riches (verse 7). This verse is a companion to Proverbs 11:24-25. Stinginess, though it may result in great financial wealth, robs one of all that is worthwhile. While generosity may deplete one's bank account, it will give him true riches.

Undesirable consequences of riches (verse 8). When a

person has money, it makes him a target for kidnappers, thieves, and lawsuits. He may be able to buy his way out of trouble with his money by paying off his enemies. But the poor person who has no money to speak of has very few concerns along these lines. He need not fear kidnappers, thieves, or lawsuits. He hears no rebuke or threats motivated by another person's desire for his money.

The righteous light and the wicked lamp (verse 9). Light emanates from a source such as a lamp. A lamp is a source of light itself. What emanates from the life of a righteous person is joyous and affects others in an uplifting way. Light bears the same relationship to a lamp as fruit to a branch. For this purpose we may compare the light of the righteous to the fruit of the Spirit. (See Galatians 5:22-23.) Such fruit is certainly joyous, having a positive impact both on the person who bears the fruit and others around him. The source of the fruit is the Spirit of God within; the Spirit is also the source of the light that shines forth from a righteous person.

While the light of the righteous is alive, vibrant, rejoicing, the lamp—the original source—of the wicked shall be put out. It will be turned off. It will fail. The wicked does what he does by the power of his own efforts. He does not have the Spirit of God within him to empower him, to give him life and light. Jesus Christ is "the true Light, which lighteth every man that cometh into the world" (John 1:9). If a person does not have Christ within Him, he does not have genuine light. (See Romans 8:9.) The lamp of the wicked, frail and feeble, is his own strength. But human efforts will fail. (See Zechariah 4:6.)

The source of contention (verse 10). Pride produces nothing but strife. Wherever there is contention, pride

125

is the source. When a person is too proud to admit he is wrong or to accept rebuke gracefully, then contention develops. The original contention between God and Lucifer was due to Lucifer's pride. (See Isaiah 14:12-14; Ezekiel 28:17.) Pride may lead a person to give a bad report about another. It may produce gossip. It may provoke rebellion. Whatever its manifestion, pride is behind contention.

Those who are well advised (those who are wise) will avoid contention. They are quick to admit error and to accept rebuke. They refuse to give a bad report, to gossip, to rebel. They have learned that the greatest secret to being used by God is humility, while the greatet hindrance to being used by Him is pride. (See James 4:6.)

Temporary and permanent wealth (verse 11). It may be possible to amass large sums of money improperly, but it will evaporate. Lottery winners and other gamblers often demonstrate this truth in a notable fashion, as do those who come into money dishonestly or illegally.

The person who works hard and honestly and who wisely handles his resources will increase in wealth over the long term. Researchers have discovered that the major difference between the poor and rich is their attitude toward wealth. The rich tend to think of the future, planning in terms of years and decades. The permanently poor, however, tend to think in terms of the immediate. They often focus on instant gratification, immediate rewards. For example, they fantasize that they will win a lottery, inherit a fortune, or otherwise stumble into wealth. People with this attitude are not future oriented, and they usually lack the patience to plan, work, and wait. As a result, they tend to rush into credit purchases that are beyond their means. They want the results of wealth without paying the price.

Deferred hope, fulfilled desires (verse 12). Disappointment comes when expectations and desires are delayed, but joy comes when they are fulfilled. Applying the thought of verse 11 here, those who wish to gain their goals quickly are discouraged by waiting. But when a person learns to wait patiently while working honestly, his desires will be fulfilled at the right time and in the right way. (See Hebrews 10:35-36.) And properly fulfilled desires are positive and satisfying, like the tree of life.

Destruction or reward (verse 13). A person who despises God's Word faces certain destruction. To despise the Word of God means more than a negative mental attitude toward it; it means failing to heed and obey the Word. If it were merely the word of men, one could ignore it and still not actually despise it. But since it is the very Word of God, the person who fails to live by it is actually despising it. His life is a public declaration of his disdain for the Word. A person declares his attitude toward the Word by the time he spends hearing, reading, and learning it and ultimately by his response to it.

The opposite of despising God's Word is to "fear" it, meaning to respect, revere, and heed it. The person who respects the commandment will demonstrate this attitude by obedience. And his reward is just as sure as the sinner's destruction.

The fountain of life (verse 14). Wisdom imparts life. It reveals the hidden snares that lead to death. A snare is a trap that is disguised or hidden, and wisdom is the only thing that pulls the disguise off.

How to gain favor with people (verse 15). A person who

127

seeks understanding—the grasp of broad principles and concepts from the Word of God and the ability to apply them to many different kinds of life situations—will have favor with people. He will be in demand, for there is always a market for understanding. But the transgressor will not have this advantage, and as a result he will struggle needlessly and fruitlessly in life. Jesus is the perfect example of someone who grew in wisdom and therefore in favor with both God and man (Luke 2:52).

Prudent dealings (verse 16). The mark of a prudent person is that he acts with knowledge. He is not satisfied to deal with people or situations with only surface information. He acts only when he has sufficient information. By contrast, a fool is content to deal without sufficient knowledge, and as a result, his folly is made public.

The importance of being a faithful representative (verse 17). If a person is unfaithful in representing another, he will cause and experience trouble. Someone who is faithful and dependable as he represents another will contribute to the well-being of his employer or superior. (See Proverbs 25:13.) This truth has important implications for our Christian witness, for we are ambassadors for Christ (II Corinthians 5:20; II Timothy 2:2).

One of the quickest and most effective ways for an employer to discover whether his employee is faithful is to give him the responsibility of representing him in some manner. As he observes the manner in which he is represented, he can tell how the employee would handle even greater responsibilities. The ideal ambassador will conduct himself exactly as his master would have done.

A key to success (verse 18). The person who refuses to receive instruction from others—one who thinks he knows it all—will come to poverty and shame. The person who appreciates and responds positively to correction will be honored. There is a close relationship between someone's attitude toward reproof and his success in life.

The price for success is too great for the fool (verse 19). To accomplish what one sets out to do is uplifting and encouraging. But fools do not achieve worthwhile spiritual goals because to do so they would have to depart from sin, and this they are unwilling to do. They actually would hate to turn away from their sinful lifestyle.

The importance of right friends (verse 20). As the apostle Paul taught, wrong friends have a corrupting influence (I Corinthians 15:33). We tend to become like the people we admire and associate with and to participate in their activities. One of the wisest things a person can do is to associate with people who personify what he wishes to become. Association with wise people imparts wisdom. Association with fools will bring destruction.

Sowing and reaping (verse 21). This verse states the law of sowing and reaping as described in Galatians 6:7-9. The sinner will find that he is pursued by the fruit of his sin. The person who does right will find that good things come to him.

The inheritance of a good person and the sinner's wealth (verse 22). It is a good person who carefully conserves, uses less than he produces, and spends less than he earns in order to leave an inheritance not only to his children but also to his grandchildren. This verse thus indicates the wisdom of saving and investing. The inheritance it speaks of probably also describes the lasting positive influence a godly person has, not only on his children but also upon his grandchildren. (See Proverbs 17:6.)

Materialism has so affected the thinking of people that a popular view of inheritance is expressed on a bumper sticker: "We're spending our children's inheritance." The idea is to use up everything one has and to leave nothing behind. But a righteous person is concerned about more than just his personal gratification. He is more interested in raising up the foundations of many godly generations. (See Isaiah 58:12.)

On the other hand, when a person disregards God and robs Him in order to amass wealth, God has a way of placing that wealth into the hands of the just. Only the righteous have an everlasting inheritance.

Industriousness and wastefulness (verse 23). There is much productivity even in the land of poor people, but injustice often causes it to be destroyed or wasted. Even though someone is poor, if he is wise he will not be wasteful. He will use all he has and make it produce the most possible. But one of the signs of a lack of judgment is senseless waste.

Tough love (verse 24). Some parents deceive themselves into thinking that they love their children too much to discipline them. But the father who refuses to discipline his children actually acts as if he hates them. He shows no concern for the development of their character. (See Proverbs 19:18; 22:15; 23:13-14; 29:15; Hebrews 12:6-11.) The parent who loves his children will chasten them early in life. (The word *betimes* means "early, promptly.") The person who receives no discipline while he is growing up will have very little self-control and will be of shallow character.

Discipline does not mean beating or abuse. We can learn how to discipline our children appropriately by noting the following aspects of God's chastening of His children. (1) He never leaves a question as to His love for His children. (2) While the discipline may be painful, the pain is never permanent. There is no injury. (3) He does not chasten in an emotional fit of anger, but out of a determination of what is best for the disobedient person. (4) He restores the offender back to fellowship with Him. (5) When the discipline has been rendered and forgiveness sought and granted, He never brings up the offense again. (6) The discipline is designed and intended to produce repentance, not rebellion.

The secret of satisfaction (verse 25). Satisfaction or dissatisfaction is not a matter of quantity, but of righteousness or wickedness. The righteous person will be content with what he has. (See Philippians 4:11; I Timothy 6:8.) The wicked person will never be satisfied. He always craves for more. But only God can satisfy the inner longings of the soul (Isaiah 55:1-3).

Chapter Fourteen

Women who build and tear down (verse 1). A woman who is wise will do things that strengthen her family by increasing her husband's devotion to her and causing her children to admire her. The foolish woman does the very things that tend to destroy her family and her marriage. The woman who usurps authority over her husband will weaken her family and marriage. (See Ephesians 5:22-24; I Timothy 2:11-12.)

The proof is in the lifestyle (verse 2). A person may make all kinds of confessions with his mouth, but in the final analysis, his love for God or his indifference toward Him is demonstrated by the way he lives. At some point, faith must be translated into action. Without works, faith is dead. (See James 2:14-26.)

The rod of pride (verse 3). The "rod of pride" here is a metaphor for foolish, vain, conceited words. The motivating factor behind most foolish conversation is pride. The rod is a weapon; and thus the rod of pride in the fool's mouth indicates that his words are dangerous and damaging. They will provoke retaliation.

The wise person, however, will speak words that will protect and bless him. A good example is found in Proverbs 15:1: "A soft answer turneth away wrath."

The value of investing (verse 4). This verse states that a good return justifies an investment. The person who owns no oxen does not have to invest in the food needed to feed them. But neither will he receive the rewards of the oxen's efforts. The ox is made strong by the food he eats, and this strength in turn enables him to produce for his owner. He will produce far more than he eats.

Throughout the Scriptures, the wisdom of investment is evident. Perhaps the parable of the talents best illustrates this principle (Matthew 25:14-30). The person who spends all he earns will never reap the rewards of investment.

Faithful and false witnesses (verse 5). People are not to bear false witness against others (Exodus 20:16). One need not be in a courtroom to be a witness. Passing along information that has not been verified can lead to false witness. A false witness is a liar. (See also Proverbs 14:25.)

Finding wisdom and knowledge (verse 6). Scorners may seek wisdom, but they will not find it, for a major key in the search for wisdom is to have the right attitude toward it. By contrast, the person of understanding will find that knowledge will come to him relatively easily. If a person appreciates knowledge and recognizes its value, research and study will be a pleasure. But if he is scornful about the value of study, his work will be dull and the satisfaction of discovery will elude him. Moreover, his contemptuous, mocking attitude will cause him to miss or reject truth when he comes across it.

Departing from a fool (verse 7). A person's foolishness is made evident by the untrue or ignorant words he speaks. Since we will be influenced by those with whom we have fellowship, it is unwise to associate closely with such a person.

Understanding why (verse 8). The prudent person displays his wisdom by his desire to understand his way, which implies knowing more than just the "what." It takes little wisdom to see what is happening, but it takes wisdom to see why it is happening. The word *ways* speaks of the "why." Fools are concerned only with what is happening, but this approach is deceitful, for nothing happens in a vacuum. There is a cause for every effect. There is a seed for every flower. Wisdom causes a person to look beneath the surface to find the source, while folly results in deception.

Mocking sin (verse 9). Sin is amusing only to fools; a wise person hates sin. This trait of the spiritually foolish demonstrates that they have a very limited view. They see only the immediate, whereas the spiritually wise have a long-range vision. The wise look beyond the short-term pleasure of sin to the sure and ultimate destruction it brings. Sin is mocked only by those who cannot see past the immediate and momentary pleasure to the destruction and death that is the final flower of sin's seed. God can extend no favor to those who love what He hates, but He does grant favor to those who love righteousness.

Private emotions (verse 10). Neither the joys nor the sorrows of one person can be wholly shared with another. No person stands in such an intimate relationship with another that he can put himself in the other person's place so entirely as to identify perfectly with what that person feels. Nevertheless Christians should strive as far as possible to identify with others in their sorrows and joys (Romans 12:15).

Insecurity and stability (verse 11). A recurring theme in the Book of Proverbs is the insecurity of the wicked.

It is important to realize this truth, for from the limited perspective of human experience, it may appear that the wicked are successful and stable. But from God's perspective of eternity, where even the nations are as a drop in the bucket (Isaiah 40:15), there is no security at all in wickedness. And regardless of what our senses tell us, the upright are not only stable and secure, but they will prosper in the way that really matters.

The way that seems right (verse 12). We must not walk by our physical senses and carnal human reasoning. The way that leads to death actually seems right to the flesh. As far as the eyes can see, the ears can hear, and the senses can reveal, it is the right path to take. But the end of this way is death. (See Matthew 7:13-14.)

How then are we to walk? We must forsake what the senses, the carnal mind, and human traditions tell us and instead walk only on the path revealed by the Word of God. (See Psalm 1; 119:105.)

Laughter and sorrow (verse 13). This verse seems to bear a relationship with the previous one. While a merry heart is beneficial, the laughter of the carnal person ultimately does not end in good. It does not lift the heart. When the laughter is over, the heart is still sorrowful and heaviness still weighs down the soul.

The backslider and the good person (verse 14). Both the backslider and the good person will reap what they sow. The backslider may put on a good front; he may fool others into thinking that everything is still right between him and God. But his problem is a heart problem. He turns from the true God and sets himself up as god. Instead of being filled with God's ways, he is now filled with his own ways. And he is a poor substitute for God.

A good person is content in the knowledge that he is doing right. He is not filled with the apprehension that consumes the person who follows his own senses. He knows God has given him the power to do right, and if he makes the choice to act on that power, God will be pleased and good things will happen.

The gullible and the prudent (verse 15). The simplistic person believes everything he hears, sees, and reads. Like a child, he is tossed to and fro, carried about with every wind of teaching. (See Ephesians 4:14.) He cannot see the violation of biblical principles. He does not recognize the telltale signs of deceit. He is a ready victim for those who would take advantage of him. But the prudent person is cautious. He does not believe something just because someone says it; he searches out the facts for himself. He goes to the source.

Taking chances (verse 16). A wise person has the good sense to know when to stop, when to draw back. He takes no chances with evil; he turns from it. The fool, in his self-confidence, blusters and boasts. He will probably pay the price for his confident raging in personal pain and injury.

Losing one's temper (verse 17). A hot-headed person will make foolish decisions. (See also Proverbs 14:29.) A person who dreams up wicked schemes to take advantage of others will be hated.

Rewards (verse 18). In keeping with the theme of cause and effect that runs throughout the Book of Proverbs, this proverb reveals that those who are simple (spiritually ignorant) will inherit folly as a child inherits property or wealth from a parent. It is the natural result of his identity. Just as a child inherits from his father because of who he is, so the simpleton inherits folly because of what he is. Folly indicates emptiness, meaninglessness, uselessness. No purpose or reason can be seen in it. To this person, life will seem to be a series of disconnected, negative events. In short, things will not go well with him.

Just as a prince will receive the crown from his father because of who he is, so those who are prudent will be crowned with knowledge. The person who chooses prudence as a way of life identifies himself with royalty. He displays kingly traits. His crown will not be a mere temporal crown; he will be crowned with something far more valuable and lasting than gold or silver or precious stones. He will be crowned with knowledge.

It has been said, "Knowledge is power." Those who have true knowledge have tapped into a divine resource, for only God truly knows all things. Humans will never have all knowledge, but to have some knowledge is a marvelous gift.

The ultimate exaltation of the righteous (verse 19). In this present world it may seem for a time that those who reject God are in a position of supremacy, but the day will come when they will submit to those who are submitted to God. For example, in Revelation 20:4-6 believers are given thrones and share in Christ's reign.

The sin of favoritism (verses 20-21). Many people treat others on the basis of their economic position. The underlying motive is personal advantage. In other words, many people ignore the poor because they perceive little economic advantage in helping them. By befriending the rich, they hope to gain economically.

But it is sinful to despise another person because of his poverty. Everyone is equal in value in the eyes of God

(Acts 10:34; James 2:1-9). The person who despises the poor is not thinking or acting like God. When the Spirit of the Lord anoints a person, he will be motivated to minister to everyone, especially the poor, as Jesus did (Luke 4:17-19). The person who thinks little of others because of their low social or economic standing will not find true happiness, but the one who has mercy on the poor will be happy. There is even an economic blessing to having mercy on the poor: those who give to the poor are actually lending to the Lord, and their gift will be returned to them (Proverbs 19:17).

Devising evil or good (verse 22). Just as some people devise evil, so believers should purposefully devise good. All human powers and abilities that wicked people turn to evil purposes, the righteous can use for good. Planning, goal setting, organizing, thinking—all can be used for evil or good. The person who uses these God-given abilities to conceive and create what is morally good will receive mercy and truth. While God resists those who devise evil by confounding their efforts (Genesis 11:6-7), He supports those who devise good.

Labor profits; talk does not (verse 23). It is common for people to spend great amounts of time talking about how they are going to achieve. But many of those who talk the most never get around to doing anything about it. If people would simply exert the same energy in working rather than talking, they would profit. Mere talking, however, leads to poverty. Rewards come from labor and effort, not empty words. Moreover, God rewards obedience, not mere profession.

Knowledge is like riches (verse 24). Verse 18 states, "The prudent are crowned with knowledge." To the wise person, this crown of knowledge is true wealth. He understands what is truly valuable. And as verse 18 also points out, the only alternative to knowledge is folly.

True and deceitful witnesses (verse 25). There is deliverance only in the truth. Deceit never brings genuine freedom. Human wisdom may suggest that a lie would spare someone from the consequences of his deeds, but even if he gained physical freedom in this way, he would still be captive to fear and guilt and would face his sin in the judgment.

True witnesses are much more concerned about delivering the innocent from trouble than in condemning others. Even when they must testify as to a person's evil deeds, it is with the motive of bringing genuine freedom to the victim. There is true freedom only in truth. A deceitful witness, on the other hand, condemns the innocent.

The benefits of revering the Lord (verses 26-27). These two verses list four benefits of fearing, or revering, the Lord. They are: (1) strong confidence; (2) a place of refuge; (3) a fountain of life; and (4) deliverance from the snares of death. None are more confident than those who fear God. Their fear of God removes their fear of all else. Those who fear God need not fear trials and temptations, for they have a place of refuge in Him. Those who fear God need not fear death, for in Him there is only life and even physical death is but a transition to eternal life.

The blessing of population (verse 28). The thing that brings honor to a ruler is how many people willingly serve him. A large or increasing population usually indicates that the government is fulfilling some basic responsibilities: the country is not being ravaged by war, massacres, famine, deadly disease, or mass exodus. A decreasing population, however, indicates severe disruptions in the society and will likely lead to massive social upheaval. A lack of people can lead to a lack of political, economic, or military strength.

Self-control (verse 29). As in verse 17, here we see the virtue of controlling the temper. Great understanding will cause a person to be slow to wrath. He realizes there is much more at stake than merely getting his way. He looks beneath the surface and behind the scenes. He is not so much interested in *what* transpires as *why*. The New Testament reinforces the value of being slow to wrath (James 1:19). A person who is quick-tempered exalts folly.

Sources of health and illness (verse 30). In the context of this verse, a "sound heart" is more than a physically healthy heart. It is sound in the sense of being pure and clean. It does not harbor bitterness, envy, pride, greed, or moral impurity. One of the greatest contributing factors to physical and emotional health is spiritual soundness. By contrast, envy contributes to physical and emotional illness. It is "rottenness of the bones," which indicates a serious condition indeed, for bone marrow to a large degree is responsible for the condition of one's health. The marrow contributes to the condition of the blood, which carries life-giving oxygen and nutrients to all parts of the body.

The right attitude toward God and the poor (verse 31). God takes note of the way people treat each other. This is why His Word repeatedly warns against the sin of respecting of persons (prejudice or favoritism). The second greatest commandment is to love our neighbors as ourselves (Mark 12:31). The commandment applies regardless of the economic status of one's neighbors; in fact, it is especially important to help people who are in need. Thus, it is a reproach to God to oppress the poor, which includes taking advantage of them or imposing unreasonable and unjust requirements on them. The person who honors God will demonstrate it by being merciful to the poor. The ideal way to help them is on a personal, individual basis.

The results of wickedness and righteousness (verse 32). The wicked person has chosen a course of life that will destroy him, but the righteous person has hope even in death. Life on earth will be the best and most pleasant experience a wicked person will ever have, but life on earth will be the worst experience the righteous will ever have.

Retaining wisdom, revealing folly (verse 33). A person of understanding will not tell all he knows; he allows some things to rest in his heart. A fool, on the other hand, finds it quite impossible to hide the thoughts of his heart. They will at some point be made public.

The exaltation of a nation (verse 34). The only thing that truly exalts or honors a nation is righteousness. Weapons will not do it, nor will negotiation. Righteousness must be in the hearts of people; it cannot be conveyed through legislation. But if a nation's laws are not founded on moral principles, then they are founded upon immorality.

Sin brings reproach or shame to any people who practice it, and ultimately it will bring down any nation. The once mighty kingdoms of the past that exist only in rubble today are a mute testimony to this truth.

How to gain favor with those in authority (verse 35). Wisdom gives a person favor with those in authority. Examples are Joseph, Daniel, and his three Hebrew friends (Genesis 41:38-41; Daniel 1:19-20). Those in authority will eventually turn in anger on servants who cause them shame by their unwise actions. An example is King Darius's treatment of those who deceived him by issuing the decree that resulted in Daniel's being cast into the lion's den (Daniel 6:24-28).

Chapter Fifteen

How to defuse anger in others (verse 1). The greatest single contributing factor to anger is the tongue. While grievous words stir up anger, soft responses to anger will turn it away. In the Sermon on the Mount, Jesus similarly taught us to resolve disputes through reconciliation, negotiation, and humility rather than by retaliation or vengeance (Matthew 5:23-26, 38-42). Pride causes a person to be extremely defensive and to respond in harshness, but humility speaks softly.

Using knowledge correctly (verse 2). It is not enough to have knowledge; one must know how to use it. There is a right time and a right place to speak. Fools not only lack knowledge, but they lack control over their tongues. Foolishness pours out of their mouths.

The eyes of the Lord (verse 3). One aspect of the fear of the Lord is the awareness that He is evaluating each thought, word, and deed. God is omnipresent and omniscient; nothing escapes His attention. People may never see or know what another has done, but God knows, and He will reward each person according to his works. He beholds and rewards both the evil and the good. (See Matthew 6:1-18; I Corinthians 3:12-15; Ephesians 6:8; Revelation 20:12-13.)

A wholesome tongue (verse 4). A wholesome tongue is a tongue that speaks wisdom, and it is a source of life. (See Proverbs 3:18.) A perverse tongue—a tongue that speaks unwise and evil things—causes a breach, or break, in a person's spirit. It can also cause similar harm to the hearer.

Handling a father's reproof (verse 5). Anyone who despises his father's instruction is a fool. A sign of prudence is to regard reproof. Even when the father is not right, it is important that the son consider his words carefully and respond respectfully. A father can be wrong, and there may be cases when a son or daughter cannot act on his or her father's instruction because it contradicts God's Word. (See Matthew 10:34-36.) But even if the father cannot be obeyed because his instructions are ungodly, he must be honored because he is the father. (See Exodus 20:12.) In general, children who are still at home under the direct authority of their parents are to obey them (Ephesians 6:1-2; Colossians 3:20). But even those who have left father and mother to establish a new family and authority structure still are to honor their parents.

True treasure (verse 6). The righteous are truly rich. They possess riches that cannot be taken away, the most important of which is eternal life. Also included in this lasting wealth are fellowship with God, peace of mind, the genuine fruit of the Spirit, purpose, and the family of God. None of these things can be stolen or destroyed. (See Proverbs 10:22; Matthew 6:19-21.) But trouble accompanies what is gained wickedly, dishonestly, or violently. There is a blessing on the income of those who honor God and a curse on the income of those who fail to honor Him. (See Malachi 3:8-12.)

Wise lips, foolish hearts (verse 7). As Jesus taught, it is from the abundance of the heart that the mouth speaks (Matthew 12:34). The lips of the wise disperse knowledge because knowledge is in their hearts. But the heart of the fool is void of knowledge; therefore his lips cannot produce it. A wise heart and foolish lips are not companions, nor are a foolish heart and wise lips.

Abominable ways and sacrifices (verses 8-9). God has no pleasure in gifts from ungodly people, for He has no pleasure in their motives (ways). (See Deuteronomy 23:18; Proverbs 28:9.) But just as God abhors the sacrifices of the wicked because He hates their ways, He delights in the prayers of the righteous because He loves their way of life. If for no other reason, this truth should be a motivation to prayer: it brings delight to God.

When correction is grievous (verse 10). Severe discipline awaits those who forsake God's way. Correction antagonizes only those who have no desire to do right; when a person forsakes the right way and refuses to be corrected, he chooses the way of death.

The omnipresence and omniscience of God (verse 11). There is nothing of which God is unaware. He is fully aware of the spirit world and the status of those who have died, and He is certainly aware of all that is in the hearts of people. There is no place where God is not; this attribute is His omnipresence. There is nothing God does not know; this attribute is His omniscience. (See Psalm 139:1-12; Jeremiah 23:23-24.)

The danger of counselling only with one's peers (verse 12). A scorner hates to be corrected, and thus he will not go to the wise for advice. He will go only to those he knows will agree with him and will approve his actions. This was the error of Rehoboam, Solomon's son, which resulted in the revolt of the ten northern tribes. (See I Kings 12:6-11.) For this reason it is extremely important that parents keep the lines of communication open with their children; otherwise their children will tend to seek and accept counsel only from their peers, which will frequently be wrong counsel.

What the countenance reveals (verse 13). It is often possible to discern the condition of someone's heart by observing his countenance. When the heart is merry, the countenance is cheerful. Cheerfulness is more than excitement; it includes peace, contentment, and joy. But the spirit is broken by a sorrowful heart, which is usually reflected on the countenance as well.

Feeding on knowledge or foolishness (verse 14). It is a sign of understanding to seek after knowledge. Fools are content, however, to mouth empty foolishness, to carry on frothy, meaningless, unproductive conversations.

Life as a banquet (verse 15). This verse appears to be a companion to verse 13. There, a merry heart is commended as the source of a cheerful countenance, while a sorrowful heart is said to break the spirit. Here, a merry heart is seen as causing one's life to be like a continual feast. This verse does not mean that a merry heart will prevent all unpleasant events from occurring but that a merry heart will cause even these events to have a positive and nourishing effect in the long run. A person with a merry heart enjoys life. He sees the bright side, he looks for and sees the good rather than the bad. This outlook is good for him physically, emotionally, mentally, and spiritually. (See Proverbs 17:22.)

By contrast, those without a merry heart see all of

life as evil. They see no point in affliction, no purpose in pain, no good in the world. The difference in the quality of life is not without, but within. The choice to have a merry heart puts a different perspective on all of life.

The relationship between possessions and the right attitude toward God (verse 16). A simple lesson, but one so rarely learned, is that the quality of life has nothing to do with the quantity of possessions. A person who serves God, though he has little, is in a much better situation than one who rejects God and has immense material wealth. A person who does not serve God will discover that material wealth is no guarantee of peace. Indeed, he will experience as much trouble as someone who is poor and rejects God. He will have not one ounce of genuine peace or happiness more than his sinner neighbor. But the person who serves God will have peace of heart and mind, though he may have little in the way of material wealth. (See Psalm 37:16.)

The relationship between possessions and the right attitude toward one another (verse 17). It is love that creates a happy home, not luxury and riches. It is love that makes a dinner a joyous occasion, not the quantity or quality of food. (See Proverbs 17:1.)

The atmosphere around the table should be one of tranquility and love. Eating should be a time of genuine fellowship and relaxation. Parents who use mealtime to correct their children or to bring up unpleasant subjects are making a mistake. Food cannot be properly digested when one is tense or angry. Mothers particularly should work at creating an atmosphere of peace for family meals.

Stirring up or appeasing strife (verse 18). A person who stirs up strife, regardless of his self-justifications, is a man of wrath. He may hide his emotions beneath a facade of concern or self-righteousness, but beneath the surface he is an angry man. But someone who has his emotions under control will demonstrate it by defusing strife.

The thorny path of the slothful (verse 19). One of the consequences of slothfulness is unpleasant, painful adversity. When the slothful person does move, it is as if he is caught in a hedge of thorns. There is trouble in every direction. But the way of the righteous is cleared of obstructions. He is able to make headway, to progress without undue difficulty.

The marks of a wise or foolish son (verse 20). To a large degree, the emotions of parents are affected by the behavior of their children. It is an unusual parent who can demonstrate gladness when he has a foolish son. A wise son will behave in a manner that makes his parents glad; anyone who despises them is foolish. Regardless of circumstances, children should show respect for their parents because of their position. A son should honor his mother, regardless of her attitude or spiritual condition.

A substitute for joy (verse 21). Someone who has no wisdom will mistake folly for joy. He is unable to see that folly is but a poor substitute. He may laugh, but the laughter is empty. (See Proverbs 14:13.) A wise person immediately sees the emptiness of folly and rejects it. In his understanding, he walks uprightly, and he will have true joy.

The wisdom of seeking counsel (verse 22). The person who acts without counsel can be sure he is overlooking something that could well bring his plans to naught. It is impossible for someone to see all the ramifications of an important decision. No individual can foresee all the potential pitfalls. It is good to have purpose in life, but for purposes to be achieved, counsel must be sought. The wise person will listen to counsel, even when he does not like it, and will apply it appropriately to his situation. By seeking out many counsellors he will accomplish his objectives.

Words are a source of joy (verse 23). When someone knows he has said the right thing, it brings him joy. Not only is it important to say the right thing, it is also important to find the right time—the due season—to say it. The right word spoken at the right time is good and satisfying, and it produces joy even in the person who speaks it.

The high road (verse 24). The wise person keeps looking up. He sets his affections (desires, goals) on things above. (See Colossians 3:1-2.) By so doing, he leaves death and hell behind. He chooses the high road.

The destroyed house and the established border (verse 25). A house is a specific dwelling place. In general, a house sits on a piece of property larger than itself; a person could lose some of his property and still have his home. God strikes at the central dwelling place of the proud. He destroys not only the periphery, but He deals with the heart of the matter.

On the other hand, God is quite concerned with the well-being of the widows and fatherless. (See Psalm 68:5.) He particularly aids the needy or helpless who trust in Him. Thus, He will not only preserve the widow's house, but He will also preserve her border, or the limit of her property. God takes notice of everything that belongs to a widow, and He will personally deal with any individual who takes advantage of her. Jesus soundly condemned the Pharisees for their wrongful treatment of widows

(Matthew 23:14). One way to measure the purity of one's religion is by his treatment of widows and orphans (James 1:27).

Wicked thoughts and pleasant words (verse 26). The wicked person does not have to express his thoughts in words for God to be aware of them. Even his thoughts are detestable to God. Since thoughts produce words and since the words of the pure person are pleasant, it is evident that his thoughts are also pleasant and appropriate.

The key to controlling one's words is to control one's thoughts. An unregenerated person may have little success in controlling his thoughts, but a person who has been born again has been delivered from sin's mastery. Now he can choose whether to yield his members, including his mind, to sin or to God (Romans 6:13). By God's grace he can overcome temptation and control his tongue.

The danger of greed and bribery (verse 27). Someone whose chief aim in life is to get money will invariably bring trouble to his home. His greed will lead him to unethical or sinful conduct, which will eventually result in problems. His own family will often hate or resent his devotion to money. He may claim to pursue money for the benefit of his family, but in doing so he robs them of what they really desire. For example, he may work two or three jobs or otherwise minimize his time with his wife and children under the guise of making life better for them. But what they really want is him, not his money. Pampered children frequently reject the lifestyles of wealthy parents, despising them for worshiping the "almighty dollar."

Those who are consumed by greed will generally stop at nothing to add to their stockpile of material goods. They often welcome or solicit "gifts" that are really bribes. The person who hates and thus rejects bribes has chosen the right path, the path of life.

Thinking before answering (verse 28). A wise, righteous person will think before he responds to others. He weighs the possible consequences of his words, and thus he does not answer quickly. The wicked person, on the other hand, has no concern for the appropriateness of his response. His words are so profuse, plentiful, and quick that they "pour out" of his mouth. The word *studieth* denotes careful consideration; the word *poureth* suggests careless babbling.

How far away is the Lord? (verse 29). Sin separates a person from God (Isaiah 59:1-2). There is no point in a wicked person—one who refuses to confess and repent of his sins—calling on the Lord. The only prayer the Lord is interested in hearing from that person is one that will lead him to repentance and salvation. While God readily hears the prayer of the righteous, He does not respond to the prayer of an unbelieving, unrepentant rebel. (See Proverbs 28:9.)

Clear vision and good news (verse 30). Jesus said, "The light of the body is the eye: therefore when thine eye is single, thy whole body also is full of light; but when thine eye is evil, thy body also is full of darkness" (Luke 11:34). Much of the spiritual well-being of an individual has to do with what he allows his eyes to look upon. Job made a covenant with his eyes not to dwell on temptation (Job 31:1). David declared that he would set no wicked thing before his eyes (Psalm 101:3). A person tends to think about what he looks at. Eyes that look upon right things let light into the inner man, the heart. Of course, it is possible to misuse the "mind's eye" as well, that is, the

God-given gift of imagination, the ability to picture things in the mind. If it is important to use the natural eye rightly, it is also important to use the mental eye correctly.

A good report has a positive effect on a person. It "maketh the bones fat," or in other words, it is healthful. What a person listens to has a dramatic impact on his physical and emotional well-being. A wise person will, therefore, control not only his eyes but also his ears.

Wise use of the ear (verse 31). The Book of Proverbs repeatedly stresses the importance of hearing and accepting instruction and reproof. One of the wise uses of the ear is to listen to reproof, specifically the "reproof of life." A wise person learns from circumstances and situations that others may reject as simply being "bad breaks." He carefully "listens" to discern the cause behind the effect.

Refusing instruction and hearing reproof (verse 32). The person who refuses to let anybody tell him what to do actually damages himself. If he would accept instruction and reproof, he would gain understanding.

Wisdom's lesson (verse 33). Wisdom teaches us, above all else, to fear God. Respecting and obeying God is the greatest lesson anyone can ever learn. The person who rejects this lesson rejects the ultimate truth that wisdom offers.

Humility precedes honor. Someone who exalts and promotes himself will come to nothing; he will be humiliated. But the person who chooses to humble himself will ultimately be honored by others, and this honor will have no evil results.

Chapter Sixteen

Guidance from God (verse 1). Humans can make their own plans, but they need God's help to provide a wise answer. Of course, it is God who initially gave us the ability to think, to plan, to set goals, to conceive ideas, to believe, to use our creative mental capacity—the "preparation of the heart"—and the ability to formulate these ideas and concepts into words that may be spoken. We may develop plans, but ultimately we need God's grace to express and implement them properly and to direct the final outcome.

Self-justification and God's judgment (verse 2). People tend to justify themselves. The human mind is extremely creative in finding ways to justify itself. No one can clearly and honestly see all his own failures (Jeremiah 17:9). But the Lord is not deceived by human self-justification. He bypasses actions and explanations and goes right to the heart of the matter by weighing, or measuring, a person's spirit. If the spirit is right, the person will be right. If it is wrong, the person will be wrong. Thus the Lord told Samuel, "Look not on his countenance, or on the height of his stature; because I have refused him: for the LORD seeth not as man seeth; for man looketh on the outward appearance, but the LORD looketh on the heart" (I Samuel 16:7).

The establishment of thoughts (verse 3). How can one's thoughts be established? How can they be solidified, brought into captivity, controlled? It can be done only as a person commits his works to the Lord. Until a person commits his works—actions, deeds—to the Lord, he will be unable to control his thoughts. He will be doubleminded and therefore unstable in all this ways (James 1:8). There is a direct correlation between what a person thinks and what he does. A person cannot long think one way and act another way. And just as thoughts tend to influence actions, actions tend to influence thoughts. So rather than recommending a cerebral exercise in right thinking only, Scripture suggests a more practical and useful approach: right action done in a purposeful, systematic manner will tend to produce right thoughts as a consequence.

All creation praises God (verse 4). In the beginning God created everything for His own purposes, and ultimately everything will work together to bring glory to God. "Thou art worthy, O Lord, to receive glory and honour and power: for thou hast created all things, and for thy pleasure they are and were created" (Revelation 4:11). God even brings good things to pass out of negative events, circumstances, and people. (See Romans 8:28.)

God is totally in control of His creation, and this proverb specifically includes the wicked as having been made for the day of evil. In God's plan, they are prepared for destruction (Romans 9:22). Asaph uttered a similar truth: "Surely the wrath of man shall praise thee: the remainder of wrath shalt thou restrain" (Psalm 76:10). Ultimately even sinful humanity will glorify God, for God's eventual judgment of human sin will reveal His righteousness, justice, and power (Romans 9:22).

The unbiblical doctrines of unconditional predestination and the restitution of all things do not follow from these verses, however. God's grace enables all people to be free moral agents; they can choose either to submit to God or to rebel against Him. Those who reject Him will have no further opportunity to submit to Him after death. And neither Satan nor his angels have any biblical hope of ever being restored to fellowship with God. Nevertheless, even the enemies of God are under His ultimate sovereignty, and even those who reject Him and fight against Him will ultimately fit into His master plan. If people submit to God, He uses them to fulfill His plan, but even when people rebel against Him, God is able to work with and around their wrongful acts to accomplish His purpose.

A practical example is seen in the crucifixion of Jesus. His enemies, including Satan, thought to destroy Him and His influence by this criminal act. But instead, God turned this terrible event into a blessing for all the world. As Paul said, "Which none of the princes of this world knew: for had they known it, they would not have crucified the Lord of glory" (I Corinthians 2:8). Likewise, in the Old Testament, God used the actions of wicked men to further His purposes, including men such as Pharaoh, Cyrus, and Nebuchadnezzar. (See Isaiah 54:16.)

The abomination of pride and the fruitlessness of uniting against God (verse 5). God hates pride, which is self-will and self-centeredness. Pride was the original sin of Lucifer, and it is the root of the other two basic sins: greed and moral impurity. (See I John 2:16.) It may be possible to portray a humble facade for a time while concealing pride in the heart, but this verse points out that it is the proud heart that God sees and rejects. He is never deceived by appearances. Indeed, Jesus urged, "Judge not according to the appearance, but judge righteous judgment" (John 7:24).

Regardless of the apparent unity that those who reject God may temporarily achieve—though they join hand in hand in their opposition to Him—they shall be punished. If all the sinners in the world united in their opposition to God, He would still judge them. Human agreement does not determine what is right. The kingdom of God does not operate as a democracy, but as a theocracy.

How iniquity is purged and how people depart from evil (verse 6). Repeatedly the Scriptures stress the relationship between mercy and truth. Neither is complete without the other. The psalmist wrote, "Mercy and truth are met together; righteousness and peace have kissed each other" (Psalm 85:10). Wherever genuine mercy is found, truth will be there also; wherever genuine truth is found, mercy will be there also. Anything that masquerades as mercy without truth is at best human tolerance. Anything that masquerades as truth without mercy is at best legalism. Iniquity—sinfulness—is purged only by the cooperation of truth and mercy.

The encounter between the prophet Nathan and King David provides an example. As David was confronted with the truth of his sin, he confessed and received the mercy of God (II Samuel 12:1-14). David's prayer of repentance included these words: "Have mercy upon me, O God, according to thy lovingkindness: according unto the multitude of thy tender mercies blot out my transgressions. Wash me throughly from mine iniquity, and cleanse me from my sin. . . . Behold, thou desirest truth in the inward parts" (Psalm 51:1-2, 6).

This proverb also answers the question of why some people do not depart from evil: it is because they do not fear the Lord. (See Job 28:28.) When people do not fear the Lord, all the good intentions they may have and all the lectures they may hear will have little positive result. People depart from evil by the fear of the Lord. Essentially, the fear of the Lord is the moment-by-moment awareness that He is judging every thought, word, and deed coupled with genuine respect and reverence for Him and His Word.

How to be at peace with enemies (verse 7). Someone who is experiencing conflict with others should first examine his own ways. "Ways" are first of all motives and purposes, followed by corresponding conduct. In general, if one's motives are right, God will cause even his enemies to be at peace with him.

The believer should not look at conflict as an isolated incident, unrelated to anything else. In every situation and circumstance in the believer's life, God is at work, trying to shape and mold the believer into the image of Jesus Christ (Romans 8:28-29). This process does not occur without conflict. Even believers are so far from pleasing God in all their ways that a certain amount of friction and pain will be involved in bringing them into conformity. The proper response to conflict is not to move to another location or to respond in kind but to change one's ways to please the Lord more perfectly.

This verse does not mean that God's enemies will always be at peace with God's children. Jesus said, "If the world hate you, ye know that it hated me before it hated you. If ye were of the world, the world would love his own: but because ye are not of the world, but I have chosen you out of the world, therefore the world hateth you. Remember the word that I said unto you, The servant is not greater than his lord. If they have persecuted me, they will also persecute you; if they have kept my saying, they will keep yours also" (John 15:18-20). He also declared, "Think not that I am come to send peace on earth: I came not to send peace, but a sword. For I am come to set a man at variance against his father, and the daughter against her mother, and the daughter in law against her mother in law. And a man's foes shall be they of his own household" (Matthew 10:34-36). Proverbs 16:7 does not focus upon enemies of God, but upon enemies of a person. When someone lives according to divine principles, as far as natural human affairs are concerned he will be able to live in harmony with others.

Right priorities (verse 8). The most important thing in life is not money but one's relationship with God. Someone who has few material possessions but who is right with God is in a much better condition than someone who possesses vast wealth without a relationship with God, especially someone who accumulates vast sums dishonestly. (See Psalm 37:16; Proverbs 15:16-17; 17:1.)

The steps of a good person (verse 9). Though we may make plans and set goals, it is God who directs our steps. As Jeremiah recognized, "O LORD, I know that the way of man is not in himself: it is not in man that walketh to direct his steps" (Jeremiah 10:23). People are helpless, apart from the gracious influence of God, to turn themselves from evil: "I have surely heard Ephraim bemoaning himself thus; Thou hast chastised me, and I was chastised, as a bullock unaccustomed to the yoke: turn thou me, and I shall be turned; for thou art the LORD my God" (Jeremiah 31:18). Repentance, which is a change of mind, heart, and will, is nothing short of a gift of God (Acts 11:18; II Timothy 2:25).

David declared, "The steps of a good man are ordered by the LORD: and he delighteth in his way. Though he fall, he shall not be utterly cast down: for the LORD upholdeth him with his hand" (Psalm 37:23-24). Thus there is no "self-made man." Anything good we have achieved must be credited to the grace of God, for it is God who works in us to give both the desire and the ability to do right (I Corinthians 15:10; Philippians 2:13).

Civil rulers are God's agents (verse 10). God is sovereign in human affairs. He directs the decisions of godly rulers, and He is even able to work through ungodly rulers. God has ordained civil government to maintain social order and well-being, and He is ultimately in control of it, regardless how godless any individual ruler may be. (See Exodus 9:16; Proverbs 21:1; Ecclesiastes 8:2-4; Daniel 4:25-26.) Thus, human rulers should not transgress in judgment.

In general, Christians are to obey the civil government, which includes paying taxes, for people in positions of authority are actually the ministers, or servants, of God in fulfilling His purpose for civil government. (See Matthew 22:21; Romans 13:1-7; I Timothy 2:1-4; I Peter 2:13-15.) We should note that the Bible taught this principle during the rule of the Roman Empire, which was certainly not a Christian government.

Scripture does offer examples of civil disobedience that God condoned. (See Exodus 1:15-22; I Kings 21:1-4;

Daniel 3:13-18; 6:10; Acts 4:18-20; 5:28-29; Hebrews 11:23, 31.) The consensus from these accounts is that civil disobedience is warranted only when human rulers prohibit the performance of God's will or when obedience to human rulers would be a sin against God. As these accounts reveal, the believer must be willing to suffer the consequences of disobedience, and even in his disobedience, he must be respectful and honor those in authority.

Honesty in business (verse 11). God is interested in honesty in the marketplace. If the weight and balance are just, or honest and right, they are said to be the Lord's. This means honesty is of Him. If they are dishonest, they are not of Him. Therefore, God cannot bless dishonesty in business, but He does reward honesty.

All the weights of the bag are His work. This statement illustrates the impossibility of separating life into separate compartments called the secular and the spiritual. God is so intimately concerned about human affairs that even the weights in the merchant's bag belong to Him; they must be handled in a way that would bring honor to Him. (See Leviticus 19:35-37; Deuteronomy 25:13-16; Proverbs 11:1; 20:10; Ezekiel 45:9-12; Micah 6:11.)

How authority is strengthened (verse 12). Those in authority are responsible to God, not so much to a political party, the people, pressure groups, or lobbyists. As a servant of God, each person in a position of civil authority will ultimately answer to God for the handling of his responsibilities. If a ruler is faithful to God, that is, if he practices righteousness, his position will be established or strengthened. If he is unfaithful, it will be weakened. All ungodly governments will ultimately collapse, regardless of their military strength, because they are built on a foundation of rebellion.

No place for "yes men" (verse 13). Wise rulers desire truthful advisors. They know deceitful counsellors have been the downfall of many in authority. (See Proverbs 14:35.) Wise rulers will not reject those who refuse to agree with them on every issue. They recognize that they themselves could be wrong.

This principle is valuable for all in authority. "Yes men" are of no worth. What is the point in surrounding oneself with those who do nothing but agree? A wise person will want advisors who are honest enough to admit differences of opinion, because he knows they may see problems he does not see. They may be aware of potential pitfalls that have escaped his attention. It is not rejection of a person to question his ideas. Indeed, the best test of ideas is to see if they will stand questioning and examination. If they will not, they would certainly fail when attempts are made to carry them out.

The anger of those in authority (verse 14). In an ancient monarchy, to incur the king's anger was tantamount to being placed on death row. A wise person would find ways to pacify, or defuse, the king's anger.

Even today, a wise person will submit to authority. Someone who rebelliously refuses to do anything that could be interpreted as yielding to those in authority is unwise and will suffer the consequences. If a person is wise, he realizes there is little value in demonstrating bravado in opposition to lawful authority.

As a modern example, corporations and businesses are weakened by those who mock at the concept of submission to authority. It seems to escape those who belittle authority that they are actually sowing the seeds of their own failure. The success of one's job depends on the success of the company. If the company prospers, so will the employee. If it does not, neither will he. Success rests essentially with the working relationship of all those employed by the company. The person who commits himself to the success of his employer will make himself successful. (See Acts 12:20.)

The pleasure of those in authority (verse 15). This verse stands in contrast to the previous one. To win the king's approval is to receive all the favor and benefits he can bestow. The relationship between Pharaoh and Joseph is a good example. (See Genesis 41-47.) Pharaoh's approval of Joseph resulted in Joseph's being placed second in command over all Egypt. When his entire family moved to Egypt during the time of famine, they were given the best land of all, the land of Goshen. It is wise to please those in authority by being committed to their success.

Wisdom is better than gold; understanding is better than silver (verse 16). This proverb applies literally as well as figuratively. The foremost application is spiritual, but it is also true economically. Wisdom and understanding are genuinely more valuable and profitable than gold and silver. The value of these precious metals fluctuates daily. It is possible to lose a great deal of money by investing in them, for no one can predict their value tomorrow. But wisdom and understanding never lose value. Someone with wisdom and understanding will find doors open to him, even in times of economic hardship, that money can never open. The use of gold and silver is limited. Basically, these metals may be used to buy things, but wisdom and understanding may be applied to all subjects in any field.

This truth leads to an important question for us to consider. We may have a piggy bank or a savings account, but do we expend equal or greater effort in pursuing and storing up wisdom and understanding as we do pursuing money and material possessions? The value we place on things can usually be determined by the efforts made to collect and preserve them.

The highway of the upright (verse 17). The high road in life is to depart from evil. The low road is to engage in it. The person who takes the high way preserves his soul; the person who takes the low way loses his.

The certain destruction of the proud (verse 18). While no one knows the future in such a way as to predict precise events, wisdom will enable a person to see trends and to forecast general developments. For example, when someone is proud, it is certain that one day he will be destroyed. It is not possible to predict on which day or how the destruction will occur, but the destruction itself is sure. Those who are haughty will eventually fall. The pattern has been repeated throughout human history. How many celebrities, rich people, and famous people have died with their integrity intact? How many have died in shame, humiliated, broken, and ruined?

Humility is better than riches (verse 19). We hear of people being "well off," or of someone being "better off" than another. This proverb puts such comparisons in perspective. The humble person who associates with common people is better off than the person who associates with the proud, even if that companionship provides economic profit. The day will come when the superiority of the former position will be evident to all.

The key to happiness (verse 20). Good will come out

of handling a matter with wisdom and in accordance with God's Word. No matter the situation, wisdom will handle it for the good. But it is impossible to handle a matter wisely unless one has previously laid up wisdom.

The person who trusts in the Lord, rather than in himself or others, will be truly happy. If confidence is placed in people, it will be disappointed. When it is placed in God, it will never be disappointed. (See Psalm 118:8-9.) People will fail; God will not.

How to improve teaching (verse 21). When someone is wise, his wisdom will be recognized by others. And a wise teacher will speak in a pleasing way, thereby vastly improving the student's ability to grasp instruction. The teacher can motivate students to learn by the words he uses, by his tone of voice, and by his attitude. The teacher who verbally abuses his students, questions their ability, or speaks harshly will hinder their ability to learn. The teacher who wishes to succeed in his task should assure his students of his confidence in them and of their ability to excel in learning. He should present the subject in an interesting manner.

This principle is important for parents in their effort to instruct their children. For example, parents should not be guilty of statements that degrade their children, such as "You'll never amount to anything" or "You'll probably wind up in prison." Such put-downs erect a barrier between parent and child that can be very difficult to dismantle, and they can become self-fulfilling prophecies.

The wellspring of life (verse 22). A wellspring is an unfailing source of water; it is continually fed. Understanding has a constant positive influence, every day, in every situation.

It is folly to attempt to instruct a fool. Only a wise person will receive instruction. The fool has no heart for it.

From heart to mouth (verse 23). If someone is wise of heart, it will be evident by the words he speaks. Words do not originate in the mouth; people speak from the heart. Words spoken reveal the condition of the heart. (See Matthew 12:33-37; 15:13-20.)

The therapeutic value of pleasant words (verse 24). A companion to the proverb found in verse 21, this verse points out that pleasant words have a positive effect both physically and spiritually. Throughout the Scripture, honey is a symbol of something good and healthy. (See Exodus 3:8; Psalm 19:10; Proverbs 24:13.) Pleasant words are beneficial, as honey is. When spoken, they produce refreshing strength in both the soul and body of the hearer.

A consistent lesson of Scripture is that words have power. They either weaken and destroy or they build up and strengthen. For this reason it is of great importance to speak pleasant, strengthening words. This is especially true in the parent-child and marriage relationships. In most cases, breakdowns of relationships and communication gaps can be traced back to negative, fault-finding, accusing words.

A simple step toward the practice of pleasant words is to practice good-finding instead of fault-finding. Nagging, pestering, or harsh criticism seldom bring about a desired change of behavior. Instead, attempts to correct undesirable behavior by ridicule or caustic disapproval often reinforce it. While there is definitely a place for correction and discipline, it must be accomplished by right words and attitudes.

The way that seems right (verse 25). This verse restates the truth found in Proverbs 14:12. While the Scripture need not repeat any truth to validate it, the reiteration stresses the importance of this fundamental truth. Many times in life a course of action will seem right, but it is wrong. The only way to determine what is right is to direct one's steps prayerfully by the principles of the Word of God.

Selfish labor (verse 26). If we view this statement in the context of the verses that follow—proverbs that describe ungodly people—it would appear to reveal the basic selfishness of human nature. While labor is a good thing, the person who labors without an awareness of or commitment to a higher purpose is performing an essentially selfish act. He works simply to satisfy his hunger. If he could satisfy his hunger in another way without labor, he would not work another day.

But the Bible teaches us to find a higher purpose in labor. We should not labor for the purpose of getting rich (Proverbs 23:4). We should not work simply to obtain food (John 6:27). Rather, we are to work as unto the Lord, in loving and willing obedience to His command to work, and as a vital part of our Christian testimony. (See Ephesians 6:5-8; Colossians 3:22-24; I Timothy 6:1-3.) This attitude toward work makes it a pleasant, fulfilling joy rather than a dull, tiring obligation performed merely to keep body and soul together. God created humans to be productive, and their productivity brings glory to Him, for He is productive.

A sign of an ungodly person (verse 27). This proverb provides a sure indication of a person's ungodliness, regardless of what he may appear to be. An ungodly person will dig up—devise or search after—evil. This verse seems to focus particularly on the evil of talebearing and gossip, for the evil affects the ungodly person's lips: they are as a burning fire. He searches for some evil to report, some negative, harmful thing to talk about, and like a fire, his use of this information is destructive. Someone may make great professions about his love for God, but talebearing and rumormongering reveal a rebellious and evil heart.

The perverse person and the whisperer (verse 28). A froward, or perverse, person despises authority, and of his chief characteristics is his practice of sowing strife. He drops a divisive word here, an innuendo there. He murmurs half-truths and subtle suggestions. One of his greatest delights is to drive a wedge between friends, and the whisper is one of his chief weapons for doing so. While whispering in a physical sense is not sinful, spreading rumors and plotting against people in a secretive manner is wrong. A good test of the appropriateness and truthfulness of a statement is whether it can be spoken aloud.

Evil influence (verse 29). A common theme throughout Scripture is the importance of doing good for one's neighbors (Proverbs 3:28-29; Luke 10:25-37). Doing so is a practical way to fulfill the second greatest commandment: to love one's neighbor as oneself (Mark 12:31). Part of doing good is to provide a good example and to be a good influence on one's neighbor.

But the violent person exerts a negative influence on his neighbors. Rather than lifting them to a higher level of morality and God-consciousness, he drags them down and entices them to do evil. Once again, we see the importance of having right neighbors and of carefully choosing our associates.

The first two steps in bringing evil to pass (verse 30). The violent person's first step in conceiving evil plans is to shut his eyes, that is, to think and imagine evil things. Before he actually performs an evil deed, he first sees it in the eye of his mind. (See Genesis 6:5.) The second step in bringing evil to pass is to move the lips, that is, to clothe the evil thoughts with words. God gives people the ability to imagine, to express thoughts in words, and to set in motion a chain of events, and we may use that ability for evil or good.

The blessing of age (verse 31). When a person has lived his life in the way of righteousness, his old age is blessed. Younger people are to respect and honor him (Leviticus 19:3). He has gained wisdom and understanding by long contemplation of scriptural principles. He has many friends gained through a lifetime of service to God. He has peace in his heart and the knowledge that all is well between him and his Lord and that the day is much nearer when he will have the blessed privilege of seeing Him face to face.

But there is nothing more tragic than an aged person whose life has been wasted in sin. He comes to the end of his days bent, scarred, and with no hope for the future. Rather than being a crown of glory, his white hair is a badge of a wasted, pointless life.

The strength of patience and self-control (verse 32). The ability to control one's emotions, particularly the temper, is far more important than physical strength or military prowess. Someone who is unable to control his spirit is open prey for the enemy. (See Proverbs 25:28.) A society that worships and serves the creature more than the Creator puts emphasis in the wrong place. (See Romans 1:25.) Such a society awards people for muscular development, admiring them for their ability to run, kick, hit, flip, or swim, but expresses little concern for their morality and strength of character. Such a society may have a "Mr. Universe," but it will not have a "Mr. Patient."

How the lot is determined (verse 33). Belief in a sovereign God precludes "chance" as people ordinarily think of it. The Bible declares that all things are in the hand of God, including what people call "nature" and "the laws of nature." Ultimately, even the lot is subject to God's sovereignty.

In Scripture, particularly before the outpouring of the Holy Spirit, people used the lot as a means of determining God's will in sensitive situations. They prayed for God to control the outcome and used the casting of lots to bring the end of contention. (See Proverbs 18:18.)

The Bible contains several examples which indicate that God intervened in the casting of lots. The wicked Haman did not realize that his use of the lot allowed God to determine the day the Jewish people would supposedly be slain (Esther 3:7). Had Haman been making the decision independently, he would doubtless have selected a date near at hand, but the lot fell on a date nearly a year away. This outcome allowed Mordecai, Esther, and the Jews sufficient time to thwart Haman's purposes. Just prior to the Day of Pentecost, the disciples used the lot to determine the replacement for Judas Iscariot after selecting two equally qualified candidates and praying for the will of God (Acts 1:26).

By contrast, gambling is evil, for gamblers do not seek

God's will, but they greedily and selfishly seek to profit at the expense of someone else's loss without trusting God or earning what they hope to acquire.

Chapter Seventeen

Peace is more important than plenty (verse 1). Human reasoning tends to equate an abundance of material things with the quality of life. But Jesus warned, "Take heed, and beware of covetousness: for a man's life consisteth not in the abundance of the things which he possesseth" (Luke 12:15). The Scriptures repeatedly teach the superiority of inner peace over material abundance.

This proverb is a companion to Proverbs 15:17. Since sacrifices had to be of the very best quality, this proverb points out that the person who has the simplest of food and peace in his heart and home is in a better position than someone who has a house full of the best food without peace.

How to earn an inheritance (verse 2). While a son has a natural advantage over a servant, he can lose that advantage if he is foolish and the servant wise. A wise father who observes foolishness in his son over an extended period of time and who at the same time observes a servant acting consistently in a wise way will, both for the sake of his son and for the good of his investments, give the servant authority over the son. This wise father knows that his foolish son could not successfully handle his business and that he would soon lose even what he had.

Thus the servant with no family ties to his master can nevertheless have hope of being included in an inheritance if he conducts himself wisely.

The Lord tries the heart (verse 3). The refining pot separates the dross from silver, and the furnace removes the impurities from gold. Similarly, the Lord tries the hearts of people to purge out everything that is unlike Him. David recognized this when he prayed, "Search me, O God, and know my heart: try me, and know my thoughts: and see if there be any wicked way in me, and lead me in the way everlasting" (Psalm 139:23-24) and "Let the words of my mouth, and the meditation of my heart, be acceptable in thy sight, O LORD, my strength, and my redeemer" (Psalm 19:14). It is necessary for the Lord to try the heart, for no one knows fully the deceitfulness and wickedness of his own heart (Jeremiah 17:9-10). The Lord uses His Word in the process of searching and purifying the heart, as Hebrews 4:12 declares: "For the word of God . . . is a discerner of the thoughts and intents of the heart."

How to tell if a person is wicked (verse 4). A person often reveals his character by what he listens to. An evildoer will himself heed falsehood; the liar will listen eagerly to a malicious tongue. But a person who is clean and pure will have no appetite for such words.

The wrong attitude toward the poor and calamities (verse 5). God is extremely concerned about the poor. (See Proverbs 19:17; 30:14; Luke 4:18; 7:22.) When someone mocks the poor, God considers it a personal affront. The proper attitude toward the poor is care and compassion. Their plight should also cause others to be thankful for their blessings, rather than smug and proud as if they somehow deserve better than the poor.

A person who rejoices at the calamities of others will himself be punished. The wise person will not rejoice even when his enemy falls (Proverbs 24:17). David's reaction to Saul's death illustrates this principle well. Though Saul had actively pursued him with every intent of killing him, David did not rejoice when at last the word came of Saul's death, but rather he mourned. Jesus demonstrated and taught love for one's enemies by doing good to them (Matthew 5:43-48).

The crown of the old and the glory of children (verse 6). Grandchildren are the crown of their grandfathers. The true proof of a man's success in rearing his children is seen in his grandchildren. It is one thing to influence one's immediate offspring; it is quite another to have an influence so pronounced that it will reach even to the second generation. In other words, it is not only how well a man rears his own children, but how successfully he prepares them for parenthood.

Children glory in their fathers. This is why young children are sometimes heard boasting, "My dad is stronger than your dad!" More seriously, this proverb reveals why it is so important that men be the fathers their children need. An uncaring, unloving, unwise father can have a devastatingly negative influence on his children. For this reason, Paul admonished, "Fathers, provoke not your children to wrath: but bring them up in the nurture and admonition of the Lord" (Ephesians 6:4). "Fathers, provoke not your children to anger, lest they be discouraged" (Colossians 3:21). Fathers should conduct themselves in such a way as to be examples, leaders, and friends to their children. The discouragement produced in children by unwise fathers who provoke them to anger is extremely difficult to surmount.

Words reveal character (verse 7). While a person can deceitfully speak words that do not accurately reflect his character—words that come from the mouth only—it will eventually be obvious to all that the words do not fit the person. Something will not ring true. Excellent speech rings hollow and false on the lips of a fool.

The initial point of this proverb, as spoken by a king to instruct his son, a prince, is that lying lips are not appropriate for a prince. The prince should speak words fitting for his station in life, considering the reputation of the royal house. Christians should remember this principle, since they also represent a royal house (Revelation 1:6; 5:10).

The use of bribes (verse 8). The word *gift* here probably refers to a bribe. (The same Hebrew word appears in verse 23.) While Scripture condemns the use of bribes (Proverbs 15:27), Solomon recognized them as a reality of life, especially for governmental officials. But they are forbidden because they pervert judgment, and God has a great concern for justice. The point of this proverb is that a person who has a bribe to give views it as being able to accomplish his desired purpose. Wherever he places it, or to whomever he gives it, it has the effect he wishes. The comparison of the bribe to a "precious stone" may be an allusion to the occultic use of such stones in an attempt to cause others to behave in a desired way.

Different responses to transgressions (verse 9). When a person loves another he will not reveal the other's transgressions. He will love his friend despite his failings, and his love will prompt him not to broadcast those faults.

Similarly, Peter said, "And above all things have fervent charity among yourselves: for charity shall cover the multitude of sins" (I Peter 4:8). Paul likewise taught that charity "thinketh no evil; rejoiceth not in iniquity, but rejoiceth in the truth" (I Corinthians 13:5-6).

This proverb does not mean love will cause a person to ignore his friend's sins. Genuine love will prompt a person to lovingly confront his friend in a spirit of meekness in an attempt to restore him (Galatians 6:1; James 5:19-20). What this proverb does mean is that someone who loves another will not publicize his friend's faults; he will keep them as private as possible.

Where there is no love, however, the news of transgressions will be repeated profusely, which will result in division even between close friends. (See also Proverbs 16:28.)

Reproof is profitable (verse 10). A wise person loves and responds to reproof (Proverbs 9:9; 12:1; 13:18; 15:5, 32). A simple spoken reproof will have a more positive effect on a wise person than a hundred stripes will have on a fool, for a wise person responds to simple correction while a fool rejects even the strongest attempts to change him. Moreover, a person himself determines what kind of correction he will receive by his wisdom or foolishness.

A messenger to the evil (verse 11). The only thing on the mind of an evil person is rebellion against authority. It is so important to refuse rebellion and to submit to authority, "for rebellion," Samuel declared, "is as the sin of witchcraft, and stubbornness is as iniquity and idolatry" (I Samuel 15:23). The essence of witchcraft is exposing oneself to the influence of evil spirits. Similarly, the rebel

177

opens himself to the destructive realm of fallen spirits, who were themselves rebels and who look for companionship in their rebellion. This truth provides a possible clue to the meaning of the latter part of this proverb: "therefore a cruel messenger shall be sent against him." As a natural consequence of his rebellion, he opens the door to punishment, demonic influence, and ultimately destruction.

Better to meet an angry bear than a fool (verse 12). A bear who has been robbed of her cubs is one of the most dangerous and fierce animals. Even so, it is safer to confront her than to confront a fool practicing his folly. The fool may be violent or he may simply be deceptive, but he is dangerous both spiritually and physically, while the bear is only a physical threat.

The danger of rewarding evil for good (verse 13). In keeping with the law of sowing and reaping, this proverb teaches that someone who returns evil for good brings unending evil on his own house. (See Galatians 6:7-8.) Those who seem to be victimized by unexplainable evil should examine themselves to see if at some point in the past they have repaid good with evil.

The momentum of strife (verse 14). Water can be a tremendously destructive force, as exemplified by major floods. When released from a dam it can sweep through valleys and canyons, tearing out of its path huge trees, gigantic boulders, and homes. Many times, after a flood has passed the terrain looks as if it has been stripped by a giant hand.

When water first starts trickling through a break in the dam it seems harmless and easy to deal with. But it soon reaches a proportion beyond containment, and destruction follows. So also strife may at first seem insignificant and almost unnoticeable, but it quickly picks up momentum until there is no stopping it and great damage is done. The only way to deal with strife is to stay completely away from it; we must refuse to participate in it at any level.

Perverted judgment (verse 15). Repeatedly the Scriptures stress the importance of true judgment. The Lord, with His pure justice, abhors perverted judgment. As a society drifts away from biblical principles, its values will begin to be warped until eventually it will call evil good and good evil (Isaiah 5:20).

The price of wisdom (verse 16). No one can purchase wisdom with money or any other commodity. The only way an individual will ever attain wisdom is to give his heart to it. That is, he must give himself wholly to the pursuit of wisdom and he must love it. Wisdom is therefore out of reach for the fool. He may read this book or that and he may try the latest techniques in meditation or dealing with people, but he will never achieve true wisdom.

The endurance of true friendship (verse 17). A true friend is consistent in his love. He is not a "fair-weather friend," available only when it is to his advantage. If we would be a friend to others, we must be willing to make a commitment of time and effort. Friendship is not always convenient (Proverbs 18:24).

Adversity provides the true test of brotherhood. Brothers (whether by birth, friendship, or new birth) should support one another, especially during times of trouble.

What pledging security for another demonstrates

179

(verse 18). Striking hands refers to making an agreement or contract, in this case assuming financial responsibility for a friend. Someone who promises to stand good for the debts of another displays a lack of understanding. He fails to understand the poor credit of the debtor and the risks involved for himself. Moreover, it is quite possible that the debtor has violated basic principles of stewardship, and the guarantor may well prevent the debtor from obeying God's leading in financial affairs and thwart God's desire to provide supernaturally. (See Proverbs 6:1-5; 11:15; 20:16; 22:26; 27:13.)

The sin of strife and the danger of self-promotion (verse 19). Strife is sin, so the person who loves strife actually loves sin. Those who fear God should seek to avoid strife at all costs. The person who promotes himself is actually seeking his own destruction. (See James 4:6.)

Results of a perverse heart and tongue (verse 20). The person whose heart is froward—deceitful, rebellious, perverse—finds nothing good in life. His heart puts an evil lens over his eyes. His wickedness causes everything and everyone else to seem wicked. What a person finds in life indicates a great deal about the condition of his heart. One who believes life as God intended it is good, that there are good people in the world, that everything will eventually turn out all right, reveals an innocent, pure heart. Rather than focusing on the work of the devil, this kind of person sees God at work.

Perverseness of the tongue is probably the single greatest cause of trouble in one's life. The reason is that the tongue acts like a rudder on a ship by providing direction in life. (See James 3:4-5.)

Foolish children and parental sorrow (verse 21). Just

as a wise son makes a glad father, a foolish son robs his father of all joy. (See Proverbs 15:20.) One of the most important ways someone can honor his parents is to bring joy to them, thereby contributing to their well-being spiritually, mentally, and physically. The fool therefore transgresses the commandment to honor his father and mother with its promise of a long and good life.

The value of a merry heart (verse 22). One of the greatest contributing factors to well-being is attitude. This proverb reveals both the positive and negative effects of attitude. A merry heart has a positive effect, like a medicine. A broken spirit has a negative effect, equivalent to drying up the bones.

Cheerfulness is good medicine physically as well as emotionally. Many medical schools now incorporate into their curriculum lectures on the value of laughter in maintaining and restoring health. Raymond A. Moody, Jr., a medical doctor, wrote in *Laugh After Laugh: The Healing Power of Humor,* "A human being's ability to laugh is just as valid an indicator of his health as are all those other things that doctors check." Dr. William Fry, Jr., a Stanford University researcher who has studied the beneficial effects of laughter for more than thirty years, stated, "When we laugh muscles are activated. When we stop laughing, these muscles relax. Since muscle tension magnifies pain, many people with arthritis, rheumatism and other painful conditions benefit greatly from a healthy dose of laughter. Many headache sufferers feel the same relief" (Nancy and Dean Hoch, "Take Time to Laugh," *Reader's Digest,* February 1988). Dr. S. I. McMillan in his book *None of These Diseases* has thoroughly documented the positive and negative effects of attitude on physical health.

This proverb indirectly indicates that there is a proper use of medicine; it is not inherently evil. Jesus Christ Himself declared that the sick need a physician (Matthew 9:12), and long after his conversion Luke was still known as "the beloved physician" (Colossians 4:14).

The statement "a broken spirit drieth the bones" speaks volumes about the negative impact of sorrow, sadness, and depression. The human body is about seven-tenths water, and this moisture is essential to health. Blood cells, which are predominantly water, are manufactured in bone marrow. Thus a broken spirit has the same effect as depriving the body of necessary moisture.

David described the effects of the guilt of unconfessed sin: "My bones waxed old through my roaring all the day long. . . . My moisture is turned into the drought of summer" (Psalm 32:3-4). When someone is in right relationship with God, when he does not struggle with the guilt of unconfessed sin, and when the joy of the Lord is in his heart, he is in the optimum mental and spiritual condition for good health.

Takers of bribes (verse 23). Those who accept bribes ("gifts") to make a decision favorable to the one who offers the bribe are wicked. Accepting bribes may be justified as "just the way business is done," but the real reason is the wickedness in the heart. Godly people refuse to be influenced by any personal advantage.

What makes wisdom near or remote (verse 24). If someone has understanding, wisdom is before him, that is, it is in his view. But a fool cannot find genuine wisdom, though he searches to the ends of the earth. The fool is restless, always searching, never finding. This description fits those who search for meaning in drugs, alcohol, illicit sex, violence, the occult, eastern mysticism, atheism, and all Christless philosophy.

The grief and bitterness of a foolish son (verse 25). This verse is a companion to Proverbs 15:20 and 17:21. Foolish children bring grief to their fathers and bitterness to their mothers. The thing that will cause a child to turn out right is wisdom, not materialism. The thing that will destroy a child is foolishness, not poverty. Parents in high-income brackets are equally as prone to have foolish children as those in low-income brackets.

Warped values (verse 26). This is a companion proverb to Proverbs 17:15. It is not a good thing to punish those who have done no wrong, especially innocent leaders.

Few words and excellent spirit (verse 27). Someone of genuine knowledge will use words sparingly. One of the signs of folly is profuseness of words (Proverbs 10:19; 29:11; Ecclesiastes 5:3). Someone with true knowledge will think before he speaks; he will be careful to use the right word to express his intent, and he will use no more words than necessary.

Someone with understanding will demonstrate it by his excellent, or calm, spirit. He is not excitable or given to ill-conceived displays of temper or fear.

The sign of wisdom and understanding (verse 28). The control of the tongue is such a major sign of wisdom and understanding that even a fool will be thought wise if he remains silent. The relationship between the tongue and wisdom is discussed more fully in James 3.

Chapter Eighteen

Gaining wisdom (verse 1). A person will never attain wisdom if he does not first desire it, and then he will never gain it unless he separates himself unto it. (See Proverbs 4:5-7; James 1:5-8.) On the other hand, a person should not isolate himself from godly people, or else he will succumb to selfish desires.

The fool's delight (verse 2). The person who is bored with the pursuit of understanding is a fool. He has no interest in understanding; his greatest wish is to express himself, or to follow his own heart. (See Proverbs 28:26.) One of the great goals of godless humanism is self-expression. But when sinful self is truly expressed, it will reveal nothing but wickedness and evil, for no one is truly good apart from Christ (Romans 3:10-12).

The company of the wicked (verse 3). Contempt travels with the wicked person, and with dishonor comes reproach. The righteous must avoid holding others in contempt or reproaching (finding fault with) others (Psalm 15:3).

What words reveal (verse 4). A person's words reveal what is deep in his heart (Matthew 12:34). Words do not come from the mouth only; their source is much deeper. When the words are words of wisdom, they are always fresh and refreshing, like a wellspring or a flowing brook.

The sin of favoritism (verse 5). Scripture repeatedly warns against the sin of partiality, prejudice, or respecting persons. (See James 2:1-9.) In particular, we must not show favoritism to the wicked or deprive the righteous of justice.

Partiality is sinful because it is contrary to God's nature (Acts 10:34-35). We must recognize people as individuals; we must not view them stereotypically on the basis of ethnic backgrounds, economic status, or neighborhoods. God created each person as an individual in His image, and each one will stand before God in the judgment as an individual. Thus, we must deal with a person on the basis of his individual wickedness or righteousness.

The fool asks for trouble (verse 6). One of the marks of a fool is that his lips enter into contention, that he is argumentative. When he opens his mouth to enter into strife, he is literally crying out for retaliation or discipline.

The destructive snare of the fool (verse 7). It is the fool's mouth that will ultimately destroy him. And this destruction will not only pertain to this present world; his lips are the snare of his soul. That is, his evil words are spiritually destructive as well.

Wounding words (verse 8). This proverb disproves the childhood verse: "Sticks and stones may break my bones, but words will never hurt me." Words have the power to do far more lasting damage than sticks and stones. Many people struggle through adulthood with feelings of inferiority and rejection over words spoken to them as children. Evil words do more than physical damage; they go down into the innermost parts of the belly, or into the spirit.

This verse specifically describes talebearing or gossip. Gossip is so vicious and damaging that those who practice it are under the condemnation of death (Romans 1:29-32). It is essential that Christians abstain from speaking wounding words; we must speak words that edify (Ephesians 4:29).

The brotherhood of sloth and waste (verse 9). Sloth and waste, or destruction, are similar evils. The slothful wastes time, energy, and opportunity. The waster squanders or destroys goods and possessions. In other words, passive laziness can be as harmful as active destruction.

The strong tower of the Name (verse 10). It is impossible to overemphasize the importance, power, and authority of the name of the Lord. Like a strong tower, the name of the Lord provides safety and protection to His people.

To the Hebrews, the name had far greater significance than it does in most societies today. A person's name represented him and was inseparable from him. The name was an extension of the individual.

The name in this proverb is Jehovah, represented here in the King James Version by "LORD." This name comes from the third person singular form of the Hebrew verb "to be," meaning "He is." When God first revealed Himself to Moses, He used the name "I am," which is the first person singular of the verb "to be" (Exodus 3:14; 6:3). Both forms of the name emphasize God's self-existence: He exists in and of Himself, with no help from any other source, separate and apart from His creation. Only God can truthfully say, "I am," without any qualification. Humans cannot make such a claim, for without God, we would not be. Thus, from God's standpoint, His name is "I am." From the human standpoint, God's name is "He is."

But as wonderful as this Old Testament revelation of the name of God was, it was still incomplete. Throughout the Old Testament, for that reason, appears the Jehovistic combinations that reveal various aspects of God's character. For example, Jehovah-Shalom means literally "He is peace" (Judges 6:24). Jehovah-Jireh means "He is provider" (Genesis 22:14). Jehovah-Shammah means "He is present" (Ezekiel 48:35). The name "Jehovah" revealed that God was, but it did not tell what He was. That is, it did not reveal His character and nature beyond His self-existence. These and other Jehovistic combinations were necessary to reveal various aspects of His nature.

The final and ultimate revelation of the name of God did not occur until the coming of the Messiah, who was actually God incarnate. He was given a name that was above every name, which of necessity included the name "Jehovah" (Philippians 2:9-10). He received this name by inheritance (Hebrews 1:4). It is the only name under heaven given among men which brings salvation (Acts 4:12). The name is Jesus (Matthew 1:21; Luke 1:31), and it means "Jehovah-Savior." Thus the most literal meaning of the name is "He is Savior."

This name is superior to all others, because inherent in the word *Savior* is all the provision God has ever made for humanity and all the attributes of God. The word *Jesus* includes every attribute of God revealed in the Old Testament, including the Jehovistic combinations. For example, as our Savior, Jesus brings us peace, provides our needs, and is present with us. When we say "Jesus" we invoke the supreme name by which God has been revealed to us and call everything in heaven, on earth, and under the earth to attention (Philippians 2:10-11). It is no accident that this proverb teaches that those who run into the name of the Lord are safe; the name includes the greatest revelation of all: that God is our Savior.

Confidence in wealth (verse 11). The greatest problem with riches is that people tend to trust in them. They begin to place confidence in their wealth to deliver them and to protect them. This confidence is misplaced, for it makes money an idol. The rich young ruler who refused to forsake his wealth to follow Jesus exhibited this problem (Mark 10:17-27).

The causes of destruction and honor (verse 12). Haughtiness precedes destruction (Proverbs 16:18). Destruction will come to a proud person, unless he confesses and forsakes that sin. Out of His love, God allows the destruction in hopes that true humility will result, for He cannot save someone who out of pride trusts in himself and not in God.

On the other hand, God will bestow honor upon the humble. Humility precedes honor.

The danger of quick answers (verse 13). It is folly to give an answer quickly, before knowing the whole story. Quick and thoughtless answers will ultimately bring shame to those who give them. One of the marks of wisdom is the ability to hear a person through before giving a response. It is good to discipline oneself to refrain from interrupting and from trying to anticipate what the other is going to say. We must not put words in another's mouth, and it is always wise to stop and think before forming a response.

The danger of a wounded spirit (verse 14). If a person has a good, strong, healthy spirit, he will survive problems and difficulties. But if his spirit is wounded, he does not have the inner strength to overcome, and he may very well be destroyed by problems that others easily overcome.

Sorrow of the heart causes a wounded spirit (Proverbs 15:13). Rejection, ridicule, and betrayal are common factors. A person who feels rejected by someone he loves or admires, or who is ridiculed by another he holds in high esteem, or who is betrayed by another in whom he has placed trust will be prone to suffer a wounded spirit. The only way a person who has a wounded spirit can be healed is for him to be willing to forgive his offender and release all bitterness. He also needs others who will demonstrate unconditional love toward him.

The heart and the ear (verse 15). There is a connection between the ear and the heart; what the ear hears will tend to enter the heart, and what is in the heart will tend to direct the ear in its listening. If someone wants a clean heart, he must guard what enters it through the ear gate. And if he wants to yield his ears as instruments of righteousness unto God, he must cleanse his heart. (See Romans 6:13, 19.) A person cannot claim inner purity if he gives his ears and eyes to evil.

This proverb teaches the importance of pursuing knowledge with both the heart and the ears. A person who obtains knowledge in his heart demonstrates prudence. Placing something in the heart, or inner being, involves study and meditation; the prudent person will meditate on true knowledge.

The wise person will seek to hear knowledge. He is

careful to listen to the right things. In an era of media saturation, it has become increasingly important to be selective in listening. So many voices cry out today, and many of them promote false philosophies. We cannot read every book, listen to every voice, or give attention to everything. A wise person will decide in advance what is worth his time and what is not, and he will waste no time with foolishness.

The skill of giving gifts (verse 16). There are two common interpretations of this verse that do not appear to be correct. The first one suggests that this proverb uses the word *gift* in the sense of a talent, ability, or even a gift of the Spirit. According to this view, a person's ability, natural or spiritual, will open doors of opportunity for him. While this concept is valid, it does not seem to be the most accurate understanding of the proverb.

The second view suggests that the word *gift* is synonymous with bribe as in Proverbs 17:8, 23. Thus, the verse would mean that a bribe will open doors and bring the giver into the presence of the great. Those who hold to this view do not suggest that the proverb condones the use of bribes; it merely recognizes them as a fact of life.

A third view, however, seems more accurate. It recognizes that the English word *gift* in this proverb is translated from an entirely different Hebrew word than in Proverbs 17:8, 23. In those proverbs the word *gift* is from the Hebrew *shachad* and suggests a bribe. It seems to have this meaning throughout the Old Testament. In this proverb, however, the word *gift* is from the Hebrew *mattan,* which seems to refer consistently to a present, with no suggestion of a dishonest bribe. Under this view, the proverb teaches the proper use of giving presents,

or gifts, a skill largely lost in our society. People sometimes give presents simply out of a sense of duty or obligation, which is an inferior motive for gift giving. At other
times they give out of generosity. While this is certainly
superior to the previous motive, it is still not the finest
use of gifts.

The finest use of gifts is based on a careful selection
of a gift to have a positive impact on the recipient's life.
A well-chosen properly presented gift can serve to
motivate the recipient to be a better person. A hastily
selected gift, chosen without a consideration of the recipient's needs, weaknesses, and strengths, can be a snare.
For example, many Christmas or birthday gifts are given
only to fulfill an obligation and so have limited value. But
a gift carefully chosen and thoughtfully given can motivate a person to greater achievement or deeper spirituali-
ty as well as cement healthy relationships between the
giver and the receiver. There is nothing evil about this
positive effect of a gift.

Two sides to every story (verse 17). Sinful human
nature practices self-justification, which is one of the
earliest evidences of sin. When God called Adam to
account for his sin, Adam said, "The woman whom thou
gavest to be with me, she gave me of the tree, and I did
eat" (Genesis 3:12). Rather than readily accepting personal responsibility, Adam first blamed Eve, and then God
Himself. When God turned to Eve, she declared, "The
serpent beguiled me, and I did eat" (Genesis 3:13). Each
wished to blame another.

According to this proverb, when someone presents
his case, he will try to put himself in the best light and
to justify himself. Consequently, it is necessary to hear

the other side of the story before making a decision. When a neighbor comes and presents his point of view, the entire episode may appear in a different light. Those who are in positions of authority should wisely refrain from making decisions before they have all the facts.

The end of contention (verse 18). The lot was a divinely approved method of making difficult decisions in cases where the Scriptures did not make a pronouncement and there was no clearly correct choice. (See Proverbs 16:33.) When people cannot agree, but they can agree to follow an impartial, unbiased decision, they can settle their differences in this way and avoid conflict.

The difficulty of winning the offended (verse 19). When a person who has had a close relationship with another is offended, it will be very difficult to restore the relationship. It is easier to conquer a strong city. The differences between two former friends are as formidable as the bars of a castle. The friendship will not be restored with a simple apology. It will rather be necessary for the offender to humble himself, confess his sin to his brother, and prove his sincerity.

It is usually insufficient for the offender merely to say, "I'm sorry." While these words suggest a certain amount of regret, standing alone they may also imply that the one offended may have been at least partly to blame for the offense. The offended party may hear this unspoken message: "I'm sorry you were offended. But if you hadn't been so sensitive it wouldn't have bothered you. I'm partly to blame, but so are you." The offended person may refuse this kind of reconciliation.

Few people would think of approaching God with such a bare apology for sin. And yet we are to pattern our approach to others after our approach to God (Matthew 5:23-24; 6:14-15; Ephesians 4:32; James 3:9-10). God resists the proud but gives grace to the humble (James 4:6). Pride prompts a person to practice self-defense and to shift the blame. Humility causes a person to fully accept responsibility for his actions and to blame no one else. So those who would find reconciliation with offended friends must accept full responsibility for the offense, confess their sin in specific terms, and prove their sincerity by their subsequent actions.

An approach that usually works well in situations like this is as follows: "God has convicted me of my sin of _____ [insert the word that best describes the nature of your offense] against you, and it would mean so much to me if you would forgive me. Will you forgive me?" After asking this question, the person should pause and wait for a response. The answer will probably be yes. If it is, he should sincerely thank the offended person and let that close the matter. If there is no response, he should ask again, "Will you forgive me?"

It is possible that the offended party will answer no. He may do so if he senses the first person is insincere, or if he realizes he was indeed partly responsible for the offense. If the latter is true he is probably trying to justify his personal sense of guilt by balancing it with his blame against the other person. If he releases his blame against that person by forgiving him, he will be left with an even more uncomfortable load of guilt. For this reason it is not uncommon to find that the offended party will answer, "Yes, I will forgive you. But will you also forgive me?" If the offended person refuses to grant forgiveness, the offender should continue to manifest humility and sincerity and wait for God to melt the resistance.

Genuine satisfaction and fulfillment (verse 20). The term *belly* in Scripture often refers to the inner person, the spirit. (See John 7:38.) The "fruit of the mouth" is words. When someone knows that he has said the right thing, that he has spoken wisely, he has an inner satisfaction. The "increase of the lips" describes the productivity of wholesome words. Genuine fulfillment comes from learning how to control one's tongue, to speak only pure, productive words.

The incredible power of the tongue (verse 21). Nothing states the awesome power of the tongue more clearly than this proverb. The tongue literally promotes life or death. (See James 3.) Those who love death will reveal it by their conversation, and they will "eat the fruit" or suffer the consequences of such evil talk. Those who love life will also reveal it by their conversation, and they will enjoy the positive consequences of the right use of the tongue.

The blessing of a wife (verse 22). In general, marriage is a blessing of God, and the man who marries receives the favor of God. In the very beginning, God recognized that man was incomplete alone, and the earliest human institution on earth is marriage (Genesis 2:18, 24.) Paul warned that demonic doctrines would arise that would forbid marriage (I Timothy 4:1-3). Though a few people may have the gift of celibacy, they are the exception and not the rule (Matthew 19:10-12).

Marriage does much more than enable humanity to obey the command to multiply and replenish the earth (Genesis 1:28). The wife completes the husband in his areas of weakness and incompleteness. Together they are stronger than either is alone. Marriage also serves to illustrate the relationship between Christ and the church (Ephesians 5:22-33).

The influence of money on personality (verse 23). People who lack money tend to learn to entreat others for their needs. Their poverty may cause them to demonstrate humility, even if it is not genuine. But the rich who trust in their money tend to be careless or harsh in answering. The rich may not be as sensitive to the needs of others due to their own affluence. Ideally, a godly person, rich or poor, will not allow his economic condition to affect his personality and the way he deals with others.

The cause and consequences of friendship (verse 24). This proverb is often quoted to illustrate the necessity of being friendly in order to gain friends, and perhaps that is a valid application. But the more accurate understanding in the context seems to be that someone who has friends will find it necessary to practice friendship with them, even when it may not be convenient. That is, the consequence of having friends is the obligation to be a friend.

The latter part of the proverb seems to bear out this meaning. Genuine friends are more loyal, concerned, and helpful than physical brothers. The test of true friendship comes when it is not comfortable, convenient, or profitable to be a friend.

Chapter Nineteen

Integrity is better than riches (verse 1). A poor person who walks in integrity is better than a rich person who is perverse in his ways and words. (This proverb is a companion to Proverbs 28:6.) The word *integrity* is translated from the Hebrew *tom,* which seems to imply moral innocence. Character is the true measure of a person, not riches.

The dangers of ignorance and haste (verse 2). The soul is the inner person, and is usually associated with the mind, will, and emotions. It is not a good thing for the inner being to be without knowledge. God created the soul with a thirst for knowledge, and this thirst will be satisfied rightly or wrongly.

In the Garden of Eden, Adam and Eve sinned when they failed to be satisfied with the knowledge of God and instead sought after the knowledge of good and evil. People would not read, listen to the radio, listen to a speaker, or watch television unless they had a thirst for knowledge. The problem is that when people do not satisfy this hunger properly, their desire for knowledge becomes perverted. Those who feed themselves on lurid literature and the immorality, pride, violence, and greed programmed over television will in time begin to crave these things. But people can break the hold that wrong knowledge has on them by mortifying it, making no provision for it, and beginning to feed themselves on the milk of the Word (Romans 8:13; 13:14; I Peter 2:2).

Haste is a sign of lack of wisdom. Things done in haste will often be wrong. Those who are wise tend to act deliberately and thoughtfully, after counsel and consideration.

The perversion of foolishness (verse 3). As a result of the sinful nature, which affects the entire human race, spiritual folly is naturally implanted in every person's heart. If he does not conquer it, it will pervert him, ruining his life. Perversion is not necessarily something of an obvious, major, gross nature. It is simply anything that veers to the smallest degree from God's perfect plan.

A person's heart by nature rages against the Lord. For this reason a person must not follow his carnal inclinations (Proverbs 28:26).

Consequences of wealth and poverty (verse 4). Those who have money will find many who want to be their "friends." But the poor person will find that even his neighbor avoids him. This state of affairs should not be, but this proverb simply illustrates the tendencies of unregenerated humanity.

The danger of giving false witness (verse 5). Verse 9 repeats the truth of this proverb, thus emphasizing the thought. It is important always to be honest. There is an inescapable penalty to bearing false witness.

Improper motives for friendship (verses 6-7). Together with verse 4, these verses reveal the wrong motives of many people in befriending others. When a person is in authority many want to develop friendship with him in order to gain some personal advantage from the relationship. Someone who is generous and freely gives gifts also finds many who wish to establish friendship with him. Again their purpose is personal advantage. But few people will purposefully befriend the poor, for they see no personal advantage to such a friendship. Even though the poor person pleads for help, those who make personal advantage the criterion for friendship ignore him. Even friends and relatives desert him.

It seems safe to say that most people, though they may deny it, form their friendships on some perceived mutual benefit. The benefit may not be financial; it may be social. But few people willingly befriend those who can offer no social or financial reciprocation. Friendships established for the wrong reasons are not true friendships, and they will be abandoned when the purpose for their being no longer exists.

Doing the soul a favor (verse 8). Verse 2 reveals that it is not good for the soul to be without knowledge. Conversely, the person who obtains wisdom does his soul good. The inner person, the spiritual nature, receives strength by wisdom. Paul expressed his desire that the church might be "strengthened with might by his Spirit in the inner man" (Ephesians 3:16). The context of this statement clearly indicates the role of the knowledge of God in this strengthening process (Ephesians 3:16-19).

Wisdom and understanding are companion virtues. The person who keeps understanding, or who conducts himself in the way that understanding directs, will discover good in life. Good things will happen to him. But even when the uncomfortable or painful events occur good will eventually prevail (Romans 8:28).

A warning repeated (verse 9). This proverb essentially reiterates the truth found in verse 5 and provides some
additional insight into the ultimate consequence for lying.
Whereas verse 5 indicates the liar will not escape, imply-
ing judgment, this proverb clearly reveals that the liar
will finally perish.

Unseemly things (verse 10). Luxury is not fitting for
a fool. The word *delight* in this verse seems to mean luxury, or delight that comes from luxurious living. The same
Hebrew word is translated as "delicate" in Micah 1:16
and "pleasant" in Micah 2:9. A fool does not and cannot
handle material prosperity wisely. He spends his money
foolishly, selfishly, and increases the possibility of a quick
death by his dissipating lifestyle. Some people know how
to handle wealth; those who do not will be destroyed by it.

It is also inappropriate for a servant to rule over
princes. People have varying gifts or talents. Some have
the ability to lead; some do not. When those who have
no ability for prudent leadership rule, by force or deception, over those who are more capable than they, chaos
results. As an example, in many nations revolutions have
overthrown governments in the name of liberty or justice
only to introduce violent, bloody regimes.

Solomon addressed this issue also in Ecclesiastes
10:5-7. It seems here as if this twisting of values is the
result of foolishness on the ruler's part. ("There is an
evil . . . an error which proceedeth from the ruler," verse
5.) When those who have the ability to exercise authority are unwise in the use of that gift, they will prompt
others without the gift to rise up in rebellion to overthrow
the ruler. But their dissatisfaction with unjust authority
does not give them the ability to lead. The result is the
exaltation of folly.

Discretion and anger (verse 11). One of the signs of discretion is deferring anger or having patience. A wise person will control violent emotions; fools are controlled by their emotions. To the glory, or credit, of a wise person, he will simply ignore or forget the wrongs that others have done to him. He is not defensive; he does not insist on revenge.

The wrath and favor of rulers (verse 12). In an absolute monarchy, the word of the king is final. It is just as dangerous to be out of favor with the king as to battle a fierce lion. But to be in favor with him is refreshing and profitable, like dew upon grass.

It is wise and valuable, as far as possible, to be in favor with those in authority. (See Romans 12:18.) Human reasoning, warped by the inherent rebellion of sin, often sneers at authority and mocks those who attempt to develop a good relationship with those in authority. But such an attitude is wrong and leads to destruction. Biblical examples of godly men who gained favor with those in authority include Joseph, Daniel, and the three young Hebrew men. Even in these cases, unwise people despised those who had gained favor with their superiors.

A person's two most painful problems (verse 13). As Proverbs 15:20 suggests, children are largely responsible for the happiness or sorrow of their parents. This proverb specifically points out the sorrow that a foolish son brings to his father.

A man who has a contentious wife will grow weary with her. The word *contention* suggests strife in words, quarreling, and angry controversy. (Proverbs 27:15 is a companion proverb.) A contentious wife is like a steady drip. One drip is not too bad, nor even two or three. Many people can tolerate a drip for a while. But finally it is too much. The legendary Chinese water torture symbolizes the steady eroding of a marriage by the continual contentions of an unwise wife. In the modern vernacular, this proverb describes a nagging wife, one who voices repeated, whining complaints.

The woman who nags often thinks it is the only way to get her husband to do something that needs doing. She has not learned that the most powerful motivator of men is gratefulness. When a man knows his wife is genuinely grateful for some small task he has performed, he is motivated to do even more for her. When he performs some task and she responds, "Well! It's about time you got around to that," he has no sense of fulfillment and accomplishment, and he loses any interest in performing other tasks.

A wise wife will tell her husband once about things that need to be done. She may even make a list and post it where he can see it, but she will say nothing more about it. When he completes even one of the tasks, she will show her gratitude.

The basic reason that leads to nagging is high expectations. She expects her husband to do certain things as his duty. When he does them, she merely thinks he has done what he should have done—long ago. This attitude frustrates the man, who also has expectations. He expects his wife to be excited and thankful for his efforts, but her attitude discourages him from exerting himself, for the more he does the more his wife expects. He will do less and less in an attempt to lower her expectations.

At this point, the stage is set for disaster. For example, the husband may work in an environment with other women. If he performs some simple task for one of them, she will probably shower gratitude upon him because she did not expect him to do it. She had not considered it his obligation, so his help seems kind and thoughtful. Her gratitude then motivates him to do even more for her, which in turn may cause her to think he is an exceptionally kind person, the kind to whom she would like to be married. If she has a husband at home who does not meet her expectations, she will begin to compare him with her new friend at work. Many times, this scenario leads to divorce and remarriage. It can all be prevented by a wife who knows how to motivate her husband by gratitude and who understands the damaging effects of nagging.

Earthly and heavenly inheritance (verse 14). Continuing the theme established in the previous proverb, verse 14 compares the inheritance left by an earthly father with the inheritance given by the Lord. Earthly fathers can leave houses and riches, but only God can give someone a prudent wife.

This proverb demonstrates again the blessings of marriage. (See Proverbs 18:22.) What greater blessing could there be than a prudent wife? A prudent wife will contribute greatly to a man's personal contentment, to his spiritual well-being, to the atmosphere in his home, to the behavior of his children, to his reputation, and to his financial success. (See Proverbs 31:10-31, especially verse 23.) On the other hand, there is no greater sorrow a man can have than a foolish wife (Proverbs 12:4).

The choice of the right life partner is so significant that it should be a matter of great prayer, deliberation, counsel, and waiting upon the Lord. The choice should never be made hastily, and it certainly should not be made primarily on the basis of what men often highly esteem: physical attractiveness (Proverbs 11:22; 31:30). Physical beauty is of no consequence at all when compared to character.

Slothfulness and idleness (verse 15). Sleep is essential, but too much is harmful. Those who, through slothfulness, sleep more than necessary will find themselves craving more and more sleep.

There is a cause-and-effect relationship between idleness and hunger. The New Testament recognizes that if a man refuses to work, he should not eat (II Thessalonians 3:10). While Christians should be concerned about the truly needy, it does not help the slothful and idle to bail them out of trouble temporarily, time and again. Indeed, such misguided charity merely reinforces habits of slothfulness and idleness.

A welfare program that does not take into account a person's character is doomed to abuse and failure. It will create professional welfare clients who will make endless demands upon the system. A welfare program should consider the recipient's willingness to work and productivity (assuming he is able to work).

Consequences of obedience and disobedience (verse 16). The person who obeys the Word of God protects his own soul. But the person who cares nothing about ordering his ways by the commandments of the Lord chooses death.

Lending to the Lord (verse 17). The person who assists the poor actually does so to the Lord. (See Matthew 25:31-46.) And the Lord will not be indebted to anyone; He will repay the blessing. Thus, there is no way a person can lose by helping those in need. Though the rich young ruler thought he knew and obeyed the Scriptures, he was either ignorant of this significant truth or he refused to obey it (Mark 10:21-22). Had he sold all and given it to the poor, God would have more than repaid him again in some form.

Discipline of children (verse 18). Parents should discipline children while they are still young and teachable; to do otherwise will likely lead to their destruction. As long as there is hope for them to turn from foolishness to God's way, a wise father will not give up.

A wise father will not allow his son's crying to prevent him from following through on the chastisement. He knows that the object of chastisement is not to get his son to cry; it is to get him to repent and change his ways. If the son learns that crying will result in less chastisement, he will cry even before the chastening begins. But he will not change; he will merely increase in rebellion as he holds his father in contempt for being so easily deceived.

The punishment due criminals (verse 19). A person of great wrath—an angry, violent person—brings punishment on himself. Misguided efforts to spare him from the consequences of his actions will fail, for they deal with the symptom, not the cause. He is reaping what he has sown, and he should be allowed to do so.

Those who intervene in an attempt to get him out of trouble will find they have to do it over and over again. The reason is obvious: they reinforce his criminal behavior when they reward him by sympathy rather than letting him be punished by justice.

One of the greatest causes of repeated criminal action is the softening of the consequences by those who have a twisted sense of guilt for being part of the society that spawned the criminal. Indeed, many consider the criminal to be the real victim. This concept is simply untrue. The criminal's real problem is sin, and it will never be cured merely by humanistic efforts to rehabilitate him without discipline or to shift the blame from the sinner to society.

The road to wisdom (verse 20). There are two simple steps to wisdom: (1) Listen to counsel. (2) Accept instruction. These are, of course, the very things a rebel hates.

The human heart and the counsel of God (verse 21). The human heart, which is deceitful (Jeremiah 17:9), is very creative. It can produce many plans, with full justification for them even if they violate scriptural principles. But all of them will come to nothing; in the end, only God's counsel and purpose will prevail.

Kindness and truthfulness (verse 22). One of the things people most desire is simple kindness. Kindness will express itself in courtesy. (See I Peter 3:8.) Kindness is more attractive to others than ambition, drive, or eloquence.

It is better to be poor and honest than to be a rich liar.

The benefits of fearing God (verse 23). The fear of the Lord leads to life. It gives life; it produces things that preserve and prolong life rather than shorten it. It will cause a person to depart from evil and will give him wisdom and knowledge. The person who fears God will be content and safe.

A characteristic of slothfulness (verse 24). A slothful person can be identified by his attitude that the world owes him a living. He refuses to do things for himself, which this proverb characterizes by his refusal to feed himself. He hides his hand in his bosom, perhaps symbolic of his self-centeredness. He is of the opinion that others should feed him. When others, out of sympathy or other misguided emotions, accommodate him, they only reinforce his behavior.

Effects of correction (verse 25). When someone receives deserved punishment, it works a positive effect on others. Indeed, one reason for discipline is for the effect it has on others. For example, when a parent corrects one child, it will often produce carefulness and sweetness in the other children as well.

While strong public discipline may be needed to teach the simple, reproving a person who has understanding will impart knowledge to him. One important sign of understanding is the willingness to accept reproof.

The foolish son (verse 26). A son who mistreats—takes advantage of, robs, or destroys—his father and rejects his mother causes shame and brings reproach. Rebellious, sinful youth delight in these very sins, which are often glorified and promoted by rock music and cheap literature. They gloat in taking advantage of their parents, stealing from them, breaking them, and abandoning them. (See Proverbs 28:24.)

Reaction to teaching (verse 27). When a person recognizes that certain teaching is designed to lead him away from truth, he should cease listening to it. We are not to learn false ways (Jeremiah 10:2). Our knowledge of evil is to be limited (Romans 16:19). A person may feel strong enough at the moment to handle falsehood, but he does not know what effect it will have on him in a moment of weakness. On the other hand, a person must not cease listening to good instruction, or he will stray from truth.

The ungodly witness and the wicked mouth (verse 28).

An ungodly witness mocks at justice. The wicked person "eats up" iniquity; that is, he has a voracious appetite for sin.

Judgment and punishment (verse 29). Scoffers deserve judgment, and fools discipline. The scornful will never overcome their sin as long as there are no consequences. Unfortunately, today's society often glorifies and promotes evil actions that would have brought censure, rebuke, and punishment in earlier times.

Chapter Twenty

The deception of intoxicating beverages (verse 1). This verse personifies intoxicating beverages as mockers and as angry, violent people. This fact alone should be enough to convince a person of their inherent evil. If a person is a mocker or a rager, that is his nature, and all of his mocking and raging are sinful. Mocking and raging are not acceptable and permissible in small quantities; they are evil no matter how small or great the degree or quantity. By their very nature, mocking and raging are deceptive.

So by their very nature are wine and strong drink. The only proper attitude toward mocking and raging is utter abhorrence, total abstinence. The same is true of all intoxicating beverages. The deception of intoxicating beverages is at least twofold: (1) The idea that one can drink and not be negatively affected is deceptive. (2) The perverted thinking produced by intoxicating beverages is deceptive.

The English word *wine* here comes from the Hebrew *yayin,* which can mean either fermented or unfermented beverages. The Bible speaks of wine in three ways: (1) simply as a matter of fact, with no implicit approval or disapproval; (2) with clear condemnation; (3) with approval. Obviously, the word means different things in different contexts. The Bible speaks approvingly of fresh, or unfermented, wine, but it speaks disapprovingly of fermented wine. (See Leviticus 10:9; Proverbs 23:20-21, 29-35; 31:4-5; Isaiah 28:7.)

Drunkenness is a matter of degree. Someone who drinks intoxicating beverages begins to be drunk with the first sip. The February 1988 *Reader's Digest,* in an article titled "Knocking Back a Few," discusses in detail the immediate effects of alcoholic beverages: "You take your first swallow. . . . White blood cells begin to mobilize to repair the insulted tongue, mouth and throat, which are immediately inflamed. . . . About ten percent of the alcohol enters the bloodstream directly by migrating in small quantities right through the folds of the stomach wall. The rest of this swallow cascades into the first part of the small intestine, where the alcohol is rapidly absorbed into the bloodstream [within two minutes]. The first molecules of this toxin reach your carotid artery and are propelled into your brain. Within a few more moments, an effect is manifest—a light-headedness, a distortion of your perceptions." The article also graphically describes the way alcohol affects the liver, causing it to create poisonous metabolites, and the way it alters the body's chemical balance, causing it to excrete such vital electrolytes as potassium, calcium, and magnesium. Alcohol makes an impact on the blood pressure, blood flow, and overall chemistry of the brain and other organs. It is certainly wrong to think that one can associate with such a mocker and rager in moderation! The Scriptures declare that no drunkard shall enter the kingdom of God (I Corinthians 6:9-11; Galatians 5:19-21).

The danger of provoking rulers to anger (verse 2). Previous proverbs have discussed the wisdom of being in good standing with the king and the danger of being out of his favor (Proverbs 16:14; 19:12). Someone who offends an absolute monarch jeopardizes his own life.

It is always foolish to provoke others to anger. It is especially foolish to provoke those in authority. Fathers are not even to provoke their children to anger (Colossians 3:21). The only time when it is proper to disobey those in authority is when obedience to man would clearly violate the will of God (Acts 5:29).

An honorable thing and the sign of a fool (verse 3). Honorable people cease from strife; they do not promote it, carry it on, or in any way encourage it, whether by conversation, personal involvement, or otherwise.

A fool is known by his meddling and quarreling. While it is good to have concern for others and to oppose injustice, it is wrong to be a talebearer or a busybody in the affairs of others (II Thessalonians 3:11; I Peter 4:15).

Excuses (verse 4). A lazy person can always find an excuse not to work: it's too cold, it's too hot, the shovel doesn't fit his hands, and so on. His laziness is the cause of his poverty, and those who rescue him out of his self-inflicted trouble do him no favor. (See II Thessalonians 3:10.)

The depth of counsel (verse 5). Many wise people are somewhat reluctant to give counsel, because it is so often unwelcome and rejected. It is a sign of wisdom to withhold counsel from those who would have no appreciation for it (Matthew 7:6). But one who has understanding and who desires counsel will make the effort to draw it out of the wise.

The contrast between self-justification and faithfulness (verse 6). Many people proclaim their own goodness, but few are truly faithful (Proverbs 18:17; 27:2). Faithful people are unassuming, honest, and hard to find.

Walking in integrity; blessing one's children (verse 7). If a person is just, or righteous, it will be evident by the way he walks, or by his daily life. He will consistently live a life of integrity. And a person's sound moral life will cause his children to be blessed.

One of the great teachings of Scripture concerns the impact of a person's life on his descendants (Exodus 20:5). God does not hold children responsible for their parents' sins, but parents' sins have lingering consequences and effects on their offspring. A father should provide spiritual protection for his family. When he fails to do so, he opens the door to unnecessary temptations for those under his authority. Frequently the greatest temptations a young man faces are in areas of sin to which his father yielded. (See I Kings 22:52; II Chronicles 22:3; Jeremiah 9:14.) Similarly, a positive parental influence may affect many generations. (See I Kings 9:4; II Chronicles 17:3; II Timothy 1:5.)

The king sees and judges evil (verse 8). When a king (someone in authority) is surrendered to the Lord and operates in the wisdom taught in the Book of Proverbs (this book was written initially to teach a prince how to rule as king), he will have insight in judgment. He will discern evil plots, intentions, and actions and will judge accordingly.

The inadequacy of human efforts (verse 9). No one can, by his own efforts, cleanse his heart or purify himself from sin. (See Psalm 51:7.) Only the blood of Christ cleanses from sin. The Old Testament saints looked ahead in faith to the coming Messiah. Their salvation depended on His atonement, and all of the sacrifices they offered in faith prefigured the cross of Calvary. (See Matthew 26:28; Acts 20:28; Romans 3:24-25; 5:9; Hebrews 9:8-22; 10:1-20; I Peter 1:18-19; Revelation 1:5; 5:9; 7:14; 12:11.) New Testament saints look back in faith to the same cross.

God's concern for an honest economy (verse 10). A common theme throughout the Book of Proverbs is God's concern for honesty in the marketplace. (See Proverbs 11:1; 16:11; 20:23.) God hears even the cries of those whose wages have been kept back by fraud (James 5:4). These frequent statements should prompt the believer to exercise the greatest honesty in all financial dealings. Moreover, those in authority have a great responsibility to be personally honest and just and to ensure that the government they administrate is also.

The moral nature of children (verse 11). Conduct reveals character to such an extent that even a child's character is revealed by his deeds. The Bible does not specifically speak of the "age of accountability," but it is apparent that at some point God begins to hold a person accountable for his sins, and this time comes earlier than many people may think. Early in life children begin to recognize their sinfulness and their need of a Savior. It is not necessary that they have a great deal of intellectual maturity to be saved but only that they have the ability to believe on the Lord Jesus Christ and repent of their sins. Children and youth who live sinful lives despite an ability to distinguish clearly between right and wrong will answer to the Lord for their deeds. (See Ecclesiastes 11:9-10.)

The ear and the eye (verse 12). Humans, with all our capabilities, are created by God. We can claim no abilities apart from our Creator. Since all human abilities are gifts from God, including the ability to see and hear, we should use them to please and glorify Him. Unregenerated people pervert these gifts, allowing things to enter the ear-gate and the eye-gate that corrupt the soul and spirit. Christians should be careful not to yield their members as instruments of unrighteousness unto sin but to yield them as instruments of righteousness unto God (Romans 6:13).

The danger of too much sleep (verse 13). While sleep is necessary (even Jesus slept), too much is as detrimental as too little (Proverbs 19:15). A love for sleep will rob a person of valuable, productive time and lead to poverty. Only those who awaken and work diligently will find their needs met. A person should experiment until he finds the proper amount of sleep that he needs on average to awake every morning refreshed and rested. He should then plan to get that much sleep and no more. Sleeping excessively after the appropriate time to get up does not add to the genuine rest received, but it does create greater difficulty in arising.

The sign of a bargain hunter (verse 14). When shopping, many people attempt to get the seller to lower his price by belittling the merchandise. They will imply that they do not really want the merchandise and that they could only justify buying it if the price were reduced greatly. They really do want it, however, and will boast of the good deal they got if they are able to get the seller to lower the price.

While it is sensible to get the most possible for our

money, we must be sure to practice honesty in all matters relating to buying and selling. We should not mind paying what an item is genuinely worth. Always looking for "a good deal" can be a manifestation of greed. Someone who falls prey to this syndrome may find himself buying things he does not actually need because they are a good deal. In boasting of a good deal, some may actually ridicule the seller by bragging about how they got the better of him.

The value of lips of knowledge (verse 15). Gold and rubies are common and plentiful when compared with lips of knowledge. So few have lips of knowledge that those who possess them are of great value to God in His kingdom. When a person truly has a contribution to make to the kingdom of God, God will not allow him to sit idle; He will open doors of opportunity before him.

Co-signing and immorality (verse 16). Someone who becomes a surety is a bad risk, especially if he does so for an immoral woman. A prominent theme throughout Proverbs is the danger of accepting responsibility for another's debt. Those who become surety for another (co-sign) are fully and personally responsible for the debt. Though the co-signer receives no benefit from the debt, he may lose even his garment to pay it. Few things are as unwise economically as becoming responsible for the debts of others. (See Proverbs 6:1-2; 11:15; 17:18; 22:26; 27:13.)

Becoming a surety is costly; so is immorality. When a man gets involved with an immoral woman, he will pay a price. (See Genesis 38:12-26.) This price will be more than just money; immorality will also take from a person peace and health (Proverbs 5:3-14; 6:26-33).

Bread gained by deceit (verse 17). Dishonest gains seem sweet at first, but ultimately they are unsatisfying and worthless. Following as it does the previous statement about the consequences of immorality, this proverb seems to be a companion to Proverbs 9:17-18. Secret immorality may seem sweet at the moment, but the sweetness soon leaves and in its place is a mouthful of gravel. The forbidden fruit never yields what it promises.

The importance of good advice (verse 18). We should not make major decisions without counsel. If a person consults with no one, he may make some plans hastily, but they will be shallow and temporary. It will be easy for him to give up on his goals. He will be quickly frustrated. When a person seeks out wise counsel, it serves to solidify and clarify his purposes. He is much more likely to accomplish what he purposes. Thus, Solomon counselled his son not to engage in warfare without seeking good counsel.

While many people pay high prices for counselling, most of the counsel a person needs is available free of charge if he is willing to ask those with experience in that area.

Talebearers and flatterers (verse 19). A person who tells secrets should not be trusted with any confidential information. A talebearer will reveal secrets; that is his nature. If he will tell someone a secret, nothing will prevent him from telling anything he knows.

Talebearers are often masters at flattery, for they know it tends to loosen up a person's tongue and cause him to say more than he normally would. A wise person will not respond to flattery; he will not involve himself with a flatterer.

There is, of course, a difference in flattery and a genuine compliment. Flattery is insincere, and it is designed to take advantage of its object. Flattery is most often given for things over which a person has little or no control, such as physical appearance. Genuine compliments are given to encourage a person, and they are generally for something the person does have control over, such as attitudes.

Those who wish to use compliments in a constructive way should concentrate their attention on character qualities, not physical appearance. Their comments will encourage others to develop those traits more fully. Generally, a man should give compliments on physical appearance only to his wife or a close relative. Flattery is dangerous because it draws attention to the wrong things, introduces wrong trends of thought, and opens the door—if ever so slightly—to wrong associations and involvements.

The penalty for disrespect of parents (verse 20). We are to honor our father and mother. Since this is the first commandment with promise, it is reasonable that there is also a penalty for its violation.

The lamp is the source of life. The person who curses his parents curses the source of his life. The person who says, "I wish I had never been born" obliquely curses his parents. From our parents we receive not only our physical bodies but our spiritual natures as well. To curse one's parents is similar to cursing the spring while drinking its water. Essentially, a person who curses his parents cuts off his own life; he turns out his own lamp. He will walk in darkness.

The danger of getting rich quick (verse 21). When money is received without effort and persistence, it will be just as quickly lost. The biblical principle is that rewards come for work (I Timothy 5:18). The discipline of the work and the character developed thereby prepare a person for the rewards; they give him wisdom to use the rewards properly.

But when a person receives the rewards without the price, he has not developed the wisdom and discipline to use them rightly. Since he did not have the wisdom to gain the riches, he will not have the wisdom to keep them or to use them in such a way as to be blessed of God. God blesses wealth gained by hard work and diligent effort, not get-rich-quick schemes, gambling, or hasty inheritances.

Research has shown that the heirs of the wealthy frequently have great trouble in knowing how to use their wealth. They often have feelings of guilt and condemnation over the unearned wealth. Rather than bringing peace and joy, the wealth brings frustration and worry. A term has been coined to describe those who find themselves in this situation: "the Golden Ghetto." Professional counselors have risen up to deal with the mental conflicts experienced by the quickly rich.

Seeking vengeance (verse 22). It is always unwise to attempt to get even with people by getting revenge. Vengeance belongs to the Lord; He will take care of His children. When someone seeks vengeance, he attempts to play God. (See Matthew 5:38-42; Romans 12:17-21.)

More about economic honesty (verse 23). Again the theme appears: God is personally concerned about honesty in the marketplace. (See also Proverbs 20:10.)

Our total dependence on God (verse 24). Some think they are "self-made men." They think they owe God nothing. But if someone has anything worthwhile, he has God to thank for it (Matthew 5:45). We actually know very little. The wisest thing we can do is to acknowledge our total dependence on God and trust Him for guidance (Proverbs 3:5-6; 16:1).

The danger of rash vows (verse 25). It is extremely dangerous to rashly dedicate something as holy and then later to reconsider those vows. In general, once a person makes a commitment he should keep it, even if it hurts (Psalm 15:4). It is particularly wrong to devour, or to use for oneself, something that belongs to God, perhaps thinking to repent or to pay it back later.

Dealing with the wicked (verse 26). A wise king will deal firmly with rebellion and anarchy by scattering the rebels. He will not allow them to congregate and form pockets of resistance. The analogy here is to the threshing of grain by a wheel and to winnowing, or separating the wheat from the chaff. The wise king will not allow the wicked to be hidden among the upright. He will detect, reveal, and judge them.

The human spirit (verse 27). The Lord uses a person's spirit to search out and reveal his inward nature. In other words, God knows our inmost character and thoughts and deals with our spirit. Our fundamental communication with God is not physical or psychological but spiritual. The new birth directly affects the human spirit. As Jesus said, "That which is born of the Spirit is spirit" (John 3:6).

Preserving the king (verse 28). Two qualities necessary to safeguard one's authority are mercy and truth. (See Psalm 85:10.) The king must be truthful and he must show mercy. Of the two qualities, mercy is more foundational; it secures the throne. (See James 2:13.)

Youth and age (verse 29). What strength is to a young man, gray hair, signifying wisdom and experience, is to an old man. This proverb is more fully understood in a society that honors age than in a society that questions whether the aged have any "meaningful contribution" to make.

Physical and spiritual discipline (verse 30). The bruise is a sign of healing. While it may look dreadful, it indicates the injury is over and healing is taking place. Similarly, physical discipline has a positive impact on cleansing the inner person. Proper correction affects a person's spiritual nature, bringing him to repentance. For this reason God will, if necessary, chasten a rebellious person. (See I Corinthians 11:27-32.)

Chapter Twenty-One

The heart of the king (verse 1). Since it is God who sets up and removes rulers (Daniel 2:21), it is evident that He can also change a ruler's heart (mind). The Lord directs a ruler's heart like a river. Just as the force of water forms bends in a river, so pressure from God turns a ruler's heart. For example, God used ten plagues to apply pressure to Pharaoh. After at first refusing to free God's people, Pharaoh vacillated and then finally relented.

In view of the sovereignty of God, we should not rebel against those in authority but allow God to change their hearts. Daniel's relationship with various authority figures illustrates this principle. The person under authority should always remember that God is bigger than the person in authority over him.

Self-justification (verse 2). This proverb is a companion to Proverbs 16:2. Humans are extremely creative in justifying themselves, even when they have committed sin. They commonly do so by shifting blame, which is at the root of much of modern psychology. But God sees more than the outward facade, and He is more concerned about a person's heart or motives. If someone's heart is right, he will do right things. But if his heart is not right, regardless of what he does, he does not please the Lord.

What God wants more than sacrifice (verse 3). Since the sacrificial system was an integral part of the law of Moses, which prevailed when this proverb was written, it may surprise some people to find that God prefers some things over sacrifice. But this theme is common even in the Old Testament. David prayed, "For thou desirest not sacrifice; else would I give it: thou delightest not in burnt offering" (Psalm 51:16). (See also Isaiah 1:11; Hosea 6:6; Amos 5:21-25; Hebrews 10:1-10.) Micah 6:6-8 sums up the Lord's three fundamental requirements for humanity: (1) to do justly; (2) to love mercy; and (3) to walk humbly with God.

God never intended for the sacrificial system of the law of Moses to be an end in itself. In and of themselves those sacrifices did not provide forgiveness, justification, or redemption (Romans 3:20; Hebrews 10:4). They were simply predictive of the coming Messiah and His atoning work (Galatians 3:24-25; Colossians 2:16-17). The Lord intended for people to perform the rituals of the law in faith, depending on God to provide salvation and looking toward the coming Messiah, who would fulfill the law as well as the prophets. (See Matthew 5:17-18; Luke 24:25-27, 44-46; Romans 3:21-22; 10:3-4.)

Those who merely went through the motions of the law without a heart of faith displeased God. As this proverb indicates, justice (doing what is right) and judgment (making correct decisions based on God's Word rather than human reasoning) were more important to the Lord than sacrifice. Even today, God is more interested in right attitudes and motives than He is in personal sacrifice done to please Him. (See I Samuel 15:22-23; Matthew 23:23.)

Three sins (verse 4). Sin is more than actions; it is attitudes. Pride and arrogance are displeasing to the Lord, whether in attitude, appearance, or actions. When a wicked person plows, or prepares to sow his evil seed, even his preparation is sinful.

The importance of thoughts to prosperity (verse 5). Diligence begins in the thoughts. Diligent plans produce diligent actions, which in turn produce profit. But the desire to get rich quick also originates in the thoughts, which produces haste, which produces poverty. God has ordained a means by which all can have plenty, but many are unwilling to follow the plan. The means to plenty is simply diligence, which speaks of faithfulness, consistency, quality work, and doing everything as unto the Lord.

The danger of dishonest gain (verse 6). The person who gains money dishonestly is actually seeking death. Money dishonestly or illicitly gained is vain and fleeting, and it results in condemnation.

The self-destruction of the wicked (verse 7). This verse expresses a similar truth to the previous proverb. The person who practices robbery or violence is laying the groundwork for his own destruction. The person who refuses to do right is choosing destruction.

The way of the unregenerated (verse 8). Because humans are sinful by nature, their ways are evil until God makes them pure (Ephesians 2:1-5; 4:17-19). The way of the guilty is perverse, but the work of the pure is right.

When it is better to be alone (verse 9). Proverbs 25:24 repeats this proverb. God created woman to complete and complement man and to be his companion (I Corinthians 11:7-11). A wife who refuses to fulfill this complementary role is a public rebuke to her husband and actually damages him (Proverbs 12:4). While it is a blessing for a man to have a wife (Genesis 2:18; Proverbs 18:22), it is better for a man to be alone than to have a brawling, contentious wife (Proverbs 21:19).

Wicked desires (verse 10). Just as grace provides the desire and power to do right, the sin nature provides the desire and ability to sin. The wicked do wrong because their desires are wrong. One mark of a wicked person is his refusal to say anything good about others or to show them mercy.

Learning from the mistakes of others (verse 11). This proverb is a companion to Proverbs 19:25. When punishment is carried out properly, it has a positive effect on others by showing them the consequences of sin. Some people, however, are wise enough not to need such an example; they learn simply by instruction.

The house of the wicked (verse 12). The righteous person is not impressed by what the wicked seem to have built. He examines the foundation of the structure and realizes their certain destruction (Psalm 73:17-19; Matthew 7:24-27). In the end, God will bring the wicked to ruin.

Sowing and reaping (verse 13). This verse illustrates the Golden Rule at work (Matthew 7:12). If someone refuses to aid the poor in their time of need, he too will not find help when he needs it.

Pacifying anger (verse 14). If a person has offended or wronged someone, it is wise to go to him privately and make amends. (See Matthew 5:23-24; 18:15.) Humbly going to that person and presenting a gift will tend to produce a positive response in the offended person.

The just person's joy (verse 15). Those who are just

enjoy doing right because it is right. Those who do wrong are sowing seeds of their own destruction.

Understanding or death (verse 16). Either someone is walking in the way of understanding or he is in the company of the spiritually dead. Only those who do God's commandments walk in the way of understanding (Psalm 111:10). Understanding comes through His precepts (Psalm 119:104).

Understanding is the path of happiness (Proverbs 3:13). A person of understanding will forsake foolishness, have a knowledge of the holy, hold his peace, be slow to wrath, seek more knowledge, walk uprightly, and heed reproof (Proverbs 9:6, 10; 11:12; 14:29; 15:14, 21, 32).

On the other hand, those who have wandered out of the way of understanding commit adultery, think it is desirable to commit secret sin, despise others, follow vanity, follow their own heart, and neglect their own responsibility (Proverbs 6:32; 9:16-18; 11:12; 12:11; 18:2; 24:30-34).

A road to poverty (verse 17). Loving pleasure and luxuries too much leads to poverty. A person who spends all his money in self-gratification will not be rich.

The last word (verse 18). The wicked may think they will escape suffering and they may even persecute the righteous, but ultimately it will be the wicked who suffer judgment instead. (See Revelation 21:8.)

Why some men leave home (verse 19). This is a companion proverb to Proverbs 21:9. It is better to be alone than with a contentious, angry woman. Although they are not justified in doing so, this is the reason many men leave their wives.

Saving and spending (verse 20). A wise person will

save and plan for the future. A foolish person will spend everything he makes as he gets it, or even before.

How to find the important things (verse 21). Someone who commits himself to a life of doing right things (by faith) and showing mercy to others will discover life in its fullest, will be righteous before God, and will receive honor.

Wisdom is greater than might (verse 22). Wisdom will enable someone to conquer the evil achievements of the mighty. Neither the physical nor the spiritual might of the wicked can stand before the wise. (See II Corinthians 10:4-5; Ephesians 6:10-13.)

How to stay out of trouble (verse 23). One of the greatest sources of trouble to the soul (mind, will, and emotions) is words. Someone who learns how to control his tongue will spare himself countless troubles. (See James 3:2-6.)

Pride and anger (verse 24). A proud and arrogant person is a scorner or mocker. He will ridicule others and consider himself superior to them. Anger will be a manifestation of his pride and arrogance. The point at which a proud person becomes angry is ordinarily when he feels his rights have been violated. He has not learned to yield his rights to the Lord.

The tension in slothfulness (verse 25). The slothful person's problem is not that he has no ambition. He has great desires; there are many things he wants. But because he is too lazy to work to achieve his goals, his desires become negative emotional pressures. He will often begin to look for unethical, dishonest, deceitful, or questionable short-cuts to fulfilling his wishes. For example, he may play the lottery or participate in chain-letter schemes, hoping to bypass God's plan of labor and reward.

The difference between the slothful and the righteous (verse 26). Greed and covetousness is a way of life for the slothful. Rather than working to achieve his goals, he spends his time plotting devious means to achieve them without effort. The righteous person, on the other hand, works an honest job not only to support himself and his family but to give generously to those in need. (See Ephesians 4:28.)

God needs no help from the wicked (verse 27). God rejects the sacrifice of the wicked, especially when he gives it with an evil intent. (See Proverbs 28:9.) God is not impressed with those who refuse to surrender their lives to Him but think to placate Him with a gift or offering. The only thing that makes anything done for the Lord of any value is faith (Hebrews 11:6).

The danger of being a false witness (verse 28). The person who witnesses falsely lays the groundwork for his own destruction. Every lying word out of his mouth is like a seed that will produce an abundant harvest of pain and sorrow in his life.

But someone who hears or observes a matter carefully will be able to report accurately, and his word will stand. People should be consistent in speaking the truth, and not just on the witness stand. If someone is called upon to be a witness, he should tell only and exactly what he personally knows to be a fact.

Controlled by emotions or controlling emotions (verse 29). A wicked person allows his emotions to rule him, hardening his position and putting up a bold front. An upright person rules his emotions, giving careful thought to his ways and making preparations.

The failure of all God's enemies (verse 30). All attempts to destroy God's kingdom are doomed to fail. No schemes against Him can succeed. Thus, humanism is self-destructive. (See Psalm 2; II Corinthians 13:8; Philippians 1:12.)

God is our only protection (verse 31). People may develop elaborate defense systems, but only God is able to protect. If He does not protect, all human efforts at defense are in vain. (See Psalm 20:7; 4:8.)

Chapter Twenty-Two

The value of a good name and favor (verse 1). Character is more important than monetary riches. A good name is not easily gained; it is earned over a period of time by honesty, courtesy, integrity, dependability, and godliness. If someone must make a choice between a good name and great riches, the choice is clear: a good name is far more valuable.

Though someone may have great riches, they will tend to dissipate if he has an evil reputation. Honest people will be reluctant to do business with him and loath to serve in his employ. He will thus find himself surrounded by those as dishonest as himself, and they will endanger his wealth. And ultimately all his wealth cannot provide love, joy, peace, and life.

Someone with no wealth but with a good name has the most important ingredient anyone could possibly have for gaining wealth: a reputation for honesty. Most people, if they have a choice, would rather do business with a person known to be a fair dealer. In short, someone should never compromise his good name for money; he will always be the loser.

Parents should recognize that the highest goal toward which they can point their children is developing godly character. They should not lead children to believe that wealth is a supreme goal. They will communicate this faulty concept even without specifically expressing it if children observe their parents' continual interest in money and frequently hear them discussing money as if it would solve their problems. Parents should praise children for their character traits and achievements rather than physical beauty, mental ability, or popularity. Children have a natural desire to please their parents, and they quickly learn where their parents place their values.

Loving favor—the favor of people—is also more valuable than silver and gold. As the boy Jesus grew, He "increased in wisdom and stature, and in favour with God and man" (Luke 2:52). Parents should teach children how important it is to learn to get along with other people and should demonstrate how to do so. The briefest and most valuable key to doing so is the Golden Rule: "Therefore all things whatsoever ye would that men should do to you, do ye even so to them: for this is the law and the prophets" (Matthew 7:12).

The similarity between the rich and the poor (verse 2). There really is not that much difference between the rich and the poor. The differences are purely external. Both are made of the same clay. Both came into the world with nothing. Both will leave the world with nothing. Both will answer to God in judgment (Revelation 20:12).

If we read this verse in conjunction with verse 1, it is evident that a poor person who has a good name and loving favor with others is in a vastly superior state to a rich person without these blessings.

The value of foresight (verse 3). A prudent person sees trouble coming before it happens and so avoids it. He does so by understanding cause-and-effect relationships. A simple person cannot see the consequences of present events, including his own actions, and he reaps the bitter results.

After discussing the importance of acquiring faith, virtue, knowledge, temperance, patience, godliness, brotherly kindness, and charity, II Peter 1:5-9 says, "But he that lacketh these things is blind, and cannot see afar off." This inspired insight explains how to gain the foresight necessary to avoid evil. (For a thorough discussion of II Peter 1:5-9, see the author's book *Insights for Christian Living* [Hazelwood, Mo.: Word Aflame Press, 1988].)

The key to riches, honor, and life (verse 4). True wealth, genuine honor, and abundant life come to those who are humble and fear God. (See John 10:10; James 4:6.) Humility means total dependence on God and the honest recognition that without Him we can do nothing. It also recognizes fully the contributions others have made to helping us become what we are.

The fear of God begins with the knowledge of God's omnipotence, omniscience, and omnipresence and with the recognition of the Creator-creature distinction established in Genesis 1:1. In a sense, the rest of the Scripture is simply an expansion of the truth revealed in that verse. Since God created the heaven and the earth and everything in them, including humans, we must recognize our total dependence upon God. When a person begins to feel self-sufficient, he is deceived and has forgotten the fear of the Lord.

Sharp reminders of rebellion (verse 5). Someone who rebels against God has chosen a path of pain and sorrow. "The way of transgressors is hard" (Proverbs 13:15). God purposefully allows obstacles in the path of those who walk away from Him in an attempt to get their attention, in hopes that the pain will awaken them to their error. (See Acts 9:5.)

Someone who submits his soul to God need not suffer these kinds of difficulties. It is very easy to choose the path away from God, but that path leads to destruction. Relatively few find the path to life. (See Matthew 7:13-14.) This does not mean the path to life is difficult to find but simply that many are unwilling to forsake their rebellion against God.

Training up a child (verse 6). Many people interpret this verse to mean that a godly parent can train his child in such a way that the child will never depart from God, or that if he does depart, he will return to God later in life. This statement has validity as a general principle; however, it is not an absolute law. If a parent could guarantee that his child would live for God, it would compromise the clear biblical teaching concerning individual free will and moral responsibility. Children are not machines guaranteed to respond in certain ways if parents press the right buttons and pull the correct levers. They are human beings, and central to being human is the power of choice. In interpreting this proverb, we should keep two main points in mind.

(1) Children are individuals, created in the image of God. Each human being is unique, gifted with an un-duplicated combination of talents and dreams. Severe problems can arise when parents try to live out their dreams through their children, or when they try to compare one child with another.

This proverb addresses one of the greatest challenges

parents face: helping each child reach his full personal potential. Parents should train up each child in the way he personally should go. Of course, parents should train every child to serve God, but more specifically, they should carefully assess each child's uniqueness and train him accordingly. They should encourage the child in the development of his personal gifts. They should not expect the child to dutifully follow what to him is a dull profession, regardless of how long a line of ancestors practiced it. The child is a miracle of creation, fearfully and wonderfuly made in the image of God. His gifts are far too precious to stifle in a musty mold made for someone else.

(2) Children are fleshly, sinners by birth. Sometimes they will fail. There is nothing a parent can do to guarantee that his children will always make right choices. The only perfect father who ever lived had two children, a son and a daughter. He raised them both in a carefully designed environment free from negative peer pressure. They did not have to struggle with television or cheap novels or heavy metal music. The father demonstrated his love for his children in a thousand ways. He spent quality time with them. Yet both children sinned rebelliously against their father. Some would have considered that a one-hundred-percent failure rate.

The father was God. The children were Adam and Eve, and they originally did not have a sinful nature. If God had arranged things so that Adam and Eve could not have failed, they would not have been human beings. They would have been puppets. But the love of a puppet is meaningless. Love is what it is only because it is a choice. All the promises of the gospel are to those who make conscious decisions to choose to serve the Lord (John 3:16; 6:37; Revelation 22:17).

This proverb focuses on the individuality of the child and the duty of the parents to help him become what God intended him to be.

The power of wealth (verse 7). In Ecclesiastes 10:19, Solomon declared, "Money answereth all things." While we should not love money nor labor to be rich (Proverbs 23:4; I Timothy 6:10), we must recognize that money is important in virtually all human affairs. Those who have money are in a position to dictate many things to those who do not have it but need it.

Likewise, a lender is in a position to dictate many things to a borrower. One of the blessings God promised to Israel if the nation would be obedient was that they would lend and not borrow (Deuteronomy 15:6). Ideally, God's people should be economically in such a position so they do not have to borrow from those who do not fear God. In general, a person should avoid borrowing if at all possible, for the more he borrows the more restrictions are imposed upon him.

Why do so many people depend so heavily on borrowing through bank loans or credit cards? Often, they exercise poor financial judgment, fail to save properly, or are unwilling to delay a purchase until it is more feasible economically. People may fail to participate in the abundant provisions that God provides because they are unfaithful in tithes and offerings (Proverbs 3:9-10; Malachi 3:8-11), give out of duty or obligation rather than cheerfully (II Corinthians 9:7), or violate biblical principles regarding the use of money. Examples are giving to the rich (Proverbs 22:16), oppressing the poor (Proverbs 22:16), stinginess (Proverbs 11:24-25), slothfulness (Proverbs 6:9-11), drunkenness and gluttony (Proverbs 23:21), failure to give to the poor (Proverbs 19:17), co-signing (Proverbs 6:1-5), a lack of diligence (Proverbs 21:5), and the desire to get rich quick (Proverbs 21:5).

The consequences of sin (verse 8). Someone who lives in sin will reap trouble, futility, and sorrow. Such a troubled, frustrated person will often lash out at others in anger, but his wrath will fail to accomplish his purpose. Eventually, he and his wrath will be destroyed.

The blessing of generosity (verse 9). Many passages of Scripture describe the blessings of generosity. (See, for example, Luke 6:38.) It is important to have a "bountiful eye," that is, to actively look for those in need rather than trying to avoid them.

How to get rid of strife (verse 10). A scoffer or mocker is the source of a great deal of contention, strife, and reproach. If he is tolerated, these will never cease. There comes a time when the only solution to negative attitudes is to dismiss the scorner. Paul recommended this course of action to the church at Corinth. (See I Corinthians 5.)

How to gain favor with those in authority (verse 11). A person whose priority is purity of heart will be known by the words of his mouth. (See Matthew 12:34.) When someone has a pure heart, he will also have lips of grace. (See Ephesians 4:29.) That is, his words will encourage people and motivate them to do right. Those who are in authority recognize the value of this kind of person, and they will value his friendship. They are so often surrounded by flatterers, slanderers, and prophets of doom that someone who speaks gracious words is a refreshing change.

Why God performs or destroys someone's words (verse 12). God is interested in the words we speak. He watches over words that are according to knowledge (in line with His Word) in order to perform them. But if words are out of line with His Word, He will destroy them.

Creative excuses for slothfulness (verse 13). One of the signs of slothfulness is the creation of excuses not to do the things that should be done. The slothful person has no lack of imagination.

A byproduct of slothfulness is procrastination. The excuse of the slothful suggests that he will be happy to go out and do his work later, when the lion is no longer a threat. A cure for this aspect of slothfulness is to do what needs to be done first, to tackle the more unpleasant tasks first. The principle God Himself established in creation is to work first and then rest.

When fear prohibits action, it is good to remember the adage someone offered: "Do the thing you fear, and the death of fear is certain." The human mind tends to focus on the negative and to magnify the dangers. But when someone takes a bold step into the unknown, regardless of the imagined dangers, he usually finds that he has vastly overrated the problems. The slothful person will never accomplish anything worthwhile, for there will always be an excuse for doing nothing. Only those who take risks achieve worthwhile goals.

A dangerous mouth (verse 14). Proverbs 6:25 declares that immoral women tempt with their eyelids. In addition, they tempt with their mouths, both by words and appearance, including makeup.

The practice of painting the face and mouth did not have its origins among the godly women of old, but among the ungodly, and the Bible never speaks of it favorably. If it were acceptable for a woman to paint her mouth, seemingly it would also be acceptable for a man to paint his, but actually it is appropriate for neither. Painting the face is artificial. It emphasizes facial features beyond the way God created them, appealing to the lust of the eyes. Godly women should be well-groomed, but they should not resort to artificial adornment or immodest displays (I Timothy 2:9-10).

Those who are deceived by an immoral woman's artificial attraction commit a sin that the Lord abhors.

The rod of correction (verse 15). Children are not "blank tablets" at birth as philosopher John Locke suggested. They have a sinful nature that will display itself increasingly over time. Proper physical discipline will help a child overcome his innate foolishness. Child abuse is sinful, but it is possible to discipline a child's rebellious will in love. (See comments on Proverbs 10:13; 13:24.)

Two steps to poverty (verse 16). Oppressing, or taking advantage of, the poor in an attempt to increase one's wealth will result in poverty. Giving to the rich will also produce poverty, for the person who does so thinks it will give him favor with the rich and that the rich will in turn favor him. But this hope will go unfulfilled, and the giver will simply be poorer. God must be the object of our trust; anything else is idolatry. Scripture teaches that we are to give to the poor (Proverbs 19:17).

Two proper responses to wise words (verse 17). To "bow down thine ear" means to listen carefully. We must discipline ourselves to listen to the right words. Foolish words tend to be much more attractive to the carnal nature, but a wise person will make a conscious choice to listen to wise words.

The phrase "apply thine heart" seems to speak of

meditation. A wise person will not only listen to the right words, he will apply his heart to them. He will think on them, examine them, and look for practical applications of them.

A pleasant result (verse 18). Meditating on words of wisdom is pleasant. But it is not an end in itself; it is merely a means to an end. The obvious result of meditating on wise words is that those words will be "fitted" in one's mouth. That is, when a person has meditated deeply on wise words, they will become the words he speaks. A wise person will speak God's words; his conversation will agree with the wisdom of God.

Another result of meditating on and speaking wise words (verse 19). The process that began with "bowing down" the ear to hear wise words (verse 17) continues to bear fruit. First, wise words are placed on the lips (verse 18). Next, they produce trust in the Lord. Those who listen to foolish words and meditate on evil reports tend to walk in fear. But those who listen to, meditate on, and speak wise words tend to trust the Lord. His Word has a soothing, strengthening, and comforting effect.

Excellent writing (verse 20). Under divine inspiration Solomon wrote these proverbs for his son's benefit, and by extension, for all of us. He did not simply speak them.

In several ways the written word is even more powerful than the spoken. It has been said that "the pen is mightier than the sword." The power of a free press is evident in the world's strongest nations. Moreover, the process of writing is an excellent discipline for the writer himself. Francis Bacon said, "Reading maketh a full man . . . writing an exact man." The process of writing forces a person to discipline his thoughts and clarify his positions. His written words will live on long after his spoken words have vanished into thin air. Of course, the written Word of God is inspired, and it is excellent in counsel and knowledge. No education is complete without a thorough study of the Scriptures. (See I Timothy 4:13-16.)

The purpose of the written word (verse 21). Solomon wrote the proverbs, rather than merely speaking them, so his son would "know the certainty of the words of truth." A diligent study of what is written is much more certain to produce genuine learning than merely listening to lectures. Moreover, this proverb is an internal witness of the truthfulness of Scripture. Solomon believed the words he wrote to be "words of truth."

Another reason Solomon wrote the proverbs was so his son would be able to "answer the words of truth" to those who asked him anything. Of course, answering with truthful words depends upon first learning them. A wise person will wish to arrive at the place where every word he speaks agrees with the truthful Word of God. (See Colossians 4:6; I Peter 3:15.)

The Protector of the poor (verses 22-23). God takes personal interest in the poor and oppressed. He will judge those who rob the poor because they are perceived to be defenseless and also those who oppress the afflicted. Those who do these things directly oppose the Messianic mission (Isaiah 61:1-3; Luke 4:16-19).

The danger of friendship with a furious and angry person (verses 24-25). People tend to learn the ways of their friends. For that reason, a wise person will not associate closely with a quick-tempered, wrathful person. Anger is a snare to the soul, and even a mild-mannered person who associates with an angry person will tend after awhile to lose his own temper. (See I Corinthians 15:33.) One of the wisest things a person can do is to decide what kind of a person he wants to be and then to make it a point to associate with that kind of person.

The danger of standing good for another's debts (verses 26-27). To the natural mind, it may seem honorable and generous for someone to stand good for the debt of another. But unless someone is willing to give this amount freely, co-signing is foolish, especially if the obligation is indefinite, unlimited, or beyond his means. A co-signer takes full legal responsibility for someone else's debt, yet he has none of the benefits for which the debt was incurred. He may very well lose his own possessions to pay another's debt, while the other person retains his possessions. (See comments on Proverbs 6:1-2; 11:15; 17:18; 20:16.)

A warning against theft (verse 28). In ancient times, landmarks marked the boundaries of property. Moving a landmark was an attempt to encroach upon and steal someone else's property. Thus the Old Testament prohibited them from being moved (Deuteronomy 19:14; 27:17; Job 24:2; Proverbs 23:10; Hosea 5:10). Moreover, God commanded the Israelites to possess the land given to their fathers forever; they were never to sell their family inheritances (Leviticus 25:23-24; I Kings 21:3).

The reward of diligence (verse 29). Diligence in business brings promotion. Diligence is so rare and valuable that those who practice it will not remain associated with obscure people; they will be associated with those in positions of great authority.

Chapter Twenty-Three

Personal conduct in the presence of those in authority (verses 1-3). Solomon, who was himself a ruler and who was training his son to be a ruler, thought it important to teach the proper conduct in the company of others in authority. And the principles that these divinely inspired words express are of general application.

The first principle is self-discipline. Even if someone has a large appetite and enjoys food enormously, he should restrain this tendency. He should eat sensibly and moderately.

Second, this passage warns against being deceived by a ruler's "dainties," or delicacies. They are "deceitful," perhaps meaning they are offered with questionable motives. This statement is possibly a warning of the danger of being poisoned by enemies who disguised themselves as friends. History records numerous attempts to assassinate rulers by poisoned food. In fact, the original task of the cupbearer was to taste the cup before the king to assure that it was safe. If someone had a large appetite and ate indiscriminately, it would be relatively easy to poison him.

Perhaps this passage teaches another lesson as well. Many people in authority have learned to tell much about a person by his eating habits. Some companies, for example, do not hire a person until they have taken him out to eat in order to observe his eating habits. Certainly, one of the chief places to test a person's manners is at the table. If he knows how to conduct himself there, he probably has a grasp of etiquette.

Verse 3 may focus on the tendency of many to admire the trappings of success and wealth without stopping to think of the price required for such "dainties." Many do not understand the price that must be paid to achieve wealth. They do not see the extra pressures upon a wealthy person, nor do they recognize the increased temptation wealth brings. They see only the "benefits" of wealth that appeal to the flesh. The point could be that a wise person will not allow himself to covet the fringe benefits that wealth brings.

Two improper goals (verse 4). This verse mentions two unworthy goals in life, which unfortunately, most people aim for: (1) the pursuit of wealth and (2) doing what seems right according to human wisdom. While God may bless someone with wealth as he works hard and honestly, wealth itself should never be his goal. If it is, he will never be satisfied with his wealth, no matter how great it is. (See Matthew 19:23-24; John 6:27; I Timothy 6:6-11; James 5:1-3.) Our greatest goal should be to bring glory to God; even our work should be done to glorify God (Ephesians 6:5-8). The moment the accumulation of wealth itself becomes the goal, wealth becomes a god. And while money makes a good servant, it is a terrible master.

The second improper, and yet common, goal is "doing one's own thing." While it is true that each person has unique gifts and interests which he should explore and develop, it is just as true that he must do so completely under the lordship of Jesus Christ. Never must the Christian slip into the error of the ancient Israelites, when "every man did that which was right in his own eyes" (Judges 21:25). As Solomon warned twice, "There is a way which seemeth right unto a man, but the end thereof are the ways of death" (Proverbs 14:12; 16:25).

The elusiveness of riches (verse 5). As further support for the warning "Labour not to be rich" in verse 4, verse 5 points out the transitory nature of riches. First, there is no real substance to riches: "Wilt thou set thine eyes upon that which is not?" True substance is found in a person's character, not in the size of his bank account or the material possessions he has amassed.

In the final analysis, the only value of riches is the confidence people place in them. If anything shakes that confidence—as frequently happens—money loses its value. For example, the only value of paper money is the confidence people place in it. There is no more intrinsic value in a piece of paper with the numeral one followed by two zeros than in a piece of paper of the exact size and color, printed with the same amount of ink, that has only the numeral one on it.

In short, riches are just about as stable as birds. Like a bird, they stay in one place only a very short period of time, and then they fly away. Those who boast in their wealth forget that their situation could be reversed within five seconds.

Having no fellowship with evil people (verse 6). Eating is an act of fellowship. Since we tend to become like those with whom we associate, it is important to avoid close fellowship with evil people. The New Testament similarly warns believers against eating with hypocrites (I Corinthians 5:11).

An "evil eye" seems to be an idiom meaning a hard, grudging, stingy, hypocritical attitude. (See Proverbs 22:9; 28:22.) Regardless of how desirable it may seem to have fellowship with such a person—he may offer delicacies ("dainty meats")—the negative consequences will outweigh any possible benefits.

Jesus ate with sinners, but He always did it with their redemption in view. In other words, His eating with them was not for the sake of fellowship and it was not a stamp of approval upon their lifestyle. Instead, it was for the purpose of bringing them out of the darkness of sin into the light of truth.

Thoughts, more than words, determine character (verse 7). In normal relationships, words reflect the thoughts of the heart. But it is possible for a hypocrite to conceal his true thoughts or motives with lying words. As important as words are, even more important are thoughts, for the thoughts determine what kind of a person one is. The root problem is not merely a person's words or habits; it is his mind. (See II Corinthians 10:4-5.)

The problem of the hypocrite of this proverb is in his mind, for he has determined in his mind to deceive with dishonest words. Although he offers food and drink, because of his stinginess he thinks about the cost and does not really want the guest to partake of much.

The consequence of having fellowship with evil people (verse 8). Whatever benefit a person may perceive in having fellowship with an evil person, he will soon forget it when he faces the consequences. His situation will be worse than if he had never eaten anything at all. When someone eats with a miser, for example, he will "vomit up" what little he has eaten and all of his compliments will be wasted.

Speaking no wisdom to a fool (verse 9). There is no need to try to share wisdom with a fool; he will simply despise it. (See Matthew 7:6.)

Another warning against theft (verses 10-11). This warning is one of a number in Scripture against moving the landmarks, the boundaries marking property lines. (See Proverbs 22:28.) But this proverb adds the warning not to take advantage of the fatherless. God takes special note of the plight of orphans and widows (Exodus 22:22; Deuteronomy 24:17; 26:12; Isaiah 1:17). He will personally take the place of the missing father (Psalm 68:5). God will provide the protection an earthly father would give his children and more. Those who attempt to mistreat the fatherless will therefore find themselves dealing with God. This matter is so important that one's treatment of the fatherless is an indication of the purity of his religion (James 1:27).

Applying the heart and ears (verse 12). This verse expresses a common theme throughout the Book of Proverbs: applying the heart to instruction and the ears to words of knowledge. (See Proverbs 2:2; 5:1; 22:17.) The heart refers to the soulish part of a person: the mind, will, and emotions. The word *instruction* suggests a systematic ordering of principles, putting individual bits of knowledge together in a complete and orderly fashion. The phrase "words of knowledge" suggests individual words, perhaps even from various individuals or sources. The wise of heart will take these words and relate them one to another, comparing, weighing, and finally formulating a sound philosophy.

The relationship between discipline and salvation (verses 13-14). No one will ever be saved simply by discipline. Salvation is by grace through faith, not by human works (Ephesians 2:8-9). But a child who receives proper discipline will tend to become disenchanted with foolishness and will develop a greater interest in what is right and wise. The ultimate wise choice, of course, is to surrender completely to God. Therefore, the Book of Proverbs repeatedly stresses the importance of proper discipline. (See Proverbs 13:24; 22:15.)

Parents do not do their children a favor by withholding instruction. If they use the rod of correction properly, it will not do physical harm, but it will do a great deal of spiritual good.

Proverbs clearly does not approve of child abuse, for verse 13 declares, "If thou beatest him with the rod, he shall not die." The "rod" was reedlike, and to "beat" here means to strike or punish. Any attempt at discipline that results in physical harm is wrong. No Christian parent will want to bring physical, emotional, or mental harm to his child. But at the same time, he will not hesitate to use physical discipline properly in order to help his child learn to have self-control and to make wise choices. For an excellent book on discipline, see Bruce Ray, *Withhold Not Correction* (Phillipsburg, N.J.: Presbyterian and Reformed Publishing House, 1978).

The thing that most pleases a father (verses 15-16). The greatest desire a wise father has is for his son to be wise. Nothing makes a good father happier than to hear his son speak the truth. (See Proverbs 15:20; 23:24-25; III John 4.)

The antidote for envy (verse 17). Wise people will never admire or envy sinners. Such an attitude is a snare (Psalm

73). Envy causes someone to focus on the object of his envy. This focus in turn causes him to become like those he envies. Rather than focusing on sinners, we should fear God every moment of the day. There is not an hour, a minute, or a second when we should not fear God; it is a full-time occupation.

The reward of fearing God (verse 18). Life is not just a meaningless jumble of events. Things in life have a beginning, development, and end. Those who fear God and thus do right will have a certain reward in the end. Their expectation will not be destroyed. They will receive what they believe for (Hebrews 11:6).

Self-control (verse 19). Wisdom comes from hearing the right teaching. Faith also comes by hearing the Word of God (Romans 10:17). It is critically important to discipline oneself to hear what is right. Those who are wise will "guide" their hearts in the right way. They will not follow the natural, sinful inclinations of the heart (the mind, will, and emotions), but they will follow the leading of God's Word and God's Spirit.

The danger of gluttony and drunkenness (verses 20-21). Since we tend to become like those with whom we associate, it is important to associate with those who exemplify the highest character qualities. It is a mistake to associate with the self-indulgent. Self-indulgence often manifests itself in drinking alcoholic beverages and an unhealthy fascination with food. But both drunkenness and gluttony will lead to poverty. They produce drowsiness, and drowsiness is one of the chief traits contributing to poverty. Conversely, one of the most important steps toward prosperity is alertness.

Honoring one's parents (verse 22). The first of the Ten

Commandments with a promise is the fifth: "Honour thy father and thy mother: that thy days may be long upon the land which the LORD thy God giveth thee" (Exodus 20:12). (See also Ephesians 6:2-3.) We should note that the command is to "honor" one's parents, not to obey. Children who are still at home under the authority of their parents definitely should obey them (Ephesians 6:1; Colossians 3:20), but when they become adults and leave home they enter a new phase of the relationship. Even then, they should honor their parents as their immediate source of life. An appreciation for life will include an appreciation for the source of life.

A wise son will seek the counsel of his father regardless of his age and marital status. He will find most frequently that his father's counsel will be right, and he will act on it. In the rare case where his father gives unwise counsel and he cannot act upon it, a wise son will continue to honor his father.

Honor is a matter of attitude. Even if someone's father is ungodly, he can still honor him for his position, though he cannot endorse his lifestyle. In short, children should never ridicule their parents or hold them in disdain. The last phrase shows that this proverb deals particularly with the proper attitude toward parents in their later years: "Despise not thy mother when she is old." A disregard for parents is actually a disregard for life itself, for parents are the immediate source of life.

Four priceless things (verse 23). There are four things we should obtain and never release, regardless of the perceived benefit of letting them go: (1) truth, (2) wisdom, (3) instruction, and (4) understanding. All four of them come from a diligent study of the Word of God. There is no shortcut, no easy route, to obtaining any of them. (See comments on Proverbs 1:2-5.)

The influence of a child upon his parents (verses 24-25). The Book of Proverbs repeatedly enunciates this principle (Proverbs 15:20; 23:15). To a large degree, a child determines his parents' joy or sorrow. One way to discern whether someone is wise is to observe the attitude of his parents. He may deceive others by a few well-chosen words or the appearance of a few wise deeds, but parents respond to a lifetime of behavior that they have observed in detail.

The danger of moral impurity (verses 26-28). Verse 26 appeals to the reader to give special attention to the forthcoming warning. Verse 27 compares involvement with an immoral woman to falling into a deep ditch or a narrow pit; there is little hope of rescue.

The immoral woman does not wait passively for her prey to come to her; she "lieth in wait." That is, she actively plans the seduction of men. While many men would fall into moral impurity anyway, she "increaseth the transgressors among men." In other words, there are some who would never have fallen had it not been for her active pursuit of them. (See comments on Proverbs 6:24-35; 7:6-27; 9:13-18.)

The momentary pleasure that someone may experience by adultery or fornication is not worth a lifetime of sorrow, pain, and conflict, much less the judgment. In the life of Solomon himself, involvement with ungodly women had disastrous results (I Kings 11:1-14, 23, 26, 40). He declared by his own observation that the consequence of being seduced by an immoral woman was more bitter than death (Ecclesiastes 7:26).

The dangers of intoxicating beverages (verses 29-35). Drinking intoxicating beverages produces woe, sorrow, contentions, senseless babbling, needless wounds, and redness of eyes. The word *wine* in the Scriptures is a generic word that can refer either to fermented or unfermented beverages. (See comments on Proverbs 20:1.) The Hebrew word for wine here, *yayin,* refers most literally to what is pressed out: the juice of grapes. Proverbs 23:31-35 show that "wine" in scriptural terminology is not always fermented, but when it is, it should not be used. It is forbidden when it turns red and sparkles or bubbles (fermentation) and when it goes down smoothly (intoxication).

The wisest thing to do is not to look at fermented wine, for its appearance is deceptive and alluring. Someone who looks at it has taken the first step toward drinking. Though it may be alluring, the result of drinking is similar to that of being bitten by a poisonous snake: it is deadly. While death itself may not come initially, the immediate results of drinking include the following: (1) moral impurity ("thine eyes shall behold strange women"); (2) loss of inhibitions ("thine heart shall utter perverse things"); (3) loss of physical control, leading to increased danger ("thou shalt be as he that lieth down in the midst of the sea, or as he that lieth upon the top of a mast"); (4) being victimized by violence ("they have stricken me . . . they have beaten me"); (5) loss of awareness ("and I was not sick . . . and I felt it not"); and (6) addiction ("I will seek it yet again"). The wise person will abstain totally from intoxicating beverages.

Chapter Twenty-Four

The danger of envy and wrong company (verse 1). Envying evil people shows wrong values and a wrong focus. (See Psalm 73.) In general, we are to avoid all envy (Romans 13:13). It is especially dangerous to envy those who are evil, for there will then be a strong temptation to mimic their ways to accomplish similar achievements. Since we tend to become like those with whom we associate, it is not good to entertain any desire to have close fellowship with evil people (I Corinthians 15:33).

Two signs of evil people (verse 2). This verse continues the theme of verse 1. The primary reasons we should not envy evil people or associate with them are that their hearts and lips are constantly centered on evil things. They contemplate ways and means of destroying others; they discuss plans for making trouble. While it is obviously impossible to sever all exposure to those who are evil, the Bible warns against close fellowship, or intimate communion, with such individuals (I Corinthians 5:9-11).

How a house is built, established, and furnished (verses 3-4). While evil people focus on destruction, wise people focus on building. Wisdom builds a house, understanding establishes it, and knowledge furnishes it with rare and beautiful treasures. Psalm 127:1 says, "Except the LORD build the house, they labour in vain that build it: except the LORD keep the city, the watchman waketh but in vain." While a literal house may be in view in Proverbs 24:3-4, clearly the truth declared here applies to the achievement of any worthwhile goal, particularly spiritual life. Purposes are built by wisdom, established by understanding, and supplied with knowledge. Strong lives are developed in the same way.

Knowledge is power (verse 5). True strength is in wisdom and knowledge. "The people that do know their God shall be strong, and do exploits" (Daniel 11:32). While physical strength wanes with the passing of years, the strength gained from knowledge should increase as long as one lives.

The secret of success in battle (verse 6). In teaching his son what he would need to know to rule wisely, Solomon told him that success in war comes not so much by superior weaponry as by superiority in wisdom. (See Proverbs 20:18.) Therefore Solomon instructed his son to seek counsel from many wise people prior to engaging in military conflict.

David, the king prior to Solomon, had said, "Blessed be the LORD my strength, which teacheth my hands to war, and my fingers to fight" (Psalm 144:1). These kings recognized their divine mandate to reign as the representatives of Jehovah over the Promised Land and to rid it of all evil influence. Since they had this divine mandate (Joshua 3:10), these kings recognized they must do it God's way. For an illustration of God's way of giving His people the victory, see II Chronicles 20:17-26.

The fool's inability to make right judgments (verse 7). A person who has no interest in wisdom demonstrates the characteristics of a fool. Wisdom is out of his reach. He may be able to speak on many subjects, but when it comes to situations that require wisdom, he is speechless. The gate was where the city rulers sat in judgment in ancient Israel. (See Proverbs 31:23.)

The person who plots evil (verse 8). Someone who plots evil is known as a mischief-maker or schemer. This verse is not speaking of a "mischievous person" in the modern sense of a child with natural curiosity who likes innocent pranks, but of someone who actually does evil.

Wrong thoughts and attitudes (verse 9). The word translated "thought" suggests the devising of evil, connecting this proverb with verse 8 and indicating that even the mental process leading to evil is itself sinful. "Foolishness" here does not refer to simple good humor or laughter; this proverb does not mandate a dour expression as essential to godliness. Rather, we must understand this word in the light of everything the Book of Proverbs declares to be spiritually foolish.

No one can prevent a fleeting thought from entering his mind. A thought can be a temptation, but temptation itself is not a sin. Even Jesus was tempted but did not sin (Hebrews 4:15). It is possible to prevent such a thought from becoming a welcome friend, however (II Corinthians 10:4-5). When someone meditates upon, fantasizes about, and ponders a wrong thought, it becomes sinful, and he must repent and forsake it.

People detest a scorner (scoffer, mocker). *Webster's Dictionary* originally defined a scorner as "one who scoffs at religion, its ordinances and teachers, and who makes a mock of sin and the judgments and threatenings of God against sinners." The Book of Proverbs offers at least ten facts about scorners: (1) A scorner delights in scorning, that is, one of his chief pleasures in life is to belittle God—to scoff at the teachings of the Bible, those who practice them, and God's warnings against sin (Proverbs 1:22). (2) Scorners will receive the same treatment from God that they give Him (Proverbs 3:34). (3) It is useless to reprove a scorner (Proverbs 9:7). (4) Scorners hate reproof (Proverbs 9:8. (5) A scorner refuses to listen to his father's instructions (Proverbs 13:1). (6) Wisdom eludes the scorner (Proverbs 14:6). (7) A scorner will not ask counsel of those who are wise (Proverbs 15:12). (8) Scorners deserve chastisement (Proverbs 19:29). (9) A scorner's pride provokes him to anger (Proverbs 21:24). (10) A scorner is a source of contention (Proverbs 22:10).

The true test of strength (verse 10). It is easy to appear strong when everything is going well. The true test of spiritual strength, however, is adversity: when things are going badly. If adversity causes someone to faint (give up), he had little strength to begin with. Repeatedly, the Scripture encourages believers not to faint, but to persevere in faith until the reward comes (II Corinthians 4:1, 16; Galatians 6:9; Ephesians 3:13; Hebrews 12:5; Revelation 2:3). When someone is doing what is right, it is always too soon to quit.

The danger of uninvolvement (verses 11-12). People who refuse to assist those in danger will answer to God for their refusal to become involved. The tendency of the sinful nature is not to get involved in personally helping those in need. But Christians must demonstrate their faith by their works and aid those who are in danger or need (Luke 10:25-37; James 2:13-26).

While humans hear spoken excuses, God examines thoughts and motives. The human mind is extremely creative when it comes to self-justification, but God cuts through all of that and goes directly to the real issue.

Christians should consider the significance of these proverbs in view of widespread abortion. By means of abortion innocent children are "drawn unto death" and "slain." Christians who refuse to make any effort to save these lives will answer to God for their apathy. For example, Christians should pray for decision makers, counsel mothers not to abort, speak against abortion, and support others who oppose abortion.

The comparison of honey to wisdom and knowledge (verses 13-14). Just as honey is both nutritious and delicious, so are knowledge and wisdom good for the inner person and pleasant to the inner person. A soul without knowledge is malnourished (Proverbs 19:2). When someone feeds his soul the true knowledge and wisdom of God's Word, there will be a positive result just as there is a positive result of eating nutritious food. His future hope or reward is certain.

The danger of attacking a righteous person (verses 15-16). Vengeance belongs to God; He never forgets to vindicate His name and His people (Romans 12:19). Those who mistreat God's people incur His wrath, which may be delayed but which is absolutely certain (Ecclesiastes 8:11-13).

Putting down a righteous person is not a simple matter; he keeps rising again. The wicked person who attacks another wicked person and observes his enemy's total destruction may think he can as easily destroy the righteous. But this is not so, for the Lord will defend and rescue His people.

The danger of rejoicing over the fall of an enemy (verses 17-18). When a righteous person has been abused and the judgment of God falls upon the abuser, the righteous person must be careful not to rejoice in his enemy's dilemma. This action displeases God. The most important goal God has in the life of His children is to conform them to the image (character) of Jesus (Romans 8:29). If the chastening of an enemy, though justly deserved, reveals a character flaw in His child, God will bring the chastening to a halt in order to deal with the weakness in His child.

The uselessness of worry about evil people (verses 19-20). Not only are we not to envy the wicked, we are not to worry about them. God is aware of their rebellion, and He will certainly halt their evil activity at the right time. Their purposes shall not be accomplished: "there shall be no reward to the evil man." These proverbs parallel Psalm 37, which gives a more extended discussion of the certain destruction of the evil and the alternative to worry, which is trust in the Lord.

Fearing God, respecting authority, and choosing right friends (verses 21-22). We should respectfully fear God, for He is the Supreme Potentate (I Timothy 6:15). We should also fear human rulers, for they receive their authority from God (Romans 13:1). We should avoid association with changeable people, those who easily shift their allegiance and values. (See Ephesians 4:14.) The kind of friends to seek out are those who are solid, the same every time we see them. People who do not respect authority, whether divine or human, and who are given to change will come to ruin; they face judgment from both God and the government.

Chapter Twenty-Four

The wisdom of unbiased judgment (verses 23-26).
Verse 23 introduces further sayings of the wise.

Since God Himself is no respecter of persons (Acts 10:34), His children must also refuse to alter righteous judgment or show partiality because of social status or friendship (James 2:1-9).

Any ruler who excuses the wicked will not long remain in favor with the people. Those in authority who administrate proper punishment to the wicked will be appreciated and blessed. (See Romans 13:3-4; I Peter 2:13-14.)

Nothing is more valuable than a right answer or right judgment. As an example, early in Solomon's career he exhibited astounding wisdom in dealing with two harlots (I Kings 3:16-28).

The value of preparation (verse 27). It is always wise to take time to think, plan, and prepare. It is foolish to rush into a project without first anticipating all the steps necessary for its completion (Luke 14:28-30). For example, before someone builds a house the outside work needs to be prepared, and before someone establishes a home the field (economic base) needs to be prepared.

The error of giving false witness and seeking vengeance (verses 28-29). One of the Ten Commandments is, "Thou shalt not bear false witness against thy neighbour" (Exodus 20:16). The Bible teaches us to love our neighbor (Luke 10:25-37) and warns against devising evil against our neighbor (Proverbs 3:29). Someone who harms his neighbor harms himself.

While someone may legitimately be called upon to witness truthfully against his neighbor, he must never witness "without cause" and he must never witness falsely. Moreover, he must never take advantage of an opportunity to witness against someone in an attempt to get revenge or to repay evil for evil.

The threefold consequence of laziness (verses 30-34). A lack of understanding produces slothfulness, which breeds drowsiness, neglect, and poverty. A lazy man may inherit a prosperous vineyard, but because he does not understand the value of diligence, he will allow it to degenerate gradually until his prosperity has fled and poverty has replaced it. All that is necessary for a house to decay is for the owner to do nothing (Ecclesiastes 10:18).

A diligent person will deal with the thorns and nettles as they appear; a slothful person will put it off until later. A diligent person will repair a breach in the stone wall when it occurs; a slothful person will postpone action. A wise person will receive instruction from the example of the slothful. He will realize that too much sleep and a tendency to procrastinate will produce poverty just as certainly as a quick traveller will overtake a slower one and just as surely as an armed robber will take one's wealth.

Chapter Twenty-Five

Proverbs of Solomon that Hezekiah's scribes copied (verse 1). This verse begins a special subsection within the book. Scholars debate the meaning of the phrase "which the men of Hezekiah king of Judah copied out." Some suggest that Solomon did not write these proverbs as he did the others (see Proverbs 22:20) but that they were spoken by him, transmitted by oral tradition, and finally recorded in writing by scribes under King Hezekiah.

But the verse does not demand this explanation. The verb "copied out" indicates that these proverbs were already in writing and were simply copied by Hezekiah's scribes. Apparently they simply copied these specific proverbs for Hezekiah's personal study.

The increased emphasis on royal authority and behavior in the remaining chapters of the book support this understanding. In the first twenty-four chapters of Proverbs, some form of the word *king* appears eighteen times. In the last seven chapters, some form of the word appears fourteen times. Apparently then, these proverbs were viewed as offering important advice to kings. Indeed, the first six verses of this chapter make use of some form of the word *king* five times, and the seventh verse uses *prince*.

A royal trait (verse 2). God's glory is evident by the transcendent, infinite mysteries that belong to Him. A king's glory is evident by what he learns and uncovers, for a king needs to know what is going on in his kingdom. Applying this principle spiritually, God displays His glory by concealing truth from skeptics and rebels, but a human receives honor by diligently searching out truth.

God has chosen to conceal many truths from humanity (Deuteronomy 29:29). He has also chosen to reveal many things, but even so they require searching out. The words of God are precious pearls, and He does not cast His pearls before arrogant unbelievers (Matthew 7:6).

Faith and spiritual desire are prerequisites to understanding the things of God. (See Hebrews 11:6; I Corinthians 2:14; Acts 28:25-28; Matthew 13:10-17.) Someone who approaches the study of Scripture in faith, desiring to understand, reveals a characteristic of royalty. In a New Testament sense, believers are kings and priests (I Peter 2:9; Revelation 1:6). The Berean Jews were more noble than those of Thessalonica, because they "received the word with all readiness of mind, and searched the scriptures daily, whether those things were so" (Acts 17:11). Paul admonished in II Timothy 2:15: "Study to shew thyself approved unto God, a workman that needeth not to be ashamed, rightly dividing the word of truth."

The unsearchable heart of a king (verse 3). No human being can read the thoughts or predict the actions of a ruler. Moreover, the Old Testament presents the king as the representative of God. If a king reigned in the tradition of David, as a man after God's own heart (I Samuel 13:14), then it was particularly appropriate to say he had an "unsearchable" heart. That is, if his heart was after

God, it was just as unmeasurable as the height of the heavens or the depth of the earth.

How a king's throne is established (verses 4-5). These verses compare the cleansing of impurities from silver, which results in a superior vessel, to the removal of ungodly counsellors from before the king. One of the most important factors in the success of someone in authority is having the right advisors. Unwise counsellors can very well result in the fall of a leader.

It has been said that those who are in positions of influence have more impact on a society than those who are in positions of power. Since those who are in authority cannot have personal knowledge of all things under their jurisdiction, they must rely on their advisors. If they receive wrong counsel and information, they will tend to make wrong decisions. Thus, Christians should pray not only for rulers but also for their advisors.

The principle taught here is that, throughout all of society, people in positions of influence have significant ability to change the opinions of those in authority. This principle holds true even in the home, where the wife has potentially life-changing influence with her husband (I Peter 3:1).

The danger of promoting self (verse 6-7). A person should not exalt himself but let others honor and promote him. Throughout Scripture, the danger of pride and self-exaltation is evident. The Book of Proverbs warns against this attitude and so does the New Testament (Proverbs 16:18; James 4:6). Jesus Himself taught the desirability of choosing the path of humility in words similar to verse 7 (Luke 14:7-11). Pride caused Lucifer's downfall (Ezekiel 28:17), and it is one of the three root sins (I John 2:16).

Haste brings shame (verse 8). There are occasions when someone should legitimately confront another person about a problem. But a person should never enter into confrontation hastily. Before he ever gets involved, he should think through all the implications and possible outcomes. He should prepare for any eventuality. Without this kind of forethought, people act foolishly, are put to shame, and then are at a loss to know what to do. Often the only action that comes readily to mind is violence.

Keeping secrets (verses 9-10). When someone has a legitimate complaint against another, he should deal with that person privately. (See Matthew 18:15-17.) Telling it to others without making an attempt to be reconciled to the offender will lead to shame and an evil reputation as a gossip. Once someone gains a reputation like this, it is extremely difficult for him to lose it.

The right word at the right time (verse 11). Nothing is more beautiful than speaking the right word at the right moment. Skill in the use of words is as valuable as artistic skill. It has been said, "A picture is worth a thousand words," and no doubt this is often true. But words can often communicate what nothing else can. For example, how could a picture ever fully express the Gettysburg Address or other great pieces of literature?

An ornament of genuine worth (verse 12). While many people are concerned with external ornamentation, an obedient person sees the value of wise reproof. He treasures it as others treasure jewelry of gold. The truly valuable ornaments are qualities of character (I Peter 3:4).

The value of a responsible employee (verse 13). In the heat of harvest season, the prospect of a cool drink is refreshing, and in ancient times snow was sometimes used to cool beverages. In the same way, a dependable, faithful messenger is refreshing to his master. One of the greatest needs in business is for responsible people, people who are willing to accept responsibility without passing the buck.

False promises (verse 14). It is useless to boast of a gift one does not have. If a person does not fulfill his promises or claims, his boasting is as empty as clouds and wind without rain.

Soft persuasion (verse 15). People are not persuaded by harsh, irritating insistence but by soft words over an extended period of time. Persistence and kindness are two of the most valuable traits that someone who wants to persuade others could have.

The value of temperance (verse 16). Honey is a nutritious food (Proverbs 24:13). But when eaten in excess, it is unhealthy. In life there are many things that, when done in moderation, are good and acceptable but when taken to extremes become dangerous and undesireable. Temperance, or self-control, is part of the fruit of the Spirit (Galatians 5:23). Of course, we must abstain totally from sin, but even in things that are acceptable, permissible, and good, we must be temperate. We must have balance.

A sure way to lose friends (verse 17). It is important to practice temperance even in fellowship with friends. It has been said, "Familiarity breeds contempt." Wise people will recognize the sanctity of their friends' homes. They will not visit too frequently, will behave wisely when visiting, and will not stay too long. They will be sensitive to unspoken signals that indicate the time for the visit is up. As a general rule, someone should not drop by to visit unexpectedly, no matter how close a friend he may feel he is. And it is better to leave while one is still welcome than to overstay one's welcome.

Sometimes a man is insensitive to his wife's need for privacy and planning, and he will unwisely invite guests without consulting with her. A man must guard his home not only with respect to what and who comes in but also in relation to the time the family has for private fellowship. Thus it is not rude if after a few moments he tells uninvited and unexpected guests, "I'm sorry, but we'll have to get together at another time." It is also wise for a man to make appointments with his wife or children. Even if these appointments are to take place at home, he can truthfully tell anyone who would intrude on this time, "I'm sorry, but I have an appointment at that time." The man who takes no positive steps in this direction often finds himself spending little or no time with his wife and children, which is one of the most regretted mistakes in marriages and families.

The danger of a false witness (verse 18). It is very destructive to testify falsely against others. For this reason, every person should carefully examine all he says about others. Before he repeats anything, he should subject it to the eightfold test of Philippians 4:8.

The disappointment of misplaced confidence (verse 19). It is a painful disappointment for someone to discover that he has placed confidence in an untrustworthy person, especially when the situation is serious. It is wise to test a person's faithfulness before trouble comes. Faithfulness is demonstrated in small, seemingly insignificant things (Matthew 25:23; Luke 16:10).

The value of empathy (verse 20). As far as possible,

we should identify with others in their sorrow and joy (Romans 12:15). When a person is suffering and is emotionally troubled, lighthearted banter merely brings more pain. It is, in other words, worse than doing nothing.

How to demonstrate love for enemies (verses 21-22). We should give food, water, and coals of fire to an enemy in need. Jesus taught in the Sermon on the Mount that we should love our enemies (Matthew 5:44), and Paul quoted this proverb in Romans 12:20. Heaping coals of fire on an enemy's head does not refer to a revengeful act but a helpful one, for the inspired explanation speaks of overcoming evil with good (Romans 12:21).

How to deal with a backbiter (verse 23). Backbiting is wrong (Psalm 15:3; Romans 1:30; II Corinthians 12:20). Thus it is also wrong to listen to backbiting. Backbiting means speaking maliciously about a person who is absent, or slandering him, and such actions cause anger.

The countenance speaks with eloquence. The backbiter can tell whether or not someone wants to hear his slanderous words.

What makes a happy home (verse 24). (See also Proverbs 21:9, 19.) It is not the size of the house ("a wide house") that causes happiness, but the attitudes exhibited within the home. The phrase "a wide house" seems to speak of the home of the wealthy. Financial prosperity does not guarantee contentment. If it did, the lady of the house would not be a brawling, or contentious, woman.

The value of good news (verse 25). (See also Proverbs 15:30.) One of the eight requirements for right thinking is that the thought must be "of good report" (Philippians 4:8). "Good news from a far country" is refreshing. By contrast, modern news media seems to focus on "bad news from far countries."

When a righteous person should refuse to bow (verse 26). Righteous people who falter, yield, or compromise values before the wicked are like polluted water. Although righteous people are to submit to authority, they are not to submit to anything that would cause them to sin against God. (See Daniel 3:16-18; 6:10; Acts 5:29.) Righteous people should always do right, regardless of what the ungodly governments say, and they should never submit to unrighteous demands out of fear. (See Hebrews 13:6.)

The danger of self-promotion (verse 27). (See also Proverbs 25:6-7; 27:2.) This verse expresses a common theme in Proverbs. Just as eating too much honey is detrimental, so it is detrimental for people to seek their own glory. When someone's "glory" is of his own making, it is not really glory, and it will quickly tarnish.

A person without self-control (verse 28). In the ancient Middle East, a community with no walls was not considered a city. The walls provided the defense against the enemy. Where there were no walls, therefore, there was no real defense; the community was open prey to any passing enemy. Likewise, a person without self-control is open to the attack of the enemy: Satan. If a person cannot control his spirit—if he tends to lose control of his temper, emotions, and actions—then he is a prime target for satanic influence and control.

Chapter Twenty-Six

An unseemly thing (verse 1). Honor is not fitting for a fool. While there are those to whom honor is due (Romans 13:7; I Timothy 5:17), honoring a fool is damaging and discouraging to those who are worthy of honor. A fool will be deceived by the honor given him; he will think he honestly deserves it and will become unbearable in his arrogance. A wise person will accept honor with gratitude, but he will never allow it to inflate his ego. When an honor is given to one who does not deserve it, the honor itself is cheapened.

A curse without a cause (verse 2). A curse pronounced upon someone without cause will have no effect. Like a flitting bird, which seems to fly aimlessly, it will not alight upon its intended victim.

The animalistic behavior of a fool (verse 3). A fool's behavior calls for correction just as much as a stubborn animal. Just as the whip and the bridle are necessary to guide animals, so discipline is necessary for fools, those who violate moral codes, laws, and decent standards of behavior.

How to answer a fool (verses 4-5). These verses show the difficulty of trying to answer a fool—someone who refuses to fear God. They suggest two opposite approaches to dealing with a fool. First, a person should answer a fool according to wisdom, to mark a clear line of separation between wisdom and folly. He should not merely argue with the fool on the basis of his folly, for arguing from the standpoint of folly brings the wise person down to the fool's level. Secondly, he should answer the fool according to his folly to reveal how inconsistent and foolish his reasoning is.

In the realm of apologetics, we must base all reasoning upon the fear of the Lord. There is no neutral ground upon which folly and wisdom meet. Neither logic, human reasoning, nor the human senses provide neutral bases for the believer and unbeliever. So the believer first answers the fool from the standpoint of his trust in God, showing clearly the difference between the two. Secondly, he answers him from the standpoint of human reasoning to show the emptiness of the circular reasoning of humanism.

The folly of placing confidence in unfaithful people (verse 6). While a faithful messenger refreshes his master, an unfaithful, foolish messenger brings disaster to his master. Some misguided people think that giving responsibility to a fool will increase his trustworthiness, but not so. When responsibility is given to a faithful person, it will increase his faithfulness. But when given to a fool, confidence is misplaced. Before someone entrusts a person with major responsibilities, he should prove him faithful in small things.

The fool's inability to teach (verses 7, 9). A parable is a means of teaching widely used in Scripture. The word *parable* suggests the placing of one thing alongside another for purposes of comparison. A fool's attempt to teach by means of parables is simply awkward; it can even be painful.

The danger of honoring a fool (verse 8). The first proverb in this chapter declares honor to be inappropriate to a fool. It is more than just inappropriate we now discover: it is dangerous. Like someone who binds a stone in a sling, a person who honors a fool sets in motion a chain of events that may very well result in damage. This truth is especially evident in a society that honors and glorifies immoral, unstable, ungodly people simply because they have the ability to run quickly, tackle effectively, sing beautifully, or act convincingly. A society reveals much about itself by the nature of its heroes.

God's involvement in rewarding fools and sinners (verse 10). It is not just that fools and sinners do senseless things that result in injury to themselves or others, even though this is often the case. But God Himself takes note of their disregard of and rebellion against Him, and He rewards them appropriately.

When a fool behaves like a dog (verse 11). What more repulsive picture could there be of a fool's behavior? Like a dog that turns and eats its own vomit, so a fool turns and engages again in foolishness. This startling picture is the subject of Peter's description of backsliders in II Peter 2:20-22. In the eyes of a wise person, folly is not in the least attractive. It is as reprehensible as the vomit of a dog.

The person who is more hopeless than a fool (verse 12). Someone who thinks he is wise separate and apart from God ("in his own conceit") has less hope of recovery than a fool. A fool may at least recognize that he is unwise, and this recognition is the first step toward wisdom. But someone who thinks he is wise has no reason to seek true wisdom. One of those who thinks he is wise is the sluggard (verse 16).

The creativity of the slothful (verse 13). (See also Proverbs 22:13.) The slothful person looks for excuses not to venture forth and perform his duties. His problem is definitely not a lack of imagination! If he gave as much effort to productivity as he does to avoiding work, he would accomplish great things.

Aimless activity (verse 14). Like a door going back and forth on its hinges without ever really going anywhere, so the sluggard turns back and forth on his bed. He may show great signs of activity, but he accomplishes nothing. He may always be "busy," but he completes no projects. One possible sign of slothfulness is turning over to go back to sleep after awaking from a reasonable period of sleep.

Another sign of slothfulness (verse 15). (See also Proverbs 19:24.) It grieves the slothful person to take personal responsibility for his survival. He would prefer to be fed by someone else. The hiding of his hand may suggest selfishness and self-centeredness. Rather than reaching out to others, he reaches inward to himself. A practical example is someone who thinks others owe him a living, that others should take responsibility for his survival.

The sluggard's assessment of his own wisdom (verse 16). (See also verse 12.) The sluggard cannot see his own folly. Nothing can convince him of his error. He thinks he is wiser than seven men who can answer sensibly.

The danger of being a busybody (verse 17). We have an obligation to come to the rescue and defense of innocent people who are in danger or need (Proverbs 24:11-12). But only a fool will become involved in argu-

270

ments that have nothing to do with him. To do so is as dangerous as grabbing a dog by its ears; the dog is certain to snap and bite. For example, peace officers testify that the most dangerous call they make is a call to a domestic quarrel. The most frequent development is that the husband and wife both unite and turn on the policeman as an unwanted intruder. Sinful human nature yearns to meddle in the affairs of others, but Scripture opposes this practice (II Thessalonians 3:11; I Timothy 5:13; I Peter 4:15).

The danger of deceiving a neighbor (verses 18-19). Neighbors should love one another, support one another, and protect one another. This practice makes for a secure and peaceful world. Someone who violates this principle and thinks he is profiting by it fails to recognize that he will hurt himself. Someone who deceives his neighbor and tries to excuse it as a joke is like a madman who plays with fire and deadly weapons. He will cause harm to himself and others. He plants seeds that will bear a bitter fruit.

The cause of strife (verse 20). Wherever strife is, one may be sure that a talebearer is at the root of it. Just as there can be no fire without wood, there can be no strife without a talebearer. People kindle and fan strife by rumors, sly suggestions, innuendoes, and outright falsehoods. When a family, organization, company, or church experiences unusual levels of strife, it is wise to search out the talebearers who are feeding the flames.

The kind of person who kindles strife (verse 21). Someone who keeps the flame of strife burning brightly is contentious. Contention is a direct result of pride (Proverbs 13:10), and it keeps strife burning. A godly person is a peacemaker (Matthew 5:9); a person who sows strife is ungodly, regardless of any sanctimonious piety.

The impact of slander (verse 22). Words have tremendous power. They can wound or heal. They can encourage or discourage. A talebearer's words have a way of penetrating to the inward parts, negatively affecting the soul.

Deceiving appearances (verse 23). An evil person may disguise his wicked intentions and purposes under a facade of apparent fervor or concern for righteousness. But this fake surface is like dross, the impurity in silver (Proverbs 25:4). Beneath it, he is as worthless as a potsherd, a broken and rejected piece of pottery of no value. A wise person will look beyond external appearances and examine the fruit of someone's life (Matthew 7:15-20).

The dishonesty of hatred (verses 24-25). Someone who hates another may cover his hatred with deceitful words (dissimulation), hiding his hatred within him. His words may seem good and positive, but he is not to be believed. In his heart there is the ultimate in abominations. A wise person will be able to look beyond mere words to discern the spirit of another. Those who are simple may be unable to do so, and they will be deceived (Romans 16:18; I John 4:1-4).

The ultimate revelation of the hypocrite (verse 26). The person described in the previous two verses will not long be able to hide his hatred. Hatred is so corrosive and so poisonous that it will eventually be exposed publicly.

The Golden Rule in reverse (verse 27). The person who plans danger and harm for another actually sets in motion a chain of events that will result in his own destruction. The drama of Mordecai and Haman in the Book of

Esther illustrates this truth perfectly. Jesus said, "All they that take the sword shall perish with the sword" (Matthew 26:52). Instead, a wise person will do unto others as he would have them do unto him (Matthew 7:12).

The alliance between lying and flattery (verse 28). The reason a person will lie against someone is hatred. Though he covers his hatred with deceit and fair words (verses 24-25), his purpose is to destroy. A flattering mouth is often the sign of hatred too; it is a false and insincere effort which, if believed, will bring ruin to its object.

Chapter Twenty-Seven

The future is unknown (verse 1). God has reserved the knowledge of the future to Himself. Human efforts to foretell the future are occultic in nature and are to be avoided. Isaiah 47:12-14 describes the folly of these attempts to look into the future.

James 4:13-16 likewise warns against presuming upon the future. There is no biblical condemnation against planning ahead; the warning is against forgetting God in one's plans. We should make all plans contingent upon God's will. Jesus taught that we should live in "day-tight compartments," refusing to borrow trouble from the future (Matthew 6:34).

The best advertisement (verse 2). Here is another warning against self-promotion, a warning found frequently in the Book of Proverbs. Someone should never praise himself; self-praise is unseemly and proud. If there is to be any honor, it should come from another.

Even in the modern age of technology and multi-million-dollar advertising budgets, companies have discovered that the most effective advertisement is still word of mouth. They attempt to use the strength of this method by hiring well-known people to endorse products in the media. But there is still no promotion as effective as satisfied users who recommend a product to friends. This principle holds true even in the advertisement of churches. A fulfilled member is the best advertisement.

This proverb does not suggest that people are to belittle and criticize themselves. Few things are more distracting than those who constantly point out their own faults in a misguided attempt to practice humility.

The heaviness of a fool's wrath (verse 3). When a fool does not get his own way, his anger is a source of great pressure to those who allow themselves to come under it. News media tend to encourage this foolish wrath by publicizing the actions and demands of fools, as in the case of terrorists who kidnap innocent people or hijack airplanes. Such crimes would greatly diminish if there were no media coverage, for the purpose of the crime would be lost.

Envy is more dangerous than wrath and anger (verse 4). Envy is a powerful, destructive force for at least two reasons. First, it often masquerades as a virtue. For example, in communism envy promotes theft as a means of redistributing wealth and reducing everyone to the same level. Second, envy is dangerous because, unlike simple covetousness which merely desires what another has, envy wishes to destroy what another has. For example, envy may prompt an evil person to pour acid in the face of a beautiful woman or handsome man, and envy may cause a person to set fire to someone's home or business.

The worthlessness of unexpressed love (verse 5). Secret love is of no value at all. Love not demonstrated is worthless. (See John 3:16.) There is more value in being rebuked (reproved) openly than loved secretly.

Faithful wounds; deceitful kisses (verse 6). A true

friend is one who loves enough to confront, when necessary. Genuine friendship is not proven by lack of disagreement. When a genuine friend must reprove another, he will do it with the right motive and attitude, with the purpose of bringing his friend to the correct position. An enemy may deceive the unwary by his kisses, but he can deceive only those who think such a display of affection is necessarily a sign of love. For example, a person who plans to seduce a member of the opposite sex will carry out his plan by obvious displays of affection, but really he is his victim's enemy. In short, wounds of reproof from a true friend are better than deceitful displays of affection from an enemy.

The power of hunger (verse 7). Someone without appetite will be repelled by the idea of food, regardless of how tasty it is. But someone who is hungry craves nourishment, regardless of the taste of the food.

Applying this principle spiritually, someone who lacks spiritual hunger will not be interested in spiritual things. But those who hunger and thirst after righteousness will gladly partake of any spiritual food available (Matthew 5:6). Some who have no spiritual hunger disdain sermons unless they are delivered in perfect homiletical fashion, with sparkling rhetorical speech skills. These people become critical of preaching; few sermons meet their unqualified approval. Those who are spiritually hungry, on the other hand, are thankful for any crumb of spiritual food.

A person out of place (verse 8). Just as a bird has a nest perfectly suited for it, so everyone has a place where he fits in life. He has certain responsibilities and roles based primarily on his abilities and interests. Spiritually, everyone has a specific place in the body of Christ (I Corinthians 12:14-31).

The pleasant fragrance of encouragement (verse 9). Pleasant fragrances have a positive influence on the emotions. The sense of smell is one of the five God-given senses that is a gateway to the soul. Similarly, the encouragement and sincere counsel of a friend is sweet to the soul.

The value of friends (verse 10). Friendship should be reciprocated. There is more to genuine friendship than enjoying common interests; genuine friendship stands in adversity. A person should not forsake a friend in a time of trouble. Neither should he forsake his father's friend; that is one way of honoring his father.

The latter part of the proverb reveals that it is possible to have a closer relationship with a friend (neighbor) than with a blood brother. In many cases, a close friend will be more helpful in a time of calamity than a distant brother.

Wise children: the best defense (verse 11). A common theme in Proverbs is the influence of children upon their parents' joy. Wise children make glad parents. (See also Proverbs 23:24-25; 29:3.) When someone reproaches a father, questioning his wisdom or holding him in contempt, his best defense is his wise children. If he has been able to rear children to walk in wisdom, then he is a success.

The value of foresight (verse 12). Someone who is prudent will be able to see the consequences of actions; he understands the law of cause and effect. This proverb does not suggest that some people have the ability to foretell the future mystically. Indeed, the first proverb in this chapter denies that suggestion. But wise people can see trends developing. They learn from history. They identify principles that when violated result in certain consequences. These people will take the steps necessary to avoid the coming disaster.

The simple person thinks life is a series of unrelated events. He sees no plan, no purpose. To him, everything happens by chance. He takes no precautions; he thinks trouble will always visit someone else, and therefore he suffers the penalty of ignorance. His most common question when unpleasant events occur is, "Why me?"

The danger of being a surety (verse 13). (See also Proverbs 20:16, which says the same thing.) A repeated theme in Proverbs is the danger of being a surety for someone. In particular, someone who puts up security for a stranger is a bad risk, especially if he does so for an immoral woman. He is engaging in a dangerous practice.

The importance of consideration (verse 14). It is certainly a good thing to bless one's friend. But there is a right time as well as a right word (Proverbs 25:11). A word should be spoken "fitly," that is, at the right time, at the right place, with the right attitude, and for the right motive. Someone who rises early in the morning and loudly blesses his friend will be resented even though his words are good. In short, it is important to consider the feelings and desires of others.

A steady drip and a contentious woman (verse 15). Several proverbs discuss the unpleasant experience of living with a loud, brawling woman (Proverbs 21:9, 19; 25:24). A contentious woman is proud and unsatisfied. She complains and argues. A man can put up with such contention for a while, in the same way that he can tolerate a drip temporarily. But eventually the constant nagging frustrates and irritates him. Many women, not realizing this truth, have destroyed their homes by their own actions. (See Proverbs 14:1.)

The impossibility of concealing or restraining a contentious woman (verse 16). It is impossible to contain the wind. It is also impossible, if one has scented ointment on his right hand, to hide the scent from those with whom he comes in contact. (Alternatively, the verse may mean that it is impossible to grasp oil with the hand.) In the same manner, it is impossible for a man to conceal for long a contentious wife or to restrain her contention. If a man has a virtuous wife, he will want everyone to know; she is an honor to him, a testimony to his wisdom and success as a husband. But if she is contentious, he wishes to conceal the truth and restrain her, for she shames him and suggests that he has failed (Proverbs 12:4).

The benefit of friendship (verse 17). In the same way that iron sharpens iron, friends should improve one another. Friendship should be profitable; both should benefit from the relationship. Friendship should elevate character. God often places people together who have strengths that complement each other's weaknesses. This is true also of husbands and wives, who should be the closest of friends.

The right to fruit; the reward of service (verse 18). The farmer who has cared for a fig tree is entitled to eat its fruit (I Corinthians 9:7; II Timothy 2:6). So the person who serves another will eventually be rewarded for that service. (See Proverbs 17:2.) Jesus taught that the servant is the greatest in the church (Matthew 23:11).

True reflections (verse 19). As water reflects an image,

so a person is a reflection of his own heart. Jesus taught that a person's heart determines his true spiritual condition (Matthew 15:10-20).

Unsatisfied eyes (verse 20). This verse compares the eyes to hell and destruction. Of course, the physical eye is not in itself evil. But the eye is a gateway to the soul, and what the eye reveals to the soul often provokes covetousness and envy. In this sense, just as there is always room for one more to be destroyed and cast into hell, so the eyes always have the ability to introduce more covetousness and lust. (See Job 31:1; Matthew 5:29; 6:22-23; II Peter 2:14.)

Many people have deceived themselves into thinking that the acquisition of some material thing will finally satisfy them. But the eyes are never satisfied. A person always tends to want what he sees. This tendency must be controlled. One important step toward control is to stop looking at what should not or cannot be obtained. Many people intend simply to look but finally justify themselves in obtaining what they see and desire.

Purified praise (verse 21). A refining pot is an instrument for purifying silver by separating the dross from the silver. Likewise, the furnace purifies gold. Similarly, people are tested by the praise given to them. When they receive praise, they should not let it alter them but they should refine it down to what they know is true.

No help for the fool (verse 22). The word *bray* means "to pound or bruise." The suggestion here is that even painful adversity will not bring a fool to his senses.

Proper delegation and oversight (verses 23-27). This passage discusses the steps necessary for the king to maintain his wealth in order to support his servants. While

281

the king cannot personally tend to his flocks and herds, and must therefore delegate that responsibility to someone else, he will inspect what he expects. He should diligently keep record of the condition of all that belongs to him. Verse 24 points out that riches and authority must be carefully preserved and guarded, for many people have lost wealth through lack of diligence. Verses 25-27 indicate that the result of diligence will be prosperity.

Chapter Twenty-Eight

Causes of fear and boldness (verse 1). Guilt produces irrational fears. One of the first things a person who is plagued by unreasonable fears should do is to examine himself for unconfessed sins. Righteousness, which is a result of openness and transparency before God, results in fearlessness.

The cause of longevity in leadership (verse 2). Rapid turnover in leadership is often a result of the sinfulness of people. Stable, long-term leadership is a blessing, but frequent coups or revolutions are a result of sin. It has been said that people get the kind of government they deserve. The more disciplined and godly people are, the less oppressive their government will tend to be; the less disciplined and godly they are, the more oppressive their government will tend to be.

The two qualities necessary for a successful leader are understanding and knowledge.

The devastation of oppression (verse 3). Contrary to Marxist theory, the greatest problem socially is not the oppression of the poor by the rich or of one ethnic group by another. The greatest problem in this area is the oppression of those on the same social level. For example, the highest percentage of crimes are performed by people against others of the same ethnic and social background.

Wrong and right values (verse 4). Those who reject the law of God embrace a false system of values. They will praise the wicked and condemn the just (Proverbs 24:24-25). It is possible to tell whether a person abides by the law by observing the object of his admiration. Of whom does he speak favorably? Those who praise the wicked reveal their own lawlessness. On the other hand, those who keep God's law will be found contending with the wicked. One of the signs of obedience to the Word of God is active opposition to wickedness. Those who actively keep God's commandments cannot coexist with wickedness without challenging it.

The source of understanding (verse 5). Evil people have rejected the only true source of judgment: the law of God. Therefore, judgment is beyond them. They cannot grasp it. But one of the rewards of seeking the Lord is that He will give understanding of all things needed.

When the poor is better than the rich (verse 6). The quality of a person has nothing to do with his social status. Character is far more important than wealth.

Wise and foolish sons (verse 7). The source of wisdom is keeping the law (Word) of God. One of the surest steps to destruction is to keep the wrong company. A wise son is a source of joy to his parents (Proverbs 23:24-25). But nothing brings parents greater shame than a foolish son (Proverbs 29:15).

God's ultimate control of economics (verse 8). God ultimately determines who will retain wealth. A person cannot make enough provisions to preserve his wealth that will guarantee it against loss. God can so arrange events that the wealth of a lifetime is lost in a day. God takes note of those who take advantage of others and increase their wealth unjustly. He has ways of removing the wealth thus gained from the hands of its possessor and placing it in the hands of those who will use it justly, especially in helping the poor.

Scripture is not against gain, profit, or interest (Matthew 25:27). But Scripture condemns unjust gain and exorbitant interest.

Abominable prayers (verse 9). For prayer to be meaningful, it must be accompanied by obedience. The person who prays hypocritically with no intention of obeying God's Word has committed an abomination. (See Luke 18:9-14.)

The law of sowing and reaping (verse 10). Some people delight in trying to corrupt the upright. They lay snares, hoping those who follow the Lord will fall into them. But those who do such things will fall into their own traps (Proverbs 26:27). Those who are upright will receive good things from the Lord (Psalm 84:11).

The "self-made" man (verse 11). Some people who are rich have an inflated view of their own wisdom. They think their riches are proof of their brilliance. But this is not necessarily true. There may be many reasons a person has amassed riches that have nothing to do with genuine wisdom. The poor man who has understanding can see past the facade of wisdom to the genuine condition of the rich man's soul.

Results of freedom and oppression (verse 12). Proverbs 29:2 points out that righteous authority produces rejoicing in the people but that wicked authority causes mourning. This proverb seems to be a companion, suggesting

285

that when the righteous triumph there is great jubilation ("glory") and freedom. But when the wicked are in authority, it is often necessary for righteous people to hide (Proverbs 28:28). This truth is evident in many nations that have adopted atheism as official governmental policy.

The barrier to prosperity and the key to mercy (verse 13). It is impossible to hide sins from God. Moreover, the law of sowing and reaping guarantees that sins will produce negative results. The person who attempts to hide his sins, practicing them in secret and refusing to admit his sinfulness to God, will suffer openly. But the person who both confesses and forsakes his sin will receive mercy from the Lord and even from other people. (See I John 1:9.)

Happy fear (verse 14). One of the greatest secrets of victorious living is to walk constantly in the fear of God. The person who hardens his heart against God will suffer the evil consequences of sin (Proverbs 29:1).

Animalistic rulers (verse 15). The lion and bear are symbols of destruction. They strike fear in the hearts of people. This verse uses them as symbols of wicked rulers. If rulers are wise and kind, their people will love them and appreciate them.

Why rulers oppress (verse 16). The reason those in authority oppress the people is that they lack understanding. Understanding reveals that the way to prosperity is freedom, but dictatorial rulers do not understand this. Tyranny may bring some short-term benefits to them, but the long-term result will be detrimental. (See I Kings 12:6-11.) The ruler who rejects tyranny and greed will enjoy a long and successful tenure in office.

The consequence of violence (verse 17). A murderer will

suffer the guilt of a capital crime, from which he will continue to run until he reaches the grave. But fleeing will not subtract from his guilt. No one should seek to spare the guilty from the consequences of his sin. The guilt is designed to motivate the sinner to repent and forsake his sin. Those who attempt to console him or aid him to escape the consequences of his action are frustrating and sabotaging God's divine plan to bring repentance.

The cause of salvation or destruction (verse 18). In the final analysis, the person who does right, that is, who lives by faith in God, will enjoy the consequences: he will be saved. He may suffer temporary trials and difficulties, but he will forget all of that when he receives his ultimate reward. But the person who departs from the right path will ultimately fall. He may appear to stand for a while, but when he falls, it will be at once. All of his apparent success will collapse in a moment of time.

The reward of work and the consequence of laziness (verse 19). As a consequence of Adam's sin, the human race must labor to survive (Genesis 3:19; II Thessalonians 3:10). People who work diligently will have their needs met. But the person who refuses to labor and instead spends his time in vain pursuits will suffer poverty. Knowingly or unknowingly, he is attempting to prove that he can outwit God, and of course, no one can do so.

The reward of faithfulness and the consequence of greed (verse 20). Faithfulness is proven first in small things, and it suggests consistency, dependability, and trustworthiness. The reward for faithfulness is blessing in every area of life. (See Galatians 6:9-10.) Someone who is hasty to be rich will bypass faithfulness; it is too slow for him. He will attempt to get his wealth as quickly as possible, even if this course demands dishonesty, and he will be punished for his greedy and dishonest ways. We should note that one of the three root sins is greed (I John 2:16).

The prejudiced person's price (verse 21). Showing favoritism or partiality is sinful (I Timothy 5:21; James 2:9). Someone who is guilty of this sin is actually looking out only for himself. If it is to his advantage, he will transgress what is right. In other words, his judgment and treatment of others is based on what they can do for him. If they can help him reach his goals, he will befriend them. If not, he has no use for them. He will do wrong merely for a piece of bread.

Greed's evil eye (verse 22). (See Proverbs 28:20.) Again, this chapter assures us that poverty is the sure consequence of greed, of the person who wants a short cut to riches. His real problem is that he has an "evil eye," that is, he is greedy and miserly. (See Proverbs 22:9; 23:6; Matthew 6:19-24.) When the eye is focused on anything other than God, it is evil.

Rebuke is better than flattery (verse 23). A person who, in love, helps someone else to see his mistakes will receive more respect than one who, for the sake of "peace," avoids all conflict by flattery. (See Proverbs 27:5; 29:5.)

The sin of robbing parents (verse 24). It is, of course, a sin to rob from anyone. But children often take parents for granted and think they are justified to mistreat them in ways they would not think of mistreating others. Since parents are the immediate source of life, the person who abuses his parents is the same as a destroyer—one who tears down, one who makes no positive contribution. Like the destroyer, the one who abuses his parents will find that the consequences of his actions will come home to him, for he actually shows disdain for his own life.

To rob one's parents can include more than just taking money from them. Children have a God-given responsibility to parents, and if they fail that responsibility in any area they rob their parents of what is due them. Jesus rebuked the Pharisees for using man-made rules to avoid providing for their parents (Matthew 15:1-9).

Results of pride and trust (verse 25). The proud person stirs up strife (Proverbs 13:10). The person who trusts in the Lord will prosper (be made "fat") (Proverbs 11:25). The first clause may be a reference to greed, in contrast to the second clause.

The foolishness of the heart (verse 26). The cry of the "me generation" is, "I want to follow my heart." But the heart is deceitful and wicked (Jeremiah 17:9). Foolishness is bound up in it and must be driven away (Proverbs 22:15). The only safe path is to follow the sound counsel of God's Word. (See Proverbs 3:5-6; 14:12.)

Avoiding lack; asking for a curse (verse 27). God will reward those who help the poor (Proverbs 19:17). He is concerned about the poor and will often prompt His children to minister to the poor on His behalf. Those who refuse, or who "hide their eyes," are rebellious against God and as a result will suffer many problems. Those who have financial problems should carefully examine their handling of money and resources to see if they have been generous with those in need.

Why good people go underground (verse 28). This proverb is a companion to Proverbs 28:12. When wicked people rise to authority, good people will often have to hide themselves in order to continue their good deeds. But when the wicked perish, as they always will, the righteous can come out of hiding and prosper in their right deeds. (See Proverbs 29:2.) This proverb shows that godly people are not in error when they disobey ungodly laws in order to worship in secret, smuggle Bibles, or spread the gospel. We must obey God, even if we must disobey human authority and worship in secret.

Chapter Twenty-Nine

The penalty for repeated rebellion (verse 1). This verse enunciates a principle that is both divine and human. Both God and man will be tolerant of stubbornness and rebellion for a time, an undetermined time. But neither God nor man will forever strive with rebellious people (Genesis 6:3). There will be no warning when the last opportunity for obedience comes, but it will come. After that, sudden destruction will fall on the rebel, and there will be no remedy.

The wise course of action is to respond immediately to reproof. Sin is deceptive, and the more one rebels, the easier it is to rebel. Rebellion is one of the worst habits someone could fall into. Instead, a person should cultivate the habit of obedience.

Righteous rulers; wicked rulers (verse 2). (See also Proverbs 11:11; 28:12, 28.) When those in authority are righteous, it produces great rejoicing among the people; when the wicked are in authority, mourning sweeps the land. Thus, one way to determine the character of a government is to observe the general attitude of the people.

This proverb reveals the desirability of placing godly people in positions of authority. Scripture definitely favors the involvement of the godly in civil affairs. Old Testament examples include Joseph, Daniel, and the three young Hebrew men in Babylon. Even in the New Testament, some believers held positions of civil authority and influence (Romans 16:23; Philippians 4:22). By implication, then, it is proper for believers to become involved in the political process of nations where they are allowed to do so, in order to place moral and godly people in positions of authority. In some cases, godless leaders have attained positions of authority by default, because godly people neglected to get involved.

Why fathers rejoice; the results of moral impurity (verse 3). A recurring theme in Proverbs is the joy that wise children bring to their parents. (See Proverbs 10:1; 15:20; 23:15, 24; 27:11.)

One of the things wisdom will do is keep a person from moral impurity. The unwise son who involves himself in moral impurity wastes his wealth. (See Proverbs 6:26; Luke 15:11-32.)

How a nation is strengthened or overthrown (verse 4). If a ruler will exercise right judgment (justice), it will contribute to stability and prosperity in the land. If he accepts bribes to pervert judgment, however, he sets in motion a chain of events that will result in the destruction of the nation. (See also Proverbs 14:34; 16:12; 20:8, 26; 29:14.)

The trap of flattery (verse 5). Flattery may seem attractive and pleasant, but it is a trap. Flattery lures one away from wisdom and sets him up for destruction. (See also Proverbs 2:16; 7:5; 26:28.)

Consequence of transgression and signs of righteousness (verse 6). A snare is a hidden trap. When an evil person sets out to sin, he does not realize there are hidden consequences. He does not see the danger until it is too late.

The righteous will demonstrate their inner joy in singing and rejoicing. We should not think it is a sign of piety to be gloomy and sad. The kingdom of God is "righteousness, and peace, and joy in the Holy Ghost" (Romans 14:17).

Attitudes toward the poor (verse 7). A common theme in Proverbs is the importance of helping the poor. (See Proverbs 19:17; 28:27.) A sign of righteousness is concern for the poor. The wicked care nothing for the poor.

What determines a city's fate (verse 8). The Book of Proverbs repeatedly addresses the importance of moral leadership in civic affairs. (See Proverbs 25:5; 28:12, 16, 28; 29:2.) The fate of a city or nation depends largely upon the quality of its leadership. Scorners (mockers) will stir up contention and lead a city into a hidden trap; wise people will skillfully direct its affairs so as to avoid and defuse anger.

The pointlessness of arguing with a fool (verse 9). It is a waste of time for a wise person to contend with a foolish person. No matter what direction the argument takes—whether it results in anger or laughter (mockery)—there will be no profitable conclusion. (See Proverbs 9:7-9.)

Attitudes toward the upright (verse 10). It is possible to determine someone's character by his attitude toward the upright. Those who are bloodthirsty (violent) hate those who do right. The behavior of the upright is a rebuke to them. One of the signs of the last days is that there will be an increase in "despisers of those that are good" (II Timothy 3:3). Those who are just are concerned about people's souls; they are interested in the spiritual well-being of others.

One difference between a fool and a wise man (verse 11). A fool will say everything he thinks, giving full vent to his anger. A wise man has self-control; he knows how to refrain from speaking until the right time. Ecclesiastes 5:3 declares, "A fool's voice is known by multitude of words." One of the greatest evidences of wisdom is the ability to control the tongue. (See James 3.)

Wicked authority; wicked influence (verse 12). If a ruler will listen to and act on lies, he will be surrounded with wicked advisors. This truth was demonstrated in the life of Ahab, king of Israel. Because he hated truth and preferred lies, he was surrounded with four hundred false prophets. (See I Kings 22.)

The common denominator between the poor and his oppressor (verse 13). A poor person and the one who oppresses him have something in common: it is the Lord who enables both of them to see. The deceitful creditor or oppressor should realize that the poor man is his equal and should treat him with respect. (See Matthew 18:23-35.)

A cause of longevity in office (verse 14). A recurring theme in Proverbs is the need for those in authority to render justice. (See Proverbs 16:12; 20:28.) Those who are faithful in judgment, particularly those who judge the poor with fairness, will enjoy a secure position.

The danger of neglecting the discipline of children (verse 15). The Book of Proverbs frequently addresses the importance of disciplining children properly (See Proverbs 13:24; 19:18; 22:15; 23:13-14.) Parents must not leave a child to himself. God places children in families so they can find direction in life. While they may complain about rules and regulations, children become insecure if left to themselves.

It is important to note that proper discipline includes two elements: a rod and reproof. Physical discipline alone is insufficient; parents need to train, correct, instruct, and explain verbally. Reproof has to do with spoken correction, which should be done in kindness and love, not in harshness (Proverbs 16:21, 24). Parents should not talk down to their children but think of how they themselves would want to be spoke to. The Golden Rule is an important principle, and it applies in family relationships (Matthew 7:12).

The rod (like a reed) refers to spanking, or the physical aspect of correction. Verbal correction alone is insufficient; without physical restrictions and correction the child will soon learn that there is no consequence of his wrongdoing. He will become increasingly bitter toward the "lectures" he receives.

The child who is neglected by his parents will eventually shame them by his actions.

The reason for a rising crime rate (verse 16). The reason trangression increases is that the wicked multiply. Society will never solve the crime problem until the sinful nature is conquered. The final solution to crime is not bigger prisons, more policemen, or advanced technology in crime detection, but the conversion of sinners.

Though the wicked may multiply, it is the righteous who are stable. They will survive to see the fall of those who rebel against God.

The blessing of correcting one's child (verse 17). Again this chapter addresses the subject of the discipline of children. (See also Proverbs 13:24; 19:18; 22:15; 23:13-14; 29:15.) While it is not pleasant to correct one's child, such an effort will result in rest and delight in later years.

The importance of vision (verse 18). The latter part of this proverb helps explain the "vision" mentioned in the first part: it has to do with knowing and obeying the Word of God. A similar usage occurs in I Samuel 3:1: "And the child Samuel ministered unto the LORD before Eli. And the word of the LORD was precious [scarce] in those days; there was no open vision [revelation]." Where there is no revelation of God and His Word, there is destruction, but when people obey God's Word happiness results. Jesus said, "Blessed are the pure in heart: for they shall see God" (Matthew 5:8).

Words are insufficient for correction (verse 19). Verse 15 points out that the correction of children has both verbal and physical aspects. This principle also has an application in the oversight of servants or employees. Words alone are not always enough to accomplish correction. Someone may understand what is said, but he may not respond positively to it. For correction to succeed, there must be adverse consequences for wrongdoing. Of course, we do not use corporal punishment for adults, but there must be sufficient penalties to make wrong behavior undesirable.

The hopelessness of someone who is quick to speak (verse 20). A recurring theme in the Book of Proverbs is the wisdom of controlling the tongue. (See Proverbs 15:2, 28; 17:27-28; 18:6, 7, 13; 29:11; James 1:19; 3.) Someone who cannot control his tongue can control nothing. There is more hope for a fool to change than there is for him. One of the most important steps in avoiding trouble is to control the tongue (Proverbs 13:3; 21:23). Someone who is hasty to speak brings unnecessary trouble upon himself.

The danger of pampering (verse 21). Someone who pampers or indulges his servant (or employee) and does not hold him accountable for his work will eventually regret it. The servant will eventually lose respect for his overseer and begin to expect many things as a matter of right even though he is not really entitled to them.

Manifestations of anger and fury (verse 22). An angry person will stir up contention by his words and deeds; the strife will become more and more intense. A furious, or hot-tempered, person will demonstrate his fury by disregarding what is right. Sin will be a way of life for him.

The results of pride and humility (verse 23). The Book of Proverbs repeatedly warns of the consequences of pride. (See Proverbs 16:18; 21:4; 28:25.) A person's pride will bring him low, for God resists the proud (James 4:6). Since the blessing of God cannot rest upon a proud person, he has no source of survival. But someone who is humble, that is, who recognizes the contributions of God and other people to his life, will be upheld and honored.

The danger of keeping the wrong company (verse 24). Someone who throws in his lot with a thief will suffer the same adverse consequences; in effect, he acts as if he hates himself. He enters into a pact with evil and refuses to reveal the sin of his partner. (The old English word *bewrayeth* means "betrays.")

The danger of fearing people (verse 25). The only one we should fear in the ultimate sense of spiritual reverence and trust is God. Those who fear people will worry about what others think. They will be unduly influenced by peer pressure or pressure from ungodly authorities. They will tend to move with the mob, even when they know it is wrong. But godly people are not to follow a multitude to do evil (Exodus 23:2). They must stand for what is right, even if they have to stand alone. The New Testament encourages believers to say boldly, "The Lord is my helper, and I will not fear what man shall do unto me" (Hebrews 13:6). God will protect those who trust in Him rather than fearing people.

The folly of trying to pull strings (verse 26). Many people try to curry favor with those in authority, hoping for favorable judgments. But in the final analysis, it is from God that we get justice. Rulers who can be swayed by personal influence are undependable. Therefore, it is better to put our trust in the Lord.

Mutual abomination (verse 27). Just as the righteous detest wickedness, so the wicked detest righteousness. Neither can tolerate the other's philosophy and lifestyle. There is no middle, neutral ground between the two. Before they can walk together, they must agree (Amos 3:3).

Chapter Thirty

The identity of the writer (verse 1). The meaning of the names in this verse has been the object of much speculation. One explanation is that Agur, Jakeh, Ithiel, and Ucal are the real names of actual men. If so, we do not know the identity of any of them.

Another explanation is that these words simply refer to Solomon, David, and two of Solomon's sons. (See the comments on Proverbs 1:1.) Agur means "the collector of wise sayings," Jakeh means "the obedient one," Ithiel means "With me is God," and Ucal means "I shall be completed." Ancient Jewish tradition identifies Agur as Solomon and Jakeh as David. And it is not uncommon for persons in Scripture to be called by more than one name, each name having significance. For example, in II Samuel 12:25 Solomon is called Jedidiah, which means "Beloved of the LORD." Regardless of the human author of this verse, it contains an internal witness to the inspiration of the passage: it is a "prophecy."

The humility of the writer (verses 2-3). The writer claims to have less than even human understanding. The word *brutish* here literally means "ignorant." He declares he has never learned wisdom, nor does he have the knowledge of the holy. Perhaps Agur genuinely expressed his human limitations apart from divine inspiration. But the following verses, especially verses 4-6, suggest that possibly he was using irony, a figure of speech used frequently in Scripture. That is, he may have been writing to someone who professed great wisdom and understanding, and his self-effacing comments may have been designed to reveal how he looked in the eyes of this self-proclaimed wise man. At any rate, the wisdom revealed throughout the chapter suggests that he was not an ignorant person at this point, and of course, the passage is divinely inspired.

Human limitations (verse 4). This verse has been the subject of much speculation. Some interpreters believe the understood answer to each question is God. Some, but not all, English translations that indicate deity by capitalizing pronouns capitalize the words *his* and *son's* in the statement, "What is his name, and what is his son's name, if thou canst tell?" Many who thus interpret the verse believe it is definite proof that there is more than one person in the Godhead and that the second person, called the Son, preexisted Bethlehem. But not all interpreters, not even trinitarians, agree on this point. Nothing can be proved by the capitalization of pronouns; it is simply a tool of the translators, with no support from the Hebrew text.

It seems better to understand the verse as referring to human limitations. The context suggests this interpretation, particularly verses 2-3, 5-6. According to this view, the verse means, "Who [what man] hath ascended up into heaven, or descended? who [what man] hath gathered the wind in his fists? who [what man] hath bound the waters in a garment? who [what man] hath established all the ends of the earth?" If the reader knows of any man who has done this, he should supply his name, and his son's name.

The answer, of course, is that no one has done or could do these things. The verse thus reveals the weakness and ignorance of humans when compared to God, especially those people who profess great wisdom, as suggested by the ironic disclaimers of verses 2-3.

If the verse is referring to God, the final question would seem pointless: "What is his name, and what is his son's name, if thou canst tell?" If it were obvious that the questions were to be answered with "God," the reader could certainly have supplied His name, for it was revealed long before this time (Exodus 6:3). But this verse presumes that the reader *cannot* supply the names: "If thou canst tell?"

At any rate, the verse cannot be reconciled to trinitarian doctrine, for under that theory the question, "What is his name, and what is his son's name" would refer to God the Father and God the Son. The grammar of the verse would then demand that each preceding question be answered with "God the Father." None of the actions described in the first four questions could be attributed to the Son; all would have to be attributed to the Father. But trinitarianism does not teach that God the Father ascended up into heaven or descended; that is the role of God the Son. For example, *The Bible Knowledge Commentary* declares of this phrase that it "remind[s] one of Christ, the Son of God."[1] Jesus said, "And no man hath ascended up to heaven, but he that came down from heaven, even the Son of man which is in heaven" (John 3:13).

It is also possible to understand this verse to be speaking of God without accepting a trinitarian explanation. If we understand that any Old Testament reference to the Son is prophetic, we can view the reference to the "son" in this verse in the same way. For example, David Bernard has said of this verse, "He was looking to the future, trying to see by what name God would reveal Himself when He would appear as the Son."[2]

The Scriptures teach that the Son was begotten at a specific point in time (Psalm 2:7). The New Testament teaches that the Son refers to the humanity of Jesus, which was born of a woman: "But when the fulness of the time was come, God sent forth his Son, made of a woman, made under the law" (Galatians 4:4). If the Son referred to a second divine person, then that person would be made of a woman! But Jesus Christ was not a second person; He was God (deity) manifest in the flesh (humanity) (I Timothy 3:16). The deity pre-existed Bethlehem; the humanity did not. We can never speak of the Son of God without some reference to or recognition of the humanity, for the Son was made of a woman.

In the Old Testament the son was still in the future: "I will [future tense] be to him a Father, and he shall [future tense] be to me a Son" (Hebrews 1:5). The Messianic prophecy of Isaiah indicated that the name of the Son would not be revealed until He was in His mother's womb (Isaiah 49:1). Thus if Proverbs 30:4 refers to God, the question "What is his son's name" would seem pointless, for the name was not yet revealed. All in all, it seems better to understand this verse not as a reference to deity at all, but to the limitations of finite humans.

The pure Word of God (verse 5). Contrary to human

ignorance and limitations, every Word of God is pure. The Word of God is the standard of truth (John 17:17). It is inspired (breathed) of God (II Timothy 3:16). We cannot separate the integrity of the Word of God from the integrity of God Himself. Indeed, as exalted as His name is, He has chosen to exalt His Word even above His name (Psalm 138:2). One reason the Word has preeminence is that the Word teaches us of God's name.

This verse places emphasis upon *every* word. No part of the Word of God is unimportant or unnecessary. Jesus declared, quoting the Old Testament, "Man shall not live by bread alone, but by every word that proceedeth out of the mouth of God" (Matthew 4:4). Those who forsake their own human wisdom and rely on God's Word will find Him to be a shield for them.

Not only is the Word of the Lord pure, but God preserves it to all generations (Psalm 12:6-7). One of the great miracles of God is the preservation of His Word down to this present day.

The danger of adding to the Word of God (verse 6). This verse warns those who add to God's Word that He will rebuke them and prove them a liar. Similar warnings appear elsewhere in Scripture. Moses warned the ancient Israelites against adding to or taking away from the Word of God (Deuteronomy 4:2). In the closing verses of the last book of Scripture, the apostle John was inspired to give a similar warning (Revelation 22:18-19). Those who dare add to the inspired Word of God are playing god, as are those who take away from it, and God will not allow such a presumptuous sin to go unpunished. The ultimate consequence of this sin is seen in Revelation 21:8.

Two requests (verses 7-9). These words indicate that

Agur was indeed a man of wisdom, for he requested of God only two things before death, both of which are wise requests. It is best to understand these verses as a prayer.

First, Agur wished to be totally divorced from vanity and lies. This verse may again be a reference and response to the pseudointellectualism of the person(s) to whom he was writing. He recognized that human wisdom was actually vain and false and wanted nothing to do with it. His desire was to walk in truth.

Second, Agur requested that he would be neither rich nor poor, but that he could live simply, with his basic needs being met. The reason for this request is clear: Riches bring unnecessary temptation to trust in wealth and so forget God (Mark 10:23-27; I Timothy 6:6-10). Poverty brings temptation to steal and so to dishonor His name, possibly blaming Him for one's lack. Jesus later taught His disciples to pray in similar fashion, "Give us this day our daily bread" (Matthew 6:11).

A warning against accusing others (verse 10). It is wrong for someone to pass judgment on a person who is not under his authority and bring slanderous accusations against that person. If he does, he can expect to be accused himself and to suffer the consequences.

Romans 14:4 teaches a similar truth with reference to the church: "Who art thou that judgest another man's servant? to his own master he standeth or falleth. Yea, he shall be holden up: for God is able to make him stand." As the context makes clear, every believer is a servant of God; therefore, individuals are not to judge one another's motives and standing before God. (See also Matthew 7:1-5; Romans 2:1.)

The implication in Proverbs is that people are not to

judge the performance of the servants of others, and this insight is important in modern society. It is common for employees to find fault with their fellow workers and try to ingratiate themselves with their employers by speaking evil of their peers. But rarely will this action produce a positive result. Ordinarily the employer will be irritated by this critical, fault-finding attitude and will at least mentally note that the informer is a troublemaker. One reason for this reaction is that a rebuke of his employees may be an indirect rebuke of the employer, for it may suggest that he is not capable of management.

The progression of rebellion (verses 11-14). It appears that the same generation is in view throughout these four verses. The first step toward the ultimate rebellion of these people is disregarding their duty to honor their parents. (See Proverbs 20:20.) But they do not just passively neglect their parents; they actively curse them.

Then these people tend to justify themselves. While they accuse their parents of being greedy and self-centered, they congratulate themselves on their pure motives. They may express a desire to overthrow the evil "establishment," but in reality they themselves are un-washed and filthy.

The next step in the development of total rebellion is a total surrender to pride: "O how lofty are their eyes! and their eyelids are lifted up." (See Proverbs 6:17.)

Finally, the rebellion degenerates into violence and destruction. They "devour the poor from off the earth, and the needy from among men." This progression has repeated itself many times during human history and con-tinues to resurface in the present day.

Personifications of greed (verses 15-16). This passage

introduces its discussion of greed by using one of the most repulsive creatures: the leech. This comparison draws immediate attention to the abhorrent nature of greed. The leech is the perfect personification of this sin; even its name has come to be synonymous with greed. The nature of greed is that it is never satisfied; it will never confess to having enough. Greed is part of the three root sins; it is included under "the lust of the eyes" (I John 2:16).

Further illustrations of the nature of greed include the grave, which continually calls for more; the barren womb, which will never be satisfied (when it is opened, it is no longer barren); the earth, which constantly craves more water (droughts can develop in a period of months, even after good rain); and fire, which constantly reaches out to consume more. All of these examples reveal the folly of greed. Greed deceitfully promises to be satisfied with the acquisition of just one more thing, but when that is obtained, it demands even more. Much of modern advertising appeals to this sinful characteristic.

The penalty for rebellion (verse 17). This proverb is based upon a phenomenon in nature. When it appears that an animal has died, vultures will first approach the carcass to determine whether it has or not. They do so by pecking at the eye, for if the victim has any life left it will make some attempt to defend its eyes. When the birds determine that the creature is truly helpless or dead, the vultures will then swoop down to begin to eat the flesh. The point of the comparison is that when a person rebels against his parents, he has chosen a path that leads to sure spiritual death. Scripture repeatedly connects the eye with the condition of the inner person, the soul (Proverbs 28:22; 30:13; Matthew 6:22-23; II Peter 2:14). Thus, the first signs of spiritual death often appear in connection with the eyes.

Thus the Scriptures sometimes symbolize evil spirits as fowls (Revelation 18:2). It is likely that the rebel will eventually fall prey to the influence of evil spirits, which will determine his spiritual death and accelerate the process of destruction (John 10:10).

"Rebellion is as the sin of witchcraft, and stubbornness is as iniquity and idolatry" (I Samuel 15:23). In essence, witchcraft is exposing oneself to the influence of evil spirits. Rebellion is the same type of sin, and it carries the same penalty.

Four amazing things (verses 18-19). These four things amazed Agur; he could not fully understand how they worked. An eagle soaring high in the sky, a serpent slipping over a rock, a ship with sails aloft slicing through the sea, and the way of a man with a maid: these things are still marvels even in a day of advanced technology. Each of them is a result of God's creation (even the ship moves because of the wind and sea), so they are all somewhat mysterious and marvelous.

Self-justification (verse 20). The immoral woman in the Book of Proverbs is portrayed as being forward and aggressive (Proverbs 6:24-26; 7:10-21). She seeks out her prey, sins as casually as she would eat a meal, and then declares her innocence. According to the normal procedure as arranged by God, a man courts a woman (verse 19), but the immoral woman instead lays a trap for a man. Much of modern literature and drama presents the adulterous woman sympathetically as a victim of circumstances who actually has a good heart. It is suggested, "She has done no wickedness." Such a distorted view overlooks the broken homes, ruined lives, destitute children, and physical and mental disease that result from her sin.

Four sources of trouble (verses 21-23). Social turmoil results when any of these four things occur: when a servant becomes a King when a fool becomes prosperous, when a hateful or unloved woman marries, and when a maidservant succeeds or replaces her mistress. A servant is not qualified to reign; he does not have the necessary training and experience, and he will make foolish decisions. A fool who prospers and has all his desires met will tend to be proud, boastful, and arrogant. He will think he deserves what he has and will rail against others whom he perceives to be not as successful as he. He will flaunt his wealth. A contentious woman will drive her husband away (Proverbs 21:9, 19). A handmaid who inherits the position and wealth of her mistress is equally unqualified with the servant who reigns.

The basic lesson here seems to be that each individual should fill the role for which he is suited and prepared. For example, a bishop (pastor) must not be a novice, lest he be lifted up with pride and fall into the condemnation of the devil (I Timothy 3:6).

Lessons from nature (verses 24-28). The four creatures mentioned in this passage are small yet extremely wise. They demonstrate the wisdom of planning ahead, compensating for weaknesses, being united, and having tenacity. Ants, though small and weak, instinctively prepare for the future: they store up their food in the summer. Proverbs 6:6-11 offers the ants as an example to sluggards.

The coney in this passage is the hyrax or rock badger,

which resembles a rabbit-size guinea pig. Since conies cannot defend themselves adequately, they live among crags so as to be less accessible to the enemy. They have built-in suction on their feet that enables them to cling to steep rock surfaces. They thus compensate for their weakness by making wise use of their strengths.

The locusts demonstrate unity, for even though they have no ruler, they work together in bands like a mighty, organized army to strip crops (Joel 1:1-12).

Over six hundred varieties of spiders have been identified in Palestine. The spider demonstrates tenacity, for it lives even where it is not wanted: in king's palaces. For many years, skeptics mocked the mention here of the spiders "hands." It was not until the discovery of the microscope that this laughter was silenced, for the microscope revealed that the spider has tiny "hands" on the end of each leg which give it tremendous grasping power.

Apparently, the reason Proverbs mentions these examples from nature is to encourage people to realize that their perceived weaknesses are no reason to accept a life of little achievement. The qualities demonstrated by these little creatures—planning ahead, compensating for weakness by making wise use of strength, unity, and tenacity—will enable any person to accomplish seemingly impossible tasks.

Four stately things (verses 29-31). In contrast to the four things that are "little upon the earth" (verses 24-28), this passage presents four things that are noble in appearance and stately in their walk. Lions were common in Palestine; there were lairs in the brush along the Jordan River. The lion, in his strength, refuses to retreat from anything. Greyhounds, used by kings for hunting, are known for their swift gait. Male goats stride with great nimbleness of foot. A king surrounded by his troops who has subdued his enemies and who rules so well that there is no dissension against him is a mighty symbol of authority. So these four examples illustrate the value of strength (courage), speed, agility, and authority. All of these qualities can be developed and improved with effort.

When a person should close his mouth (verse 32). The Book of Proverbs frequently warns against self-promotion (Proverbs 17:19; 25:6, 27; 27:2). It also warns against wrong thoughts (Proverbs 15:26; 23:7; 24:9). A person who is guilty of either of these evils can minimize their detrimental effects, however, if he will lay his hand upon his mouth, that is, refuse to put his thoughts into words. When someone clothes thoughts with words, they take on strength and force, for they are embraced, enunciated precisely, and communicated to others. Thus words are extremely important. (See Matthew 12:36-37; James 3.)

How to handle anger (verse 33). Just as certainly as churning milk produces butter and wringing the nose causes it to bleed, so forcing wrath produces strife. This verse illustrates the law of cause and effect. Since strife is undesirable, we should avoid it by not forcing anger. In other words, we should not stir up anger. We should not pursue it, that is, we should not retaliate, either verbally or physically, against another. Paul explained, "Avenge not yourselves, but rather give place unto wrath" (Romans 12:19). He also taught that it would be better for a Christian to allow himself to be defrauded than to pursue a matter in secular court with another Christian (I Corinthians 6:7). Anger is fueled by an angry response; it is defused by soft words (Proverbs 15:1).

Notes

[1]John F. Walvoord and Roy B. Zuck, *The Bible Knowledge Commentary Old Testament* (Wheaton, Il.: Victor Books, 1985), 969.

[2]David Bernard, *The Oneness of God* (Hazelwood, Mo.: Word Aflame Press, 1983), 50.

Chapter Thirty-One

The identity of the writer (verse 1). We should note the similarities of this verse with Proverbs 30:1. Both begin with "the words of" and both claim that what follows is "prophecy." This verse identifies the words that follow as those of King Lemuel, which his mother taught him.

If Lemuel is the actual name of a king, we have no knowledge of his identity. The name Lemuel means "devoted to God," so, as with Agur, it is possible that this name is actually a term for Solomon. If so, the mother was Bathsheba.

The Book of Proverbs discusses the importance of a mother's teaching (Proverbs 1:8; 6:20). The high regard of this king for his mother's counsel is evident by his description of it as prophecy.

What counsel can a mother give? (verse 2). When a mother considers giving her son counsel for life, what should she say? The king's mother apparently gave much thought to this question; thus, the following counsel is the most important advice she could offer. The phrase "the son of my vows" may indicate that the king's mother made vows to God concerning her son either before or after his birth.

A warning against immorality and destructive behavior (verse 3). The first warning this mother gave was against moral impurity. She understood fully the weakness produced in a man who succumbs to immorality. If the mother counselling her son was indeed Bathsheba, this advice is extremely interesting, for she saw firsthand, and was personally involved with, the near destruction of Israel's greatest king, David. While she was certainly not innocent, David took the initiative in the sin by calling her to him. When Bathsheba reported to him her conception, she saw him turn from the kind, wise king he had been to a conniving, scheming despot. If the mother was Bathsheba, she testified from bitter firsthand experience, which included the death of the son born of the illicit union, and she wanted to be certain that her son Solomon did not fall into the same trap. Perhaps Solomon's explicit warnings elsewhere stemmed in part from the teaching he received from his mother (Proverbs 2:1-19; 5:1-14; 7; 22:14; 23:27-28).

The king's mother continued by warning her son against things that destroy kings.

A warning against intoxicating beverages (verses 4-5). After warning her son against immorality, this mother warned him against drinking intoxicating beverages. The drinking of wine or strong drink is not fitting for those who would rule. The reason is clear: intoxicating beverages cloud the mind, causing the ruler to forget the law and make unwise and unfair judgments. Similar warnings appear elsewhere in the Book of Proverbs (Proverbs 20:1; 23:20-21, 29-35).

The word translated "wine" is the Hebrew *yayin,* a generic term that can refer to the juice of the grape both in unfermented and fermented states. Thus, the word is similar to the Greek *oinos*. The context determines the meaning of the word. In this case, the Scripture clearly forbids fermented wine, for fresh grape juice would not cause anyone to forget anything or to pervert judgment.

The words "strong drink" are translated from the Hebrew *shakar,* another generic term that refers to the juices obtained from dates and other fruits (excepting grapes) as well as barley, millet, and other grains, which were dried, scorched, and mixed with honey.[1] Like "wine," "strong drink" apparently can refer to fermented or unfermented beverages. The context determines the usage.

Anyone who wishes to be a responsible leader in any area of life must avoid intoxicating beverages. This principle applies to fathers, mothers, employers, teachers, pastors, governmental leaders, lawyers, and doctors. In short, anyone who wishes to have any influence at all and who wishes to make right decisions must avoid intoxicating beverages.

The deception of intoxicating beverages (verses 6-7). Perhaps these verses mean that intoxicating beverages are fit only for people on the verge of death or those under great depression. If so, the beverages are recommended only for medicinal purposes. Of course, in our day medical science has certainly progressed to the point where far superior medicines and anesthetics are available.

But even if this interpretation were true, it would apply only to the ungodly who are on the verge of death or in great sorrow, for the righteous should not be heavy-hearted and in misery at the prospect of death, nor should they rely on a drink in times of sorrow; instead, they are

to trust in the Lord. Someone who fears God will not call
for liquor at the hour of death; he will call on the Lord.
If a believer is heavy-hearted, he will not ask for a glass
of intoxicating drink—he knows that will solve nothing—
but he will encourage himself in the Lord.

It appears, however, that the most reasonable interpretation of these verses is that they were spoken in irony.
Would a wise mother seriously suggest to her son that
he give intoxicating beverages to those with "heavy
hearts" so they could drink, forget their poverty, and
remember their misery no more? Would alcohol solve their
problem? Would they awaken from their drunken stupor
with glad hearts and riches? Would intoxicating beverages
rescue a person who was perishing?

It does not seem consistent to tell a king to abstain
from intoxicating beverages because of their tendency to
cloud the mind and produce irrational thoughts but to give
these drinks to others. If an ungodly person is dying, he
does not need to be intoxicated to forget his trouble; he
needs someone to speak to him about his soul. If there
were ever a time in his life when he needed to think ra-
tionally, it is on his deathbed! If a person has a heavy
heart, drunkenness will not solve his problems. He needs
someone to explain to him the love of God and the Lord's
desire to supply his needs.

Again, if the king's mother was Bathsheba, she saw
firsthand the evil of intoxication, for it was David's tool
in his failed effort to deceive Uriah. (See also Habakkuk
2:15.)

These verses seem to reinforce the warning given in
verses 4-5. Intoxicating beverages are unfit for those who
wish to act responsibly, who wish to live, and who wish

to solve their problems. These verses satirically state that intoxicating beverages are fit only for those who are ready to die and those who are in the depths of despair. One thing is clear: these verses do not conflict with the abundant teaching of Scripture forbidding the use of intoxicating beverages. They certainly do not give dying or downcast believers an excuse to become inebriated.

The importance of righteous judgment (verses 8-9). Following the strong warnings against immorality and intoxication, this chapter next stresses the importance of speaking on behalf of those who cannot defend themselves, of judging righteously, and of defending the poor and needy. These actions will cause the common people to love a leader and support him (Proverbs 24:23-26).

The virtuous woman (verse 10). This verse begins a discussion of the virtuous woman, which continues through the end of the chapter. It is interesting that a woman, the king's mother, introduced this subject (verse 1). She, more than anyone, understood the importance of the king having a virtuous wife. Women tend to be more successful than men in discerning motives and character in other women.

The truly virtuous woman is rare; she is worth far more than rubies. In other words, she is more valuable than material wealth, regardless of how great. Choosing a wise and virtuous wife is far more important to a man than amassing wealth.

Subsequent verses describe the character and activities of a virtuous woman. Perhaps not every good wife will engage in every one of these activities in the same way, but she will embody the wisdom, strength, and diligence that they portray.

A trustworthy wife (verse 11). The husband of a virtuous woman is able to trust her in all areas. Specifically, he can trust her management of household affairs, as described in following verses. She will manage wisely and conserve resources so that he will lack nothing of value and will have no need of spoil (unjust gain).

A wife who does good (verse 12). The virtuous woman is a helper suitable for her husband (Genesis 2:20). She does him no evil; she harms him in no way. All that she does is good for him. Moreover, she is consistent: she brings him good all the days of her life. He is made better because of her. She complements, completes, and strengthens him.

A wife who works willingly (verse 13). The virtuous woman does not have to be told what to do. On her own initiative, she selects wool and flax for clothing. She does not have to be cajoled or threatened into working; she works willingly. She does not think she is too good to use her hands. It is not a drudgery to her to work; she enjoys it. It gives her a sense of accomplishment and fulfillment.

A wife who shops wisely (verse 14). Like the merchants' ships that sail to far ports and return with valuable cargo, so the virtuous wife ventures forth, conducts the business of shopping, and returns home with her purchases. If necessary, she brings her food from afar. That is, she shops wisely, not buying a product simply because it is convenient. She will search until she finds what she actually needs.

A wife who gets an early start (verse 15). The virtuous wife does not squander the day in bed. She does not wait for someone to serve her, even though she may have servants. She rises before the sun does to begin preparations for the day's meals and to provide for her maidens.

A wife who engages in business transactions (verse 16). Some in the feminist movement have wrongly thought the Bible belittled women and limited their potential. Instead, the Scripture exalts the woman and points out her value and importance. (See Galatians 3:28.) This verse portrays the woman considering and making a major purchase: a piece of land. Then with the profits of past investments and enterprises, she plants a vineyard. This example shows her business acumen and active involvement in the free enterprise system.

A strong wife (verse 17). The virtuous woman is not "weak." She works vigorously. She strengthens herself for work in order to accomplish her goals.

A wife who does quality work and plans ahead (verse 18). The virtuous woman knows the value of her merchandise. She cannot be deceived by unscrupulous businessmen. She makes sure that her work is good and she plans ahead, for she works into the night. (See Matthew 25:4.)

A wife who works with her hands (verse 19). Verses 13, 19, 22, and 24 describe weaving and sewing. Much of a woman's work for the family takes place in the home. (See I Timothy 5:14; Titus 2:4-5.)

A generous wife (verse 20). The virtuous woman is sensitive to the needs of others and reaches out to help them personally. Her interest in making a profit does not prevent her from giving freely to those in need.

A wife who is prepared (verse 21). The virtuous woman is not caught unprepared by cold weather. She has plans ahead and provides quality clothing that is warm enough to protect her family from the elements.

A wife who makes many necessary items (verse 22).
While the virtuous woman knows how to shop wisely
(verse 14), she does not necessarily rely on the marketplace for all her needs. She develops and uses the skills
necessary to make some household furnishings and
clothing. The "scarlet" clothing of verse 21 and the "silk
and purple" of this verse indicate the prosperity of her
family.

*A woman who is a public crown to her husband (verse
23).* The city gates were the place where the esteemed
elders (leaders) of the community gathered for discussion,
decision, and judgment. The husband of the virtuous
woman is so blessed by her wisdom and diligence that he
is well thought of among the wise. (See Proverbs 12:4.)
It is obvious that she does not belittle or denigrate her
husband. Her diligence and skill complement him; they
do not detract from him.

A productive wife (verse 24). The virtuous woman
makes items for sale in the marketplace. For example,
she regularly delivers belts or sashes to merchants. She
is in the wholesale business. She figures her costs,
estimates the value of her products, and conducts her
business.

A wife's strength and honor (verse 25). The word
clothing here refers metaphorically to her character; she
is clothed with strength and honor (dignity). She is a
morally strong, honorable person. She does not worry
about the future. The preparations she has made enable
her to enjoy life; she can look forward to the future with
eager anticipation instead of fear or despair.

A wife's words (verse 26). The virtuous woman's
wisdom is reflected in the words she speaks. She is not

a gossip; she is not known for a multitude of empty words. When she speaks, wise and kind words come out.

An observant and busy wife (verse 27). The virtuous woman is always alert to the needs of her family. She knows what is going on and can anticipate future needs and plan for them. While she knows how to relax, she is not an idle person. She is always engaged in some worthwhile, productive pursuit as she oversees the affairs of her household.

A wife's commendation (verses 28-29). One of the surest ways to determine the character of a woman is to observe how her children and husband speak of her. The virtuous woman's children "arise up," that is, they honor her presence. They speak of her with respect and reverence. Her husband praises her. Specifically, he says, "Many woman have done well, but you have done better than all of them." Each husband should be convinced that his wife is the best of them all!

The genuinely important thing (verse 30). Since people tend to place so much emphasis on physical attractiveness, it is revealing to note that outward charm is deceptive and that outward beauty is fleeting and ultimately worthless. (See Proverbs 11:22.) Physical beauty is dangerous because those who are physically beautiful are tempted to rely on their beauty to gain favor with others. But physical beauty can be taken away in a moment of time. If a woman has not developed character, she is an empty shell. Women should not be praised primarily for their physical appearance; this emphasis tempts them to put their priorities in this area. They should be praised for their character, for their fear of the Lord.

A wife who has earned her reward (verse 31). A virtuous woman deserves to reap the benefit of her labor. She should be treated as an individual in her own right, and she should have the privilege of reaping the reward of her efforts. She gains a good reputation for the quality of her work and of her life. Even community leaders who sit at the gates of the city (verse 23) notice her noble qualities and commend her.

It is fitting that the Book of Proverbs, which frequently discusses the danger of involvement with immoral women, should conclude with a detailed discussion of the blessings of having a virtuous wife.

Note

[1]William Patton, *Bible Wines* (Oklahoma City, Ok.: Sane Press, n.d.), 56-57.

Conclusion

The principles found in the Book of Proverbs are timeless. They will guide any person, of any generation, to true success.

All of the insights in the book begin with the fear of the Lord (Proverbs 1:7). Without this starting point, all else is at best weak human effort.

The person who reads this book carefully, thinking deeply about its principles, will discover that he gradually begins to think differently. His mind will begin to be transformed and renewed. (See Romans 12:2.) He will no longer respond hastily and automatically to situations by human reasoning; he will look for cause-and-effect relationships. He will learn to control his tongue, his thoughts, and his eyes.

It is a good form of discipline to read the chapter from the Book of Proverbs that corresponds to the day of the month. If a person starts by reading the first chapter on the first day of the month, he will read the entire book once each month. When someone faithfully practices this habit for some time, the wisdom of the book will begin to sink deep within his mind and heart.

This wonderful book of wisdom, written by a king initially to prepare his son for the throne but inspired by God for every person in every age, addresses almost every area of life. Those who consult this work will spare themselves many bad decisions and actions, and they will tend to prosper in everything they do.

Topical Reference Index

We can identify over three hundred themes in the Book of Proverbs. This index presents these themes by noting the specific chapter and verse where each is found. Many of these topics occur repeatedly throughout the book. In other cases, a theme or subject may appear only once.

This section is not merely a concordance to the Book of Proverbs, although it may serve that purpose to some degree. It is rather a topical reference to the book.

This index seeks to group related themes together under one topic, using the following format. The topics are listed alphabetically. In some cases, the word itself may not appear in any of the verses listed, but the idea is there. Under each topic, the chapters where that topic appears are listed, followed by each verse in the chapter that deals with the subject.

Boasting
20:14
25:14
27:1

Bones
3:8
12:4
14:30
15:30
16:24
17:22

Brawling woman
21:9
25:24

Bread
4:17
6:26
9:5, 17
12:9, 11
20:13, 17
22:9
23:6
25:21
28:19, 21
31:27

Brokenness
3:20
6:15
15:13
17:22
24:31
25:19, 28

Brutishness
12:1
30:2

Business
22:29

Calamity
1:26
6:15
19:13
24:22
27:10

Character
28:6

Chastening
13:24
19:18

Child rearing
13:24
19:18
22:6, 15
23:13-14
29:15

Children
4:1
5:7
7:24
8:32
13:22
14:26

15:11
17:6
20:7, 11
22:6, 15
23:13, 24
29:15, 21
31:28

City
1:21
8:3
9:3, 14
10:15
11:10, 11
16:32
18:11, 19
21:22
25:28
29:8

Co-signing
(surety)
6:1
11:15
17:18
20:16
27:13

Commandment
2:1
3:1
4:4
6:20, 23
7:1, 2
8:29
10:8

14:12, 27, 32
16:14, 25
18:21
21:6
24:11
26:18

Deceit

11:18
12:5, 17, 20
14:8, 25
20:17
23:3
26:24, 26
27:6
29:13
31:30

Delight

1:22
2:14
8:30
11:1, 20
12:22
15:8
16:13
18:2
19:10
24:25
29:17

Desire

3:15
10:24
11:23
12:12
13:4, 12, 19

18:1
19:22
21:10, 25
23:6
24:1

Destruction

1:27
10:14, 15, 29
13:3
14:28
15:11
16:18
17:19
18:7, 12
21:15
24:2
27:20
31:8

Devices

1:31
12:2
14:17
19:21

Dying

5:23
10:21
15:10
19:16
23:13
30:7

Diligence

4:23

10:4
12:24, 27
13:4
21:5
22:29
27:23

Discord

6:14, 19

Discretion

1:4
2:11
3:21
5:2
11:22
19:11

Drowsiness

23:21

Drunkard

23:21
26:9

Ear

2:2
4:20
5:1, 13
15:31
17:4
18:15
20:12
21:13
22:17
23:9, 12

22:14
24:16, 17
26:27
28:10, 14, 18
29:16

False balance

11:1
20:23

False witness

6:19
12:17
14:5
19:5, 9
21:28
25:18

Father, fatherless

1:8
3:12
4:1
10:1
15:20
17:21, 25
19:13, 26
20:20
23:10, 22, 24, 25
28:7, 24
29:3
30:11, 17

Favor

3:4
8:35
11:27

12:2
13:15
14:9, 35
16:15
18:22
19:6, 12
21:10
22:1
28:23
29:26
31:30

Fear

1:26, 27, 33
3:25
10:24
20:2
29:25

Fear of the Lord

1:7, 29
2:5
8:13
9:10
10:27
14:26, 27
15:16, 33
16:6
19:23
22:4
23:17
29:25

Feet

1:15, 16
3:23, 26

4:26, 27
5:5
6:13, 18, 28
7:11
19:2
25:17, 19
26:6
29:5

Flattery

2:16
6:24
7:5, 21
20:19
26:28
28:23
29:5

Flesh

4:22
5:11
11:17
14:30
23:20

Flourishing

11:28
14:11

Folly

5:23
13:16
14:8, 18, 24, 29
15:21
16:22
17:12

Glory
3:35
4:9
16:31
17:6
19:11
20:29
25:2, 27
28:12

Gluttony
23:21

Gold
3:14
8:10, 19
11:22
16:16
17:3
20:15
22:1
25:11, 12
27:21

Goodness
2:9, 20
3:4, 27
4:2
11:17, 23, 27
12:2, 14, 25
13:2, 15, 21, 22
14:14, 19, 22
15:3, 23, 30
16:20, 29
17:13, 20, 22, 26
18:5, 22

19:2, 8
20:18, 23
22:1
24:13, 23, 25
25:25, 27
28:10, 21
31:12, 18

Good name
22:1

Good news
25:25

Good report
15:30

Good word
12:25
15:23

Government
20:28
28:2
29:2, 4, 14

Grace
1:9
3:22, 34
4:9
22:11

Greed
1:19
15:27
30:15, 16

Hands
6:10, 17
12:14
14:1
17:18
21:25
22:26
24:33
30:28
31:13, 16, 19, 20,
   31

Happiness
3:13, 18
14:21
16:20
28:14
29:18

Harvest
6:8
10:5
20:4
25:13
26:1

Hasty
14:29
21:5
29:20

Hate
1:22, 29
5:12
6:16
8:13, 36

Promotion
3:35
4:8

Prudence
8:12
12:16, 23
13:16
14:8, 15, 18
15:5
16:21
18:15
19:14
22:3
27:12

Punishment
11:21
16:5
17:5, 26
19:5, 9, 19
27:12

Quietness
17:1

Rage
6:34
14:16
29:9

Ransom
6:35
13:8
21:18

Rebellion
17:11
30:17

Rebuke
9:7, 8
13:1, 8
24:25
27:5
28:23

Recompense,
repayment
11:31
13:21
20:22

Rejoicing
8:30, 31
11:10
13:9
15:30
29:3

Reproach
6:33
14:34
18:3
19:26
22:10

Reproof
1:23, 25, 30
5:12
6:23
10:17

12:1
13:18
15:5, 10, 31, 32
17:10
29:15

Reputation
22:1

Respect of
persons
24:23
28:21

Revenue
8:19
15:6
16:8

Reward
11:18
21:14
24:14, 20
25:22

Riches
3:16
8:18
10:4, 15, 22
11:4, 16, 28
13:7, 8
14:20, 24
18:11, 23
19:14
21:17
22:1, 2, 4, 7, 16

24:5, 10
31:3, 17, 25

Strife
3:30
15:18
16:28
17:1, 14, 19
20:3
22:10
25:8
26:17, 20, 21
28:25
29:22
30:33

Stripes
17:10
19:29
20:30

Strong drink
20:1
31:4, 6

Stumbling
3:23
4:12, 19

Substance
1:13
3:9
6:31
8:21
10:3
12:27

28:8
29:3

Subtilty
1:4

Summer
6:8
10:5
26:1
30:25

Surety
6:1
11:15
17:18
20:16
27:13

Sweetness
3:24
9:17
13:19
16:21, 24
20:17
23:8
24:13
27:7, 9

Talebearers
11:13
18:8
20:19
26:20, 22

Talk
6:22
14:23
24:2

Tenacity
24:10
30:28

Thief
6:30
29:24

Thoughts
12:5
15:26
16:3
21:5
23:7

Tongue
6:17, 24
10:20, 31
12:18, 19
15:2, 4
16:1
17:4, 20
18:21
21:6, 23
25:15, 23
26:28
28:23
31:26

Training
22:6